Persephone's Fall
Tiago Lameiras

Epic Poetry

Persephone's Fall
Composed & Edited by Tiago Lameiras

© 2018 Tiago Lameiras

The right of the editor to be identified as the author of the editorial material, and of the author for his individual chapters, has been asserted in accordance with sections 77 and 78 of the Copyright, Designs and Patents Act 1988.

All rights reserved. No part of this book may be reprinted or reproduced or utilized in any form or by any electronic, mechanical, or other means, now known or hereafter invented, including photocopying and recording, or in any information storage or retrieval system, without permission in writing from the publisher.

Persephone's Fall – Edited by Tiago Lameiras.
Includes a table of contents, images, and footnotes.

Printed and bound by CreateSpace Independent Publishing Platform.

ISBN–10: 1978275331
ISBN–13: 978-1978275331

Typeset in Sabon Roman
by Linotype

Charleston, SC, United States

*To Maria, living proof
divinity is earthly*

"Perfer et obdura,
dolor hic tibi proderit olim"*.

— Ovid

---

* "Be patient and tough, someday this pain will be useful to you".

Table of Contents

Winter **17**
    Canto I 19
    Canto II 33
    Canto III 45
    Canto IV 57
    Canto V 69
    Canto VI 83

Spring **97**
    Canto VII 99
    Canto VIII 113
    Canto IX 129
    Canto X 145
    Canto XI 159
    Canto XII 173

Summer **191**
    Canto XIII 193
    Canto XIV 209
    Canto XV 221
    Canto XVI 235
    Canto XVII 249
    Canto XVIII 265

Fall **287**
    Canto XIX 289
    Canto XX 297
    Canto XXI 305
    Canto XXII 311
    Canto XXIII 317
    Canto XXIV 329

The Island of Sicily[**] in Ancient Greece

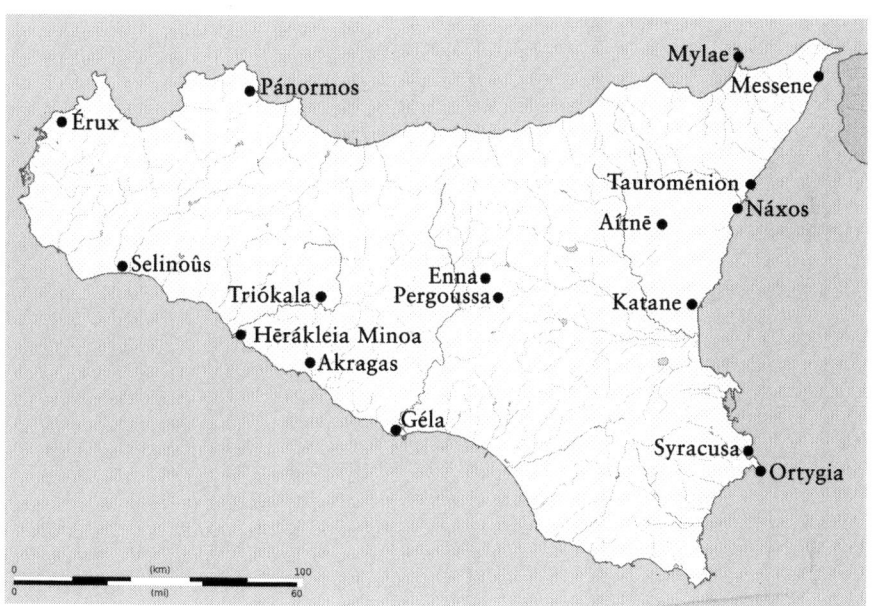

[**] Originally named "Trinacria" because of its triangular shape.

Winter

Canto I

    Nearly three months had passed since the daughter
of Demeter, goddess of agricultural tenure and natural
fertility, and Zeus, ruler of the Olympians and widely
renowned for his «bearer of the aegis» epithet,
5 had been taken from the earthly domain where both,
mother and child, would oversee the annual
sowing of the seeds – a cult spoken of by the
practitioners of the tradition held in Eleusis, Greece,
which, in all honesty, was a depiction of the cycle
10 the various worldly lifeforms, including fauna and flora,
necessarily experience across their lifespan.

    Phoebus Apollo, the all-seeing deity in charge of driving
the golden chariot across the skies for each daily
revolution by Man celebrated, all the way from the
15 Crescent to the Pillars of Herakles, began to rapidly
decline as the missing goddess – Persephone she was
called – would simply not turn up, to her mother's
painful sorrow, one an ever-caring parent could only
imagine, while attempting to avoid in their mind
20 the dreadful reality of such a woeful scenario,
unless, of course, the three Fates had decided
it was meant to be, just as they had already paved
the path for the deity of springtime and rebirth,
or any living being feasting under the roof of Hades,
25 which was to permanently remain in Tartarus,
regardless of either a human or divine complexion,
for not even father Zeus could repel the contract
implied in the ingestion of pomegranate seeds.
From the shores of Pergoussa Lake, in Sicily, an insular

30   portion of the Italian Peninsula, about sixteen stadia away
     from the mainland's toe, separate from each other
     by the Strait of Messene, bathed by the Ionian Sea
     to the East, the Mediterranean to the South and West
     and, finally, the Tyrrhenian to the North side,
35   there was no trace at all of the large fissure
     in the ground into which Persephone had been
     taken by an invisible figure who also drove
     a golden chariot, but certainly not as bright as Helios's.
     On the contrary, the sable-black horses drawing it
40   would unmistakably consume the light of Man
     and cast the human soul into perpetual obscurity;
     Phoebus dared not contradict his own kin,
     for Underworld affairs were not his concern.

     Demeter had promised herself she would not withstand
45   the rape of her daughter so lightly, having begun
     a long search which lasted for nine whole days.
     Depending on who you ask, Persephone might have been
     either seen by Apollo, during his antemeridian journey,
     or Hekate, the titanic goddess of magic, who helped
50   the desperate mother in her ordeal at nightfall,
     lighting candles wherever she went, longing to find
     her lost child, deliberately taken underground,
     far below her natural habitat, the land of blooming flowers.
     It was precisely when Demeter had told Persephone
55   to go paint the petals of a perpetual spring that
     the presiding judge of the dead's fate saw her for
     the very first time, instantly falling in love.
     Who would have guessed, you may ask, an entity
     as dark-hearted as Hades, used to dealing with pestilence,
60   was capable of embodying a feeling as enriching
     as love? Perhaps Eros had secretly struck his great-uncle

Persephone's Fall

with an arrow so powerful, that even ethereal deities
like himself could not avoid the consequences of being hit.
Now, Zeus, of course, did not require the couple maker's
65 services, for there was no romance involved in his
constant cheating on Hera, the queen goddess.
All of his conquests were merely carnal satisfactions;
the problem was he often generated offspring
his wife and sister, both the same woman, bedeviled
70 and wished could annihilate as soon as possible.
There is, for instance, the widely spread story
of Herakles, by Alcmene borne, while her husband-to-be,
Amphitryon, was seeking revenge for the slaying
of her brothers (all but one) against the Taphians.
75 It was certainly not Alcmene's fault she had copulated
with Zeus, nor did the latter force her to do so.
Via the power of metamorphosis, «the bearer of the aegis»
turned, one night, into Amphitryon, making the woman
believe her fiancé had returned sooner than expected.
80 As a result of this stand, twins were given birth to –
the mortal Iphicles, son of Amphitryon, and the
demigod Herakles, far too strong for a regular infant.
Hera knew of all the bastards left behind by her spouse,
and smitten as she had been with the greenest jealousy,
85 she sent two snakes through a statue made in her image,
placed inside the couple's home in Thebes, to poison
or perhaps strangle their illegitimate son.
Little did she know her vipers would be the ones
to suffer the asphyxiated demise for Herakles intended.
90 The boy eventually grew to become a famous hero,
which is all great Mycenean warriors aspire to;
Their deeds, fights, conquests... that is their legacy,
never to be forgotten across the annals of History,
and proof to that is still today we learn of their feats.

95   Though Hades was Zeus's brother, he did not sustain
any carnal desires at all – Persephone was to be the one.
No ordinary woman would satisfy the undisclosed
desires concealed in his immortal transfiguration,
which is why, perhaps not so subtly, the goddess
100 was taken away from the company of Artemis,
Athena, and the Oceanids, grabbed by the wrist
and the waist, leaving the flowery shores
of Pergoussa Lake abandoned to their eventual death.
That is how the end to spring (which included summer)
105 came to its end, for Demeter could not bear
the loss of her child, who had already been neglected
by her father as soon as she left her mother's womb.

Crops require constant care, and both Demeter
and Persephone were there to provide it, preventing
110 Humanity from starving to their death, helping them
stay in one place alone, without the constant need
for nomadic practices, forced to move along
after all resources available had been exhausted.
Furthermore, the inhabitants of Trinacria
115 were isolated and, even though they had mastered
the ways of the sea, defying Poseidon's rule,
you would think it to be impractical, heading to
the mainland of Great Greece and just keep walking
all the way to a new oasis, leaving the previous
120 ravished, never to be intelligently reused again.
The gift of agriculture meant, therefore, Man's very survival.
Without any reference as to where Persephone
might have been taken (neither Athena, nor Artemis
had had the opportunity to understand the complexity
125 of the abduction events, having occurred with such speed),
Demeter could only rely on Hekate's share of light,

clearing the path for her, while promising she would
engage in her own search party, should Persephone's
apparently inexistent trace lead somewhere else
130 having nothing to do with the earth or the Olympus,
which, in this case, could easily be reached via
the frequently active Mount Aitne, spewing lava and ashes
from beneath the surface toward the atmosphere.
The locals associated the volcano's wrath to that
135 of Hades himself, whenever he felt so lonely, that
he mandatorily had to remind humans to fear death
and enjoy their life as much as they could, for what
came next would not comprise the same chances,
especially for those who took pleasure in the suffering
140 of the innocent, so often making them spill
their own blood, out of sheer despair, lacking
a viable solution to their issues, worsened by the mind.

It just so happened, however, that one day, below
the ground, where Hekate lived, this one found
145 the girl who had gone missing – a remarkable feat,
at that, for in the Underworld, the fires of damnation
were the only available light source to depend on,
and though many souls were subjected to an eternal
burning, they were not scattered all over the place.
150 As soon as she realized Persephone was restrained
to the Dark Lord's manor, located on the pinnacle
of Tartarus, Hekate ran all the way above ground
to warn the distraught mother, who had given up
on everything she was supposed to look after,
155 no matter the end of the Myceneans being at stake.
That is how it was done – either the gods were happy
and appeased, or an entire people could be wiped out,
as literally as the Atlantians, overseen by Poseidon,

who could not, to their misfortune, prevent an overnight
160 earthquake that swallowed their island whole,
leaving an insuperable mud-like sort of debris in the ocean.
Their attempted slavery over Athens might have been
too much of an ambition for Athena to withstand,
and when a god sees their will done, it cannot be
165 undone by another, except for a slight compensation,
similar to the blindness Hera made Tiresias endure,
somewhat dimmed by Zeus via the gift of clairvoyance
(not to mention the multiple gender changes
he was submitted to for causing disagreement among
170 the Olympic couple, masters of the entire pantheon).

Young Persephone pretty much kept to herself;
no wonder, it is rather difficult to set your spirits up,
when you have been napped against your will,
to the likes of any napping I have ever heard of.
175 The girl who had once made the spring of Sicily
a true blessing for sore eyes and dented souls
had had the misfortune of having her own heart broken,
shattered for not knowing whether she and her mother
would ever meet again (eternity is too long a time
180 to wait, being as immortal as deities are in fact).
If blood ran through her veins, she would have
likely torn her wrists open, dampening the unfruitful
soil of the land of the dead, permanently thirsty
for another soul brutally stabbed away from its body.
185 Were it to taste a stream of slowly gushing red waters,
the ferryman would perhaps start bringing human
sacrifices across the Styx, tainting it with the color of life,
as its origin became whiter by the minute, rigidly
turning into marble, exactly like the victims of Medusa.
190 Man was created to the gods' own image, though made

powerless for obvious reasons, and still I cannot help
but feel moved by the need of sacrificial rituals
to have his will done; butchering, greasing and roasting
animals is an already gruesome picture to imagine,
195 but to distinguish one man from another, making
the first a tyrant and the second an offering to the gods,
is purely appalling and outrage-igniting; I would have to say
men are not created equal at all – the gods have their pets.
For the moment, Ilion stands… but will it in the future?
200 Only the gods can tell, after they have gambled the lives,
not just of heroes (whose killing sprees precede them),
but also of innocent women and children who could not
stand their ground and defend themselves, witnessing their
marital and parental guardian, respectively, be slaughtered.

205 Fortunately for Persephone, Hekate approached her
subtly, addressing her these winged and honeyed words:
'Hush, now, child; sheathe your tears, for you are
no longer alone in this enterprise. I am here to look out
for you. I have free passage between this realm and above,
210 and will let your mother know of your whereabouts'.
The grain-maiden, inevitably caught by surprise,
whispered unto the goddess of witchcraft like so:
'Who are you?! How do you know my mother?
Why am I here, shackled to the Tribunal of mortal souls,
215 as if a notorious crime I had emphatically perpetrated?
And how do I know you are to be trusted, revealing
yourself as a part of a monstrous place such as this?'.
Hekate did not falter before these numerous questions,
replying only: 'All in good time, daughter of the fair-haired.
220 I helped your mother for the entirety of the nine days
she sought your location, after you mysteriously vanished.
It had never occurred to me I would find you in Tartarus,

and yet, here you are, held a prisoner to Hades' affections'.
The sound of that name, synonymous with her surroundings,
225   made Persephone instantly shiver as much as the folk
above her, who had never felt what freezing was like.
'Please, I beg of you! Never mention his name in my presence.
If he were not as divine as I am, I would kill him myself.
Although I cannot comprise what death is, the emptiness
230   I feel in my heart, its hollowness… they are slowly
driving it to a full stop. The chariot that once sprang
through the green leaves, up in the canopy of trees,
leaving a rainbow behind it with which to color the flowers
lying by their feet, is now no better than a rotting carcass'.
235   Hekate then asked: 'Has the Judge of Death been mistreating
you in any way at all? Are you hurt, or injured, child?',
to which Persephone replied: 'my wounds scar me beyond
my flesh… they are all but visible to the untrained eye.
Other than that… the only occasion I was touched was
240   when he grabbed me by the wrist and waist. Since then,
he has merely tried to reason with me, though unsuccessful'.
The daughter of Perses, watching the newfound as she spoke,
addressed her again like so: 'you would be wise to appease
Hades for as long as you remain here. Your mother shall
245   intercede, she is powerful enough, but there is no guarantee
the Screech Owl will heed the Hummingbird's calling
lightly. I am Hekate, and I have now befriended you.
I shall not leave you alone to your misery, though time
has come for Demeter's anguish to be dimmed.
250   I must ascend back to the earth and rest her spirits'.
Persephone held her chest in her hands, sighing these words:
'Please… please, do what you can to get me out of here,
so I can rejoin my mother in rebirthing Nature…
there is too much darkness in the pit of the damned'.
255   The cloaked goddess promised both the lost child

and the unresigned mother would soon reunite,
immediately departing to the intertwined domain.

Having nearly lost all hope, Demeter stopped caring,
not about Persephone, but rather all of civilization.
260 Regardless of the countless hecatombs performed
in her honor, the fields could not grow the smallest
weed, let alone the crops that fed the Grecian city-states
to their remarkable prosperity, now long-lost.
Without the gift of agriculture, all that could be done
265 was hunting and breeding, though none of this
was ever enough to overcome slowly ravaging famine.
The animals kept could not reproduce instantly, and those
hunted down were only around because they had not yet
found their way out of the snow and ice, plain shelterless.
270 There was also another problem which had not been
faced before: how could people protect themselves
from the freezing cold temperatures brought in by
the seas and Boreas, together with Euros and Zephyros?
Aeolos, the ruler of winds, did try sending Notos,
275 the Southern wind, to ease the incoming wintery chaos
(thought to have been destroyed in its primordial form),
but survival was at stake, and something had to be done.

The goddess of witchcraft arose as fast as she could
by Demeter's side, as if she had worn Hermes' winged
280 sandals, bringing, like him, the divine news, as was his duty:
'Sacred sustenance of Mankind, hold your wrath within,
for I bring you the word you have long sought'.
Gasping because of the unexpected visit so late
in the day, considering the search had been suspended
285 for a long period of time, now, Demeter grabbed
her fair hair and grievously pulled a few strands out.

She had taken shelter in Hekate's cave above ground,
hiding from the begging men, women and children
freezing and starving simultaneously; both damnations
290 kept betting which one would strike the strongest
blow first and take the life away from bodies left to be
cremated, consequently remaining stuck on the shores
opposite to Tartarus, for Kharon could not traverse
the irate river with souls still attached to flesh and bone.
295 Besides, there was, of course, the question of payment.
An obol per soul was how much the ferryman charged.
It was up to someone else, usually a family member,
to put the coin in the dead body's mouth, but judging
from the state of the land, too cold to sow anything,
300 let alone reap, entire bloodlines were vanishing.

After realizing it was her loyal friend, thus spoke Demeter:
'Please tell me you have found my child, or, should the Fates
decide otherwise, tell me at least that you have some leads!'.
Hekate pulled down the hood from her cloak and said:
305 'The life-weaving trio have decided in your favor,
caring mother of earth and all its creatures walking upon it.
Your enterprise has revealed itself to be fruitful;
I have located your once lost daughter, Persephone'.
Two waterfalls streamed down the mother's cheeks,
310 only these were joyful waters, demonstrative of the
happiness the poor goddess had been overwhelmed by.
Who ever said being divine and immortal was a gift?
If you are to live forever, then there has to be something,
or, more importantly, someone you need to live for.
315 A real mother will always live to care for her children,
regardless of their age or condition (ethereal, in this case).
'Where is she? Take me to her, now!', begged Demeter,
with an understandably hoarse and outworn throat.

Persephone's Fall

     Sighing in disappointment, the sorceress replied:
320 'It cannot be done... your daughter has become
     a prisoner of Hades. He was the one who emerged
     through the still waters of Pergoussa and, leaving
     a whirlpool behind, took Persephone across the soil,
     into the unknown depths of the fearful Underworld'.
325 Attentively listening to Hekate's report, the Lady
     of the Golden Sword leaned against the cave's wall,
     in an effort to stand, though her legs had gone numb
     because of the prolonged sitting and crouching.
     The ghoulish goddess tried helping her friend up,
330 but an incisive hand wave was enough to turn her down.
     Demeter's eyes began shimming sideways in a sort of craze.
     The hand used to support her weight was grabbing
     the rock wall like a piece of soft cloth meant for a tunic,
     such was the rage taking over the mother's troubled spirit.
335 As if the wrath consuming her were giving her strength,
     the same strength she had always had before these events,
     thus she echoed and thundered inside the trembling cave:
     'My own brother! Her uncle! How dare he, the wretch?!
     If only he died, I would rip his head apart this instant!'.
340 Locking her sight to the ground, Hekate remarked:
     'Yes... Persephone somewhat shares your feelings...
     but you cannot risk entering the world of the dead,
     not even with my help; I would have brought the girl
     myself, if I could... justice will need to be done,
345 only not the way you want. The God of Thunder must
     intervene and be the judge of this unsavory ordeal'.
     Though they had become like family, Demeter looked
     Hekate in her eyes with a burning, piercing sight, saying:
     'Zeus never cared for his own child! He has got bastards
350 distributed all over Greece and only cares for a few.
     My daughter does not fill the requirements of that lot!

He left that clear when he abandoned the both of us'.
The sorceress understood Demeter's reasons perfectly,
though she added: 'Still, Mother of Spring, the bearer
355 of the aegis is the king of all living creatures, mortal or not.
The final decision relies upon his will. Surely, he will not
be so complacent regarding this matter – it is one thing
to abandon a child and leave them to the care of another
parent; it is different, however (and cruel), to leave
360 a child to their own luck, once you are bestowed
unanimously with the power to change the course of events
by all the other Olympians. Truth be told, Persephone
is one of them, just like you are, as one of Zeus' siblings
and mother of one of his offspring... would you not agree?'.
365 Discoursing as wisely as only the gods could, inflating
poets with their unmistakable omniscience for centuries
to come, Hekate hoped she had talked at least some sense
into the wheezing Demeter, so she could make a decision
after having pondered all elements for and against
370 her actions. Regaining her breath, her thoughts matched
the words of the goddess of moonlight and magic:
'Yes... you are right, of course, my sister-in-arms.
Even though I dare not look him in the eye, Zeus
might well be my only hope to retrieving Kore.
375 I shall depart to Olympus via Aitne as soon as rosy-fingered
Dawn opens its gates to the Sun's golden chariot.
Hades is but a lackey, he will inevitably have to yield'.
And so, during the remaining hours until sunlight,
both Demeter and Hekate summoned Morpheus
380 to accompany them in their voyage through sleep.

Canto II

    O Calliope, my perpetual Muse of reference,
    I beg of you, speak on my behalf to the gods,
    spare not your input, address them wisely and
    convince them with your rhetoric that my own tongue
5   must not be refrained from claiming the truth,
    as Hades' affections for Persephone are but
    the result of the flammable passion traversing his aura,
    and as far as love is concerned, my lips must avoid
    any attempt at being padlocked, or justice
10   will not have been otherwise properly served.

    Not every man will speak his heart lightly to
    the woman he so fondly desires, divine or not,
    and, to be fair, according to my proposition regarding
    this story, in which Astraea has a pivotal role
15   in blindly holding the scale under the constellation
    of Virgo, into which she was transformed by Zeus,
    on account of her innocence and spite for lawlessness,
    that does not mean the male in question would dare
    disrespect or mistreat the female; input will often
20   be at fault, in such occasions, for love treads softly
    on the grounds of Reason, who Persephone was
    accompanied by in the moment of the rape, no less,
    in the figure of Athena, her half-sister on the paternal side.

    Hades's approach to his niece and better half,
25   chivalrously speaking, was most certainly not the best,
    and the actual gentleman will bear that in mind
    and reckon when he is out of line; it is not a question
    of protocol or etiquette, but rather civilized mannerisms,

applicable also to the gods ruling the fate of Mankind,
with a few exceptions that act quite the contrary,
not setting the example for others, mortal or immortal.
I have already spoken of Zeus, who would always leave
his self-righteousness to the side (if any at all he had)
and betray his faithful wife exclusively for the libidinous
kind of satisfaction; Aphrodite, for instance, being the
goddess of love, and the mother of Eros, did not care
much for faithfulness; born from the foam cresting
toward the shores of Cyprus (generated by the amputated
testicles of Ouranos, overthrown by his son Kronos
in the context of the Titanomachy, under Gaea's orders,
together with the impregnation of Thalassa, personification
of the sea), the deity of beauty became a referral to the men
coveting the excellence of physicality in women and
to the women who dreamed of becoming like her,
so they could feel free to choose from a wide range
of suitors, as would happen with Penelope, in a near future,
though she was the symbol of fidelity and would never
betray Odysseus, no matter how long she had to wait.
Aphrodite also became an Olympian, fabled to actually
be another daughter of Zeus, though no one thought it
to be true; Hephaestus, on the other hand, was the son
of the bearer of the aegis with Hera, making him legitimate.
Riddled with so much imperfection, ugly and crippled,
he was the male opposite of his wife; indeed, the lustful
beauty Aphrodite had been gifted with, especially in the
midst of the Olympians, had become a reason for Zeus
to force her to marry the god of metallurgy, so she
would not be disputed by other gods, including the
ruler himself. After he was cast off Mount Olympus
by his own mother to the island of Lemnos,
in the Northern Aegean Sea, Hephaestus grew into a

Persephone's Fall

     remarkable blacksmith, producer of the majority
     of divine weapons (Zeus's signature weapon, the
     lightning bolt, was everlasting and cyclops-made).
65 Hera came to acknowledge via Thetis, a sea goddess,
     leader of the Nereids and future mother of Achilles,
     that her son's specialty was not weapons alone,
     for he could also produce fine pieces of jewelry.
     Demanding her son's return, Hephaestus refused
70 to heed the goddess of marriage's calling, tricking her,
     instead, into accepting a chair made of both silver and gold.
     The trickery of the act revealed itself when the seat
     was sent to Olympus, Hera sat on it and locked her
     in place for three whole days, preventing her from
75 all sorts of movement; the ingenious god of volcanoes
     had finally had his revenge as far as his mother's hubris
     against him was concerned; not even Zeus could persuade
     him to unlock the gripping gadget, and that was the time
     the ruler of gods thought uniting his son to Aphrodite
80 would be enough to talk him into releasing the irate Hera.
     The goddess of love did not care much for the idea,
     but she had no other choice (not a legitimate one, at least).
     Long after the incident between mother and son,
     Hephaestus gifted his consort with the most beautiful
85 gifts he could think of, though his faltering outlook
     was always a case of repudiation from Aphrodite.
     She then started seeking the company of other
     personalities, most frequently that of Ares, god of war.
     One day, nestling in the hall of the craftsman's abode,
90 the adulterous pair was sighted by all-seeing Helios,
     who warned Hephaestus; being the god of fire,
     his heart was set in flames, his entire body was smoldering
     with rage, disgust and, naturally, disappointment (for who
     could ever be happy about the feeling of betrayal?).

95　Because of this embarrassing episode, Hephaestus fashioned
　　an invisible and unbreakable chain-like net and waited
　　for their next encounter, hoping to bluntly capture them,
　　which he did, then taking them back to Olympus
　　for their shaming of the other gods, who burst into tears
100　from the uncontrollable laughter possessing them
　　(though they would not have minded switching places
　　with Ares, but only with respect to their carnal cravings).

　　Back to the central plot of this literary production
　　the Muse has inflated me with in good time,
105　charming this humble poet into loving her unicity,
　　thus loosening the intellect secluded in the back of my mind
　　(sometimes not even remembered by myself),
　　we have already uttered Hades did not share the promiscuity
　　of the Olympians, or any other kind of deities, come to that.
110　All he wanted was to love, and be loved in return;
　　Only Persephone could eradicate his melancholy,
　　for no other woman, regardless of her feminine wiles,
　　was good enough for him; every day the Master of Death
　　held Kore captive, all the more he was risking losing
115　her, without even having won her heart, yet,
　　unlocking the purity of her chest with his own honor.
　　The ruler of the Underworld knew little about courtship,
　　but there had to be something he could do to appease
　　Persephone and gradually convince her of his
120　innocuous intentions; conversing would be a starter,
　　though he was mostly gifted in judicial rhetoric,
　　sentencing cruel men's souls to a painful eternity.
　　Crime, of course, was not exclusive to men,
　　for in Tartarus there lay forty-nine infamous women
125　known as the Danaids, daughters of Danaus,
　　who had each been sentenced to perpetually carrying

jugs of water they had to fill their own bathtub with,
so as to cleanse themselves from their common sin,
mariticide, though they would never be able to do so,
as the tubs were either leaky or bottomless, without
any chance of a makeshift restoration that made them
usable, freeing them at last from their punishment.

It all began when the women's progenitor fled with them
to Argos, in mainland Greece, in an attempt to avoid
having them marry the fifty sons of his twin brother,
Aegyptus, King of Egypt; even though they were all
family, betrayal was at the corner and underway,
for Danaus had devised a deception that hopefully
would spare his daughters from their fate, unknowingly
assisting the actual Fates in their own weaving,
which was a great deal fairer and less brutal, as far as
the girls' actions were concerned. Their father had agreed
to give them away to his nephews, should they come to
Argos and help defend the local population from any
possible threats, and so they did, accompanied by Aegyptus.
The fifty weddings took place and, on their first night
together, the Danaids were instructed by Danaus
to kill their husbands in their sleep, after copulating.
Only one of them, Hypermnestra, refused to obey
the order, considering her husband, Lynceus, had been
chivalrous enough to respect the maiden's wishes
of remaining a virgin, therefore sparing him from the
acute burning of the blade, unlike his brothers.
That is why, out of fifty, forty-nine women were sent
to Tartarus to serve their sentence in the fashion of an
infructuous task, permanently begging for forgiveness.
Discontented with Hypermnestra's defiance, Danaus
vowed to seek justice in the courts of Argive rule,

which he did, but not in the manner he had expected.
160 Lynceus himself sought vengeance and rightfully killed
his uncle, ruling Argos together with the surviving Danaid,
producing a dynasty of their own under the same name.

As the monarch of the realm of the dead, Hades could
subject his inmates to whichever activity he wanted them
165 to perform; the Screech Owl thus made the maidens
into maids, mostly serving him food, accompanied by
the delectable nectar no respectable god could do without.
Because he wanted Persephone to feel at home, something
she found to be despairingly hard and appalling, the ruler
170 of Tartarus would send some of the Danaids to feed
his prisoner, even though all she claimed for was freedom,
the only gift he would not grant her; in his mind,
Hades sooner or later would have to wed the goddess
of springtime, ultimately putting an end to his loneliness.
175 But what of her free will, I dare ask? Should she not
have the right to speak her own desire, weakly yielding
to the power of a male without any sort of confrontation?
Persephone had too much of a free spirit to be kept
locked away wherever, let alone in that hellish place,
180 overlooked by a weird figure who would not even face her.
Apart from taking her hunger and thirst away, Hades
also showered his womanly love with other sorts of gifts,
such as jewelry, commissioned directly from Hephaestus'
hands, and such a great talent he had, the blacksmith.
185 No matter how beautifully crafted, however,
the missing daughter to a distraught mother refused
selling herself to the pleasures of a male companion
over precious metals; she would rather give up hope
and embrace her imprisonment with both body and soul,
190 than turning into something she had never been:

a superfluous, materialistic goddess, whose dedication
lay with the people and the cyclical revival of Nature.

Gathering all the boldness he could to set his heart free,
Hades had finally come to the conclusion that a three-month
confinement to a bedroom (though in a luxurious palace,
having everything at her disposal) was enough.
Persephone would not give up easily, but perhaps
she would be willing to confront her Nemesis,
only in the form of a judge, whose line of thought
he hoped Persephone would follow, after breaking her.
On her turn, the offspring of Demeter would not mind
asking the original Nemesis for a rightful revenge
on Hades, but in Tartarus, the ruler was untouchable.

Moreover, the gates to afterlife were well guarded
by a three-headed watchdog named Kerberos,
which could not be easily fooled into letting danger
go beyond the crystal-ornamented doors, perhaps
as rigid as those which protected Troy on earth,
along with its impenetrable high walls, capable of
withholding all sorts of menacing from other men.
Only a cunning mind of a thousand resources
could transpose such barriers, fallible alone to the power
of an inflated intellect, and not bronze-made weaponry.
Clearing his throat and preparing to address Persephone
as gently as he thought was his best, Hades knocked on
the bedroom door, assessing Kore's aura at the time:
'Who is it?!', she abruptly asked, waking her enraged,
tearful face from her knees, as she sat in one of the corners,
pulling her hair and scarring her chest with anxiety.
The master then said: 'It is I, Milady. Hades, son of Kronos,
judge of the dead and ruler of the Underworld realm.

May I please come in and speak with thee? It is a matter
of urgency, monumental proportions and great importance'.
As the discourse traversed the frame of his teeth and swept
225 the floor under the door's narrow gap, Persephone
held her breath, tainting her face with drips from
the markings on her breast, undeniably shocked.

In her three months of captivity, the goddess of rebirth
had never once heard the voice of her raptor; somehow,
230 she was sure he would sound horrifying, once he uttered
a syllable. However, that was certainly not the case.
On the contrary, it was quite gentle, as if it had been
deliberately oiled like skin after a bath, to soften it.
In a way, Hades was indeed putting an effort to it,
235 so he could minimize the damage caused until then.
Nonetheless, and no matter how delicate his voice was,
Persephone could not help but take a golden bowl
with grapes and ram it against the door, cautioning
the trespasser of her little patience for sudden reasoning.
240 'Sir, I advise thee not to force thy entrance in these
chambers! My judgement is steadfast at hurting thee
by all means necessary, at my disposal within these walls'.
Hades gulped at the craze present in Kore's words.
He obviously did not fear he might get hurt, it could
245 not be done, but he did consider it had been foolhardy
of him to stay away from the girl for so long, thinking
only of his own interest in succeeding, without caring
enough to providing an explanation for the rape
he had performed in the beginning of Nature's decline,
250 the first time in History such an event took place.

Regardless of one's condition, bound to die or eternally
live without the faintest chance of wrinkling,

somehow, there has to be meaning, purpose in life,
and that, I cannot stress enough; it would be maniacal
255 not to share our soul (for, in the end, we all are
ethereal) with another, but not just any other.
Our mate in spirit must complete us, the missing pieces
must join and generate one fortified being alone.
None of them should lose their personal identity,
260 listlessly yielding to the other's will and desire;
on the contrary, dialoguing is essential to the
sustainability of a relationship, if it is meant to last,
and that is the reason why the Lord of Tartarus
did not plan on giving up, albeit he was at fault,
265 which was something he was perfectly aware of.
It was not just the men who had to fight for honor,
in order to be remembered by through the annals;
in fact, fighting for honor needed not become
a petty excuse to have other men slain, lying
270 on the ground, their throat slipped, their heart
pierced, their wielding hand cut off, along with
the enemy's morale, represented by the flag now
torn, lying on the ground, stepped on, marked by
a concoction of blood and dirt, made pasty by the Sun.
275 There is no such thing as honor in killing or destroying,
let alone the innocent, undeserving of capital punishment.
Women and children have been killed before, because of
men's bloodthirst, and the more a man tastes blood,
the more he becomes addicted to it, in search for the
280 trance he experienced the first time, never finding it again.
Females may be physically weaker than men, but it is
their heart that pumps the necessary strength for a man
to stand, and not only as mothers or nursing maids,
but most importantly as partners, companions, or wives.
285 Only true lovers will understand what sharing is,

building each other together, indifferent to gender.
The weaker sex is the product of a fool's imagination;
the aphorism is clear – behind every great man, there lies
a great woman (perhaps even greater than himself).

300 Hades knew he was great; he was one of the three gods
who had inherited one of the three domains ruled by
the Titans, and his was precisely the latter's prison.
The Screech Owl had taken part in the annihilation
of tyranny, by helping Zeus and Poseidon defeat Kronos,
305 bursting from his insides after being eaten, for fear
of being overthrown by his children, just as he had done
to his father before him, during the Titanomachy.
Simultaneously, being great for such an accomplishment,
or even for delivering proper sentences to his inmates,
310 made him think little of himself, perhaps unworthy.
As he leaned his back against the outer bedroom wall,
grape juice was pouring from underneath the door,
widening as it spread across the marble floor,
bathing his sandals; he could see his reflection
315 in the blood-like liquid, bearing a stern look on his face.
His oratory afterward was infallible, hinged with wings:
'Milady, I do not intend to break into thy berth.
Had I the will to do it, I would already be inside.
I came to thee to seek forgiveness for raping thee
320 from the earth thou walked upon, gently sowing
seeds and painting flowers with the precision
a great many deal of artists aim for their entire life
and, yet, cannot reach, as they lack thy delicate hands.
I do not mean to flatter, I just speak what the heart cannot.
325 I am unquestionably aware there was nothing chivalrous
about my courting thee... I did not court thee whatsoever.
Cowardice took over, it is my only explanation.

Persephone's Fall

  Thou shalt regard me as being weird, uncommon, perhaps,
  but I will have thee know that, those of us who seem
330 to be the weirdest are, in fact, the purest, hiding disquiet
  within our heart, revolted by the mask of falsehood,
  which I cannot bear; that is the reason I fell for thee,
  that is the motive Phantasos, one of the Oneiroi,
  took thy feminine form and comforted me in my dreams,
335 by Morpheus induced, at last appeasing my spirit
  with the awareness of thy delightful existence in this world.
  Eros could have pierced my heart with an arrow
  soaked in hemlock and take my immortality away;
  it would not have been paralyzed without beating,
340 begging for thy love at least once, despite thy reply.
  Yes, I have unjustly taken thee, and must now repent,
  but only thy forgiveness will have washed my sin away.
  Thou shalt not be laid a single finger upon thy skin,
  thou hast my word; be assured, however, that although
345 thou art not a prize to be won, thy love is to be conquered.
  Now that I have stated my intentions, I must leave.
  Thou wilt have gained plenty of food for thought; goodbye'.

  The discourse had been long, but Persephone had outdone
  herself by holding her breath for nearly the entirety
350 of the time she spent listening to the ruler of the
  Underworld's love swearing for her, binding both souls.
  The goddess of rebirth was in awe from the honeyed
  words she had just been delivered by the unknown
  assailant, causing her to silently weep, though
355 it was unclear what she felt in that moment.
  A mixture of sadness and unexpected joy was dripping
  from her eyes into her half-open mouth, a bittersweet
  waterfall replacing the familiar taste of ambrosia
  with that of both a salty and confused judgment.

Canto III

    As soon as Hekate ordered the Moon to set, yielding to
    rosy-fingered Dawn, who cleared the path for Helios's
    golden chariot, Demeter woke, immediately dismissed
    the Oneiroi and walked out of her loyal friend's cave,
5   decisively stomping the ground in great virtue;
    the day she would retrieve her daughter had finally come,
    and the Mistresses would be once again reunited.
    The mother's least concern was bothering Zeus
    so early in the morning; Persephone was his daughter,
10 he was bound to do something about it, otherwise
    civilization would become extinct, breaking the balance
    between sky, earth (the sea included) and the Underworld.
    Without any surviving men, women or children,
    the world would likely fall into the hands of Chaos
15 again, ridiculing the Olympians' efforts to establish order
    throughout a series of epic battles others have sung better.

    Outside, the scenario showed the result of carelessness.
    All was white, which somehow signified purity,
    as if the soil were hibernating, waiting for its rebirth,
20 hoping its cleansing would soon come, so it could
    become useful and impregnated with fertility itself,
    saving the mortals from their freezing and starving demise.
    The eldest of the Thesmophoroi felt sorry for abandoning
    what she loved the most – agricultural enlightenment…
25 however, without the youngest's presence and assistance,
    she felt it was all in vain; her grief often turned to rage,
    deliberately disregarding the fate of Mankind, on account
    of her own concerns, for a mother will always care
    for her children, no matter how independent they are.

30　And so, from the province of Enna, Demeter departed
　　to the border between Katane and Messene, toward Aitne,
　　discarding her physical form, in order to travel faster.
　　When she arrived at the top of the stratovolcano,
　　she felt the irrational urge to just plunge in and
35　confront Hades, deciding, however, following Hekate's
　　advice was a great deal wiser, taking the marble-crafted
　　stairway the opposite way, visible only to immortals.

　　The gods could never be too careful as to what they offered
　　humans, and Prometheus was the best lesson to be learned.
40　Being one of the greatest benefactors to Mankind,
　　the titan, who had fought alongside Zeus, against his kin,
　　had provided Humanity with fire, exclusively divine,
　　together with defiance, teaching men to keep the best parts
　　of animals sacrificed in hecatombs to themselves,
45　offering the gods the worst pieces; not only that,
　　the wisest of titans also provided humans with hope,
　　the only remaining item in Pandora's jar, after she
　　peeked into it, spreading all that was bad and evil,
　　thus giving Zeus an excuse to swallow the earth
50　in a great flood, saving just those he found to be worthy.
　　Before he was rescued by Herakles, Prometheus suffered
　　a severe punishment, being beaked every single day
　　by the Kaukasios Eagle, summoned by the bearer of the aegis
　　to eat his liver out, which regrew overnight, while bound
55　to a rock in chains, given the sour taste of hubris.

　　Mount Olympus had been physically erected in mainland
　　Greece, Southwest of Salonika, with multiple gorges
　　housing each of the twelve Olympians' palaces.
　　Close to the top, there lay the Throne of Zeus, from which
60　the thunderous ruler would cast his lightning bolts.

Persephone's Fall

Only he could sit in that chair, and no one else,
not even Hera, his wife, sister, and queen of the skies;
anyone daring to do otherwise would experience
a dreadful wrath and perhaps be fulminated instantly.

65 That is how certain city-states across the Hellenic world,
such as Thebes, by Cadmus founded, often switched
between aristocracies, oligarchies, timocracies, and
tyrannies, rarely choosing democracy as a fair regime.
The concept of having the richest and most powerful
70 in government had been inherited from divinity, as Zeus
was indeed above all living and non-living creatures.
It thus became an excuse for tyrants to hold their place
under the will of the gods, therefore holding the will
of the people in their hands, mostly until their death,
75 either by natural causes, or cathartic assassination.
Having power or riches was not always required;
making good use of a rhetorical ability by conveying
a credible logos in favor of the contenders' ethos
was usually enough to drive out of the people
80 their ingenuine pathos, blindly offering their trust.

The Pantheon, on the other hand, was the theater where
divine councils took place, rallying all deities for the most
assorted discussions and (often) heated arguments,
resolved alone by either Zeus's consent or disapproval.
85 Now, Demeter was an Olympian herself, together with
Persephone (depending on the cult of your preference).
It had been long since the eldest of the Mistresses
had sat down in her place, among the hemicycle, though
it was exactly as she had left it, before the rape events.
90 Certain gods were savage as far as some of their attitudes
are concerned, but at the same time respectful in many ways;

leaving others' seats untouched was one of them, a sadly
inapplicable principle when it came to women, divine or not.
Next to her seat was her daughter's, together always.
95 Hades did not have a seat in the Pantheon; living below,
he rarely paid his siblings a visit, perhaps because
Apollo's sunrays were too aggressive to his sight,
accustomed to the gentle brightness of Underworld torches.

Although she could have taken her place that instant,
100 Demeter was unaware of any scheduled plenaries.
Maybe the gods would not reunite at all, that day;
the Great Goddess thus decided she would get Zeus's
attention by sitting on his throne, in order to rattle him.
The least of her concerns was her brother's wrath,
105 for it was him who carefully had to choose his words
and actions; Demeter would not give in lightly
to a sibling and former partner who cared not for their child.
Helios was, naturally, the first to see her, up above;
other gods could afford sleeping late, ignoring daylight,
110 but not the twin of Artemis, as taking a break would mean
incessant darkness across the earth, causing a cataclysm
among humans, brutally sacrificing each other as a gift
to the Sun's expected return, aboard its golden chariot.
Being the all-seeing god, Apollo understood her intentions;
115 he thought of warning his father of the outrage, though
he did not wish to be delayed in his journey, nor did he
want to be the one causing Zeus's tempestuous awakening.
Helios simply rode away, leaving it to the others.
The moment Demeter sat on the Olympian throne,
120 putting down her forearms on the chair's armrests
and accommodating her legs and feet on the marble ottoman,
thunder was cast from behind it, up to the celestial dome,
as if it were some sort of an alarm, warning of an intruder.

Persephone's Fall

  The bearer of the aegis was fast asleep, dreaming of
125 his latest conquests, while Hera was drowning in jealousy,
rolling on herself multiple times, trying to ignore
his uttering and mumbling about other women.
She became so tired, that she eventually started to yield,
allowing Morpheus to do his work and take her to sleep.
130 However, when the lightning bolt was sent to the sky,
outside, its collision with the stars reverbed loudly enough
to wake the whole of Greece, as well as Ilion, across the sea.
The Goddess of Heavens thought for moments
her husband had dropped one of his rays in ecstasy,
135 thus abruptly addressing him: 'For your own sake and mine,
consort, can you not let me rest in peace, without you
making all this annoying and unbearable racket?!
I have been awake all night, let me at least enjoy
the morning, before Apollo reaches his noon zenith!'.
140 Because he had woken so suddenly, Zeus' eyes
were forced open and, consequently, bloodshot;
rubbing them only made it worse, like he was in
some sort of craze, which was not at all far from the truth.
He knew what the thunderous sound meant; Hephaestus
145 had been commissioned to install the system himself,
though he never thought someone would actually dare
sit in his throne, which was not equipped with any sort
of entrapment, unlike the one Hera had been offered,
for there was nothing as punishing as the ire of the Father.
150 He quickly got up and enragedly looked at his wife,
enouncing these dreadful vocables: 'Silence, woman!
Did you not hear the thundering echo outside the palace?!
Someone dared sit in my throne! A death wish has arisen
early in the morning!', Zeus said, stomping the marble floor
155 as his laurel wreath was magically produced atop his head,
together with the majestic tunic covering his naked body.

Hera lay goggling at him quietly, dropping her head back
on the pillow; surely, her husband had had a nightmare,
and was now gobbling for having his dream taken away.
160 'Good!', she thought, 'that will teach him not to bring
others to this bed, even if they are no more than oneiric'.

As soon as the God of Thunder traversed the palace hall
and stepped outside, he covered his eyes with his hand,
for daylight was becoming stronger each minute,
165 looked straight at the peak where his throne lay,
and tried to make out who the criminal was indeed.
After a few seconds, Zeus recovered his visual acuity
and still could not believe what his eyes showed him;
there she was, the eldest of the Mistresses, long gone
170 from Olympus, now returned, though to an unlawful seat.
To the likes of his own bolts, Father Zeus became a flash,
taking back his human (but imperial) shape before Demeter.
'What are you doing here, sitting there, by my own beard?!',
he asked, thundering his voice as much as lightning.
175 Demeter looked him in the eye passively, replying like so:
'Hold your peace, brother; we must talk about our daughter'.
Caring about Persephone's fate as much as before, Zeus said:
'Get out of my chair! Does your nerve know no bound?!',
a question to which the goddess responded assertively,
180 leaving the royal chair behind in one jump alone:
'Dare not defy the lioness when she has lost her cub!'.
Within, Zeus trembled before his sister's piercing eyes,
but he naturally had no intention of showing it.
Forgetting about what had been a personal insult,
185 having his throne at the mercy of another, despite
their divinity, the thunderous god focused on the words
Demeter pronounced in a cocktail of agony and rage,
feeling puzzled: 'what are you talking about, woman?'.

Persephone's Fall

The fact that her daughter's own father did not realize
190 face value what she meant by such impaling words
left the eldest of the Thesmophoroi's nectar boiling
a great deal more, nearly vaporizing from her veins.
Though her desire was to strike the bearer of the aegis
across his face, Demeter withheld her rage, as she had
195 to try and reason with Zeus, if their offspring was to return.

Taking a deep breath and holding her tears within,
the goddess of harvest looked down to the cloudy soil
and clarified: 'Persephone has been gone for three months.
She was abducted by Hades from the shores of Pergoussa,
200 and has not come back since; he is holding her in Tartarus'.
As Demeter ended her explanation, she looked back up,
meeting the gaze of a rather confused Zeus, who then spoke:
'Hades...? Our brother has taken our daughter, his niece?
On what grounds? And why does he not let her go?!',
205 he exclaimed, undoubtedly surprised by the eerie revelation.
The goddess replied: 'I am still not sure, but such a daring
move suggests she has won his heart – unintentionally.
There is yet one more riddle to this wounding story;
Hekate informed me Persephone ate pomegranate seeds,
210 though I cannot be precise as to how many, exactly.
Regardless, you know what it means, brother; the prophecy
is clear – one month underground per each seed ingested'.
The thunderous god remembered what had been decided
by the Fates, though he had never thought it could happen.
215 Despite being the supreme ruler of all living creatures,
Zeus had no power whatsoever over the three sisters;
they were independent and could decide the fate of gods
themselves, as it had happened to unknowing Persephone.
The Father of Gods walked to the empty throne and sat in it,
220 empowered again, grabbing the left armrest with his hand

and placing his right elbow on the opposite side,
while supporting his chin, displaying a pensive look.
After a few moments of silence, during which he remembered
he had never cared for either his sister or his daughter,
225 Zeus enquired: 'What, then, do you expect me to do?
You know I do not command the Fates; whatever they weave
cannot be undone and woven again differently; besides,
we know not whether Persephone has eaten enough seeds
to keep her in the Underworld for the course of a whole year'.
230 Demeter thus kneeled, holding her brother's shins, begging:
'Please, brother! It might not have been so, there is still hope!
You may not be able to undo the sisters' prophecy, but you
have the power to order Hades to return Persephone to the
earth below the glowing sky and above that crooked place!'.

235 Even though the three realms the world was divided in
were autonomous, each of them governed by one god
(Zeus in heaven, Poseidon in the oceans, and Hades below),
the latter two mandatorily responded ultimately to Zeus;
it had been agreed like so after the defeat of the Titans.
240 However, and considering the Lord of the Underworld
always kept to himself and was not even an Olympian,
the bearer of the aegis was reluctant about talking to his
brother, even though it could mean his daughter's freedom.
And so, he made his decision: 'I shall not speak to Hades.
245 Tartarus is his domain, I will allow him to hold Persephone
for as long as he wishes; the thunderous Zeus has spoken'.
The agrarian goddess, who had laid her sobbing eyes
on her brother's tunic, appealing to his good humor,
immediately let loose of his legs and stood up, wiping
250 the tears that had streamed down her rubicund cheeks.
She looked Zeus in his eyes as if setting them afire,
leaned over the divine throne (nearly crushing

Persephone's Fall

the armrests with her hands) and asked the begging:
'Have I heard this correctly…? Are you telling me that,
255 by your grey beard, you will do nothing to release
my daughter from that barbarian's clutches…?
Am I to understand that is your intention and none other?'.
Listlessly, the brother nodded and spoke no more,
which was the perfect cue for Demeter to retaliate:
260 'Hear this, then, O mighty Zeus, bearer of the aegis!
If you do not force Hades to return Persephone to the
living world, I shall inflict upon that very ground
you see below your feet a thousand years of drought
and famine, putting an end to your most prized creation!
265 Each and every human will die of thirst and hunger,
and green will no longer be cast across the horizon,
for I will leave all soils frozen and nothing will ever
grow from them again; heed my warning – Mankind
will cease to exist, and no more shall you abuse
270 honored women, either virgin or happily wedded!
I, goddess of sustenance, Demeter, over you have spoken!'.

I believe that, in the end, it is true one cannot (or should not)
dare defy the lioness when she has lost her cub, for her wrath
shall be far worse than that of a rattled Zeus himself.
275 The difference between a progenitor and an actual parent
is henceforth set clearer than the bluest of skies above.
Zeus knew pleasure; love, on the other hand, was a mystery,
regardless of its kind, whether marital, fraternal, or parental,
of course; he had never raised any of his children, let alone
280 those who were a product of a one-night liaison, except for
Dionysos, of course, whom he secretly sewed to his thigh
until he was born, after accidentally killing the mother,
Semele, daughter of Cadmus, the founder of Thebes,
with a spectacle of lightning and thunder no mortal could

285 witness by looking directly up to the gods, resulting in
instant incineration, which is what happened in this case.
That is the story behind the «insewn» and «double-born»
epithets utilized by poets to address the god of Theater Arts.

Confronted by an irate Demeter he had never seen before,
290 the bearer of the aegis gulped as much as when he had been
devoured by his own father, though he never really gave in.
Blushing all over with nectar rushing to his rigid face,
he stood up from his chair, imposing himself before
his sister, who let go of the throne and stepped back
295 to give him space, though she did not drop her guard.
Zeus then stated, bluntly: 'Very well. I shall not sacrifice
Mankind once more on account of your womanly caprices'.
Stepping down from the peak and headed to the Pantheon,
the voice of the Father echoed across the ether, saying:
300 'I now declare the Council of Gods to be in session!'.
From the palaces in the gorges, the remaining Olympians
withdrew from their rest and promptly obeyed the order
to gather in their rightful place among the hemicycle.
Behind the thunderous god's back, Demeter grinned
305 for getting back at a coward who abandoned his offspring,
careless about whichever fate they faced, were they eternal
or simply bound to die, like a lamb in a hecatomb.
As Calliope has whispered unto my ear only just now,
love does not comprise letting go, regardless of the obstacle
310 lying ahead, even if it takes the shape of a taciturn god.

Canto IV

    Six months were soon to be gone since Persephone
    had been forcibly taken to Tartarus by Hades, its ruler.
    Nonetheless, the sobbing goddess of spring remained
    reluctant to leaving the room she had been confined to.
5   Thinking her mother had spent all that time roaming
    from Syracusa to Érux, perhaps even crossing the strait
    to the mainland, made her feel all the more worse,
    disgusted about a rapist who, deep down, possibly
    felt the same great deal of sorrow she was carrying,
10 for not being able to make her happy; no wonder,
    a woman's heart cannot be bought, whichever the fee,
    as Hades had likely become aware of by that time.

    One day, however, as the youngest of the Mistresses
    lay in her bed, sonorously crying, as usual, the door,
15 which had been previously opened by a few Danaids
    doing the regular cleaning and food-serving, failed
    to stay shut, unable to lock the commotion coming
    from the exterior of the Underworld Palace, where
    the inmates did their time, either freely or under torture.

20 Hades himself was responsible for overseeing the prisoners,
    and would often let his rage loose as a form of punishment,
    far greater than that which they had been sentenced to.
    Struck with curiosity, Persephone heard loud cries
    for either help or mercy, though no one ever heeded them.
25 As trapped as she were, the goddess of rebirth felt some sort
    of a rebellion brewing within her, wishing to get back
    at the perpetrator of her misery by aiding other convicts.
    The goddess of maidenhood then approached the door

and peeked from the catch, in order to find out if it was
not all a trick to make her leave the room and be assaulted.
Apart from the apparent desolation reverbing outside,
which she had had a chance to witness the day she was raped,
while Hades firmly held her by the wrist and waist
as he drove his chariot, the palace itself seemed to be quiet.
Persephone escalated on her daring enterprise and popped
her head out, looking both ways of the corridor, making
her believe she definitely had her way clear of any snares.

Even for someone who was scared, her pace really was
embellishing; it nearly felt like each and every step
was being either walked upon a cloud or a water lily.
There was something natural about her composure
that would not let her falter, regardless of the fear
she had been living in (or sentenced to) for so much time.

When she reached the end of the corridor, the youngest
of the Mistresses realized she had been staying on the top
floor, for she found a grand staircase which led to the hall.
Come to think of it, the home of Hades did not seem like
the house of pestilence and misery at all; on the contrary,
Persephone understood the Lord of the Underworld had
excellent taste in decoration, with several works of art
scattered across the enormous entrance; she did not know,
however, whether they had been commissioned or created
by Hades himself, during his time away from the inmates.
Beyond beautifully crafted vases, urns, marble statues,
bronze warrior arms, elms, spears, shields, Doric columns,
murals made of mosaic, and tables of the finest oaken wood
laid down with detailed silverware and pottery, there was
something larger than life that had caught her attention,
especially because it was covered with a drape, tied around

the structure, preserving, perhaps, the most precious
of treasures, or simply secrets, which could also be
highly valued, often more than a chest filled with gold.
The ruler of Tartarus clearly did not want anyone to see
what lay underneath the long piece of cloth, harboring
its content in a corner of the room, hiding its relevance.
Judging from the shape, Persephone thought it could be
a statue, maybe of Hades, just to polish his ego a bit more.
There was a seal carved into the center of the entrance
floor, depicting men and women praising and bowing
toward an orifice that was left to be filled by either a tile
or, perhaps, the nearby secluded sculpture; some people
painted on the floor carried instruments such as the plough,
a few spades, whereas others had crops of barley and wheat,
and a third group was spreading and sowing seeds.
Bluntly put, it resembled an agricultural cycle – rebirth.
Being the goddess of Nature's cycle, precisely, Persephone
could not help but shed a few tears, reminded of her mother.
The plinth incrusted in the base of what she thought to be
a statue indeed was only partially covered, thus revealing
writing carved into the marble; however, from where
the goddess was standing, it turned out to be illegible.

Marveled as she was with the ingenious craftsmanship
surrounding her, the youngest of the Thesmophoroi
progressively lost focus on what had moved her out
of her room in the first place – the engendering of payback.
It was then the perpetual cries of sufferance came back,
sounding a lot stronger, now that the exterior was closer.
Not only that, coming from one of the windows to the side
was some sort of flame-toned flashing light, giving
the impression of an unstoppable, repetitive event.
As curious as she was to see what lurked underneath

the drape, Persephone's original intentions were enlightened
once more because of what she feared to be a gruesome,
horrendous, if not sordid display, accompanied
95 by endless screams of inhuman pain infliction, even though
the inmates of Tartarus were already dead and bodiless.

As opposed to the Elysian Fields, where heroes chosen
by the gods are rewarded with a happy and quiet afterlife,
the isles Persephone saw from the main doors of the mansion
100 mirrored scenes that were, mildly put, stomach-churning.
Everything that was unknown to humans or gods themselves,
all that was contrary to the ideals of comfort and happiness,
to the goddess's horror, was right in front of her, making her
impulsively drive both her hands to her chest, afflicted,
105 nauseated and repulsed by the grossness of the scenario;
it was only because she had not eaten for so long that
there was nothing for her to regurgitate, apart from bile,
which was even worse than having an indigestion,
or spitting out blood from a lethal wound in the battlefield.

110 Now, because the Underworld was indeed below ground,
magma ran in tributary streams surrounding the isles
where the inmates' cells were located (in a manner of speech,
considering bars were not required to detain them;
their punishment already worked as their imprisonment).
115 Bridges made of solid rock connected the portions of terrain,
leading to the central isle, where the palace had been set;
the layout to this part of Tartarus was in many ways
similar to that of Atlantis, the city Poseidon was a patron of.
It was either too much of a coincidence, or straightforward
120 intentional, reminding the prisoners what kind of hubris
lay behind their own cathartic moments of evildoing.
The goddess of spring felt so deranged that she nearly fell

Persephone's Fall

  into the bottomless pit in which the magma kept falling,
  endlessly; the grounds of the palace were suspended
125 on top of the pit, avoiding contact with the waterfall
  from every single corner, preventing erosion, perhaps.

  In a flash, the goddess of the Moon, Hekate, showed
  by Persephone's side; she would have been scared to death,
  if such were possible, like with all the others in sight.
130 Demeter's friend was also the goddess of ghosts;
  spooking Persephone had not been so much of a surprise.
  The companion from above enounced these words,
  hinged with wings: 'Do not be afraid, child, it is I, Hekate.
  What are you doing out of the palace? Did Hades
135 show compassion for you and set you free?', to which
  the goddess of spring replied, while holding her heart
  in her chest: 'Oh!, I am ever so glad it is you, my friend.
  I thought the king himself had spotted me out here.
  No, he did not let me out, I escaped by myself; the door
140 to the bedroom I have been trapped in was left unlocked.
  I naturally suspected it was all his doing, some kind of test.
  So far, however, nothing has yet happened', she concluded.
  Hekate had been holding her while she eloquently spoke,
  then adding some more, as she stood: 'I wanted to see
145 what it was like, what kind of suffering all these people
  have to endure for eternity, hoping I could save some,
  help them get away from these fires and into Elysium'.
  The goddess of magic grabbed Persephone by the arms,
  gently, and spoke with caution: 'My young friend,
150 it is not only the gods or Hades himself who choose
  the sentencing these inmates are condemned to; coming here
  means what they perpetrated while living was nothing short
  of brutality, inflated with rage, a craving desire for revenge.
  Man is exactly so, unpredictable, though mistrust is often

155 mirrored in their eyes, disguised by greed and ambition,
the greatest of falsehoods the world has ever known.
Come, let me show you why some of these people
were denied perpetual peace in the Elysian Fields, where
both good men and women are found in abundance',
160 Hekate explained, taking a confused Persephone across
one of the connecting bridges, to where Ixion, former king
of the Lapiths, was bound to a spinning wheel in flames.

'Oh!, dear…', the goddess of rebirth exclaimed, nauseated.
The wheel's continuous loop, together with the heat,
165 formed an unbearable concoction of motion sickness,
which begs the question – if third-parties could easily
experience the feeling of regurgitation, then how sick
could the inmate be, rotating endlessly while burned?
Despite the inexistence of actual flesh, Ixion bore
170 exactly the same physiognomy as when he had lived.
Nonetheless, he never took a charred appearance;
instead, his skin kept regenerating (like Prometheus's liver),
only to be instantly reburned, thus inflicting constant pain.
His hair just set itself aflame, as if it were a candle wick,
175 while his eyes melted like beeswax, dripping on the ground.
Screaming for ages, he had gone hoarse long, long ago.

Horrified with the insurmountable scene of desolation,
Persephone questioned Hekate about Ixion's actions:
'What has this man done to deserve the unthinkable?!',
180 to which Hekate replied: 'he defied the bearer of the aegis'.
Kore felt repulsed, seconding her first question
with the following: 'Was that it? Zeus defies everyone
and everything, my mother and myself included;
such is my father figure, to my bitterly great misfortune…'.
185 The goddess of the Moon further explained: 'there is more

to it – before punishing Ixion, the thunderous god took pity,
which is rather rare, to the best of both our knowledge.
This former king of the most ancient tribe of Thessaly
was the first man to ever kill one of his own kin, even though
190 they were not related; Dia was the woman they shared –
a wife to Ixion, and a daughter to Deioneus, the victim.
The latter had been promised a good price for Dia's hand,
but Ixion did not keep his word, insulting his father-in-law.
Deioneus then took revenge and stole the king's horses.
195 He was deranged for having been duped, though he had been
the first to engage in the betrayal enterprise; nevertheless,
the son-in-law had already made his mind as how to ensnare
Deioneus, stacking yet another damning layer on his fate.
Ixion invited him to a feast in Larissa and pushed him
200 into smoldering coal and fire the moment he arrived'.

Attentively listening to Hekate while observing the burning
man, Persephone interrupted her friend, cathartically asking:
'Is that why this man was sentenced to being aflame...?'.
The goddess then addressed her these motherly words:
205 'Do not be so quick to feel sorry for him, dear child.
That was the moment Zeus intervened, looking to redeem
the criminal of his sins, for the neighboring princes refused
to perform cleansing rituals on him, who had violated xenia.
Ixion was thus ostracized, never to return to Thessaly.
210 Although killing one of your own is a horrendous crime,
the treacherous act soon wiped the cold-blooded killer
within him, driving him mad on account of his conduct.
As I was saying, the fatherly god came to him and invited
the outlaw to a feast in Olympus, introducing him
215 to the other gods (you and your mother were absent).
Instead of thanking the Olympians for their hospitality,
Ixion insulted the host by growing lust for his wife, Hera.

Eventually finding out about his intentions, Zeus picked
a cloud, Nephele, and gave it Hera's appearance, tricking
220 the guest into copulating with the goddess's double.
Although it was a cloud, from their union rose Centaurus,
founding father of the new breed known as Centaurs
(or Ixionidae), after mating with the mares of Mount Pelion.
Knowing the ways of males, Zeus was allowed to covet
225 other men's women, whereas Hera was forcibly only his.
Ixion was kicked out of Olympus and hit by a lightning bolt.
Immediately after, the thunderous god ordered Hermes
to tie the traitor to a spinning wheel set afire, miming
his burning desire; he stayed in the sky, at first,
230 but Zeus eventually grew tired of his screaming and remitted
him to the care of Hades, forever bound, forever burned
without trial, far away from either human or heavenly sight'.

Once Hekate was finished with the tale of treacherous Ixion,
Persephone tried staring at the prisoner, slowly gulping.
235 Though she was sure the punishment was rather harsh,
there was no way of denying kin-related homicide
(or any other kind, come to that), together with betrayal,
were inexcusable and, therefore, Ixion had earned his fate.
'Please, take me away from here, show me someone else,
240 I beg of you', Kore asked, nauseated, not only from the scene,
but also the background that had led to it in the first place.
The goddess of magic heeded her friend's request,
and helped her walk across yet another bridge lain over
the molten rock flowing back toward the palace.
245 Hekate thought she should show Persephone a less painful
punishment, though she knew Demeter's daughter
would still experience pain, one of a different sort,
directly related to what the Mistresses did above ground.
Both goddesses approached another small isle, where a man

250 stood in the middle of a pool with fresh water
around his waist, having a tree right in front of him;
its branches were garnished with fruit, and raising
an arm's length would be enough to grasp one of them.
Once they reached the edge, Tantalus, the inmate,
255 begged Persephone for water to drink and food to eat:
'You, there! Please…! Grab some of that fruit for me
and hold your hands in a conch with water, please!'.
The youngest of the Thesmophoroi felt confused
by the request, asking the former monarch: 'My good man,
260 the fruit is hanging just above your head and the water
surrounds you, why should you require my help…?',
to which Tantalus replied: 'Because of the witchcraft
I have been bedeviled with! The branches rise every time
I try to reach them, and the water drops when I kneel!
265 Here, watch closely', he said, piercing through Kore's heart.
It was true, the man tried reaching the fruit, but the tree
stood upright, reclining again only when he had lowered
his arm; afterward, he kneeled in order to have a sip of water,
but failed in doing so, for it nearly looked like the pool
270 was being emptied like one of the Danaids' tubs.

There was no possible comparison between Tantalus
and Ixion as far as punishments were concerned,
though Persephone felt horrified all the same by the weird
spell, exclaiming: 'I will give you fruit and water, come!'.
275 As soon as she stretched to reach the abundant branches,
the tree did not stand upright, but it did open a clearing
in its canopy, revealing an enormous piece of rock aligned
with Tantalus's head, hanging from a stronger branch.
Ceasing the attempt, the goddess pulled her arm back,
280 and the clearing was no more, hiding the rock again.
She then kneeled and tried to gather water in her hands,

granted the pool did not lower as before; nonetheless,
the concealed rock produced itself a second time,
threatening to freefall on the deposed king's head.
285 'What are you doing, you stupid woman?! I am already dead,
so what if that rock falls on me, what of it?! Go on!',
said Tantalus, exploding with rage before Kore's caution.

Hekate, who had stood still for the duration of the event,
promptly said: 'I would not advise it, Tantalus. You are dead
290 on earth; this is your afterlife, it goes on for eternity.
That is why you will forever experience hunger and thirst.
If you insist Persephone give you what you want, that rock
is bound to crush your skull repeatedly, poisoning this
fresh water with your filthy blood, thus killing the tree.
295 Your frustration would never cease, should you yield
to temptation; that is the price to pay for your crimes'.
As if trying to set Hekate's eyes alight, the man said,
gnashing: 'Sorceress…! Witch…! If only you died,
I would strangle you for eternity! Then you would suffer!'.
300 Persephone then asked the obvious question: 'Which crimes
were those?', as she stepped away from the madman's pool.
The goddess of magic bluntly stated: 'He maimed his son,
boiled him and served him as food to the gods, taking
advantage of the banquet to steal ambrosia and reveal
305 its secrets to his people; honestly, filicide and cannibalism
are far more gruesome than robbery, and yet, Tantalus
shows no regret for his actions, which brought him here'.

There was more to Hekate's words than those uttered,
but she did not want to shock Persephone with the truth.
310 Hades, however, who had been watching her every step,
decided to take shape by both goddesses' side, startling them.
Angrily facing the banned king, he revealed what Hekate

Persephone's Fall

had deliberately concealed: 'Thy mother inadvertently ate
Pelops's left shoulder, distraught as she was because of thy
315 absence; the others, though, found out about the plot in time
and did not dare eat any part of the young man's body.
Tantalus was immediately sent to Tartarus as punishment,
and Pelops was reassembled and revived, with an ivory
shoulder replacing the original, crafted by Hephaestus.
320 I personally made sure this obnoxious creature spent
his eternity looking for untamable satisfaction; dost thou
still think of me as a monster, or rather a fair referee?'.

Kore had put her hands in front of her mouth, remaining
speechless for the following moments, absolutely deranged.
325 Regardless of having been duly sentenced to the Underworld,
Tantalus had only succeeded in feeding Demeter a part
of his son's body because of the suffering she was riddled
with, after failing to locate Persephone's whereabouts.
If Hades had not gotten away with his selfishness, the eldest
330 of the Thesmophoroi surely would not have been duped.
The goddess of springtime felt split in both her mind
and heart, knowing not whether to appreciate or condemn.

Canto V

    All Councils of Gods were presided by the bearer of the aegis,
whose word was final in matters concerning the fate
of those under his direct rule; Zeus's power, however,
was not absolute, as it would have been usual to consider.
5 Clotho, Lachesis and Atropos, otherwise known as the Fates,
were autonomous deities, and though they paid their respects
to the almighty, the thread of life was ultimately woven
by them, especially as far as Mankind was concerned.
Nevertheless, should any god fall foul to any of the sisters,
10 they would have to pay the rightful price in some way
other than death, as per definition, gods do not die,
no matter the age they take in their human-like shape.

    Persephone's situation, of course, was quite different;
Hades was the one to blame for her rape, together with
15 tricking her into eating Underworld pomegranate seeds.
Still, it was the goddess's future that was at stake,
as innocent and unaware as she might have been,
digesting her misfortune, to the Screech Owl's pleasure.
He has already admitted himself it had not been
20 the best approach, adding he was not the monster
Kore had constructed in her mind, during her tenure
in Tartarus, but it was hard to believe his candor,
for his actions were exactly the opposite of his words,
and, if there is no reason to trust in the first place,
25 bandaging the wound becomes a great deal more difficult.

    In the Pantheon, Zeus, of course, had a seat at the center
of the hemicycle, binding both sides of the plenary.
To his left, there sat his wife and queen of deities, Hera,

followed by Phoebus Apollo, who had been forced
to abandon his golden chariot to heed the call, leaving it
to his four horses (Aethon, Pyrois, Phlegon, and Eous)
to pull it on their own; naturally, his twin sister Artemis
was next, having by her side Hermes, the divine messenger,
who was immediately seconded by Aphrodite, far away
from those who had both a legitimate and an illegitimate
claim to her, as they will soon be remembered, opposite.
Dionysos, the «insewn», was the one closing this side.

To Zeus's right, there sat Athena, born out of his head
fully grown, after having it cracked by Hephaestus
to let her out, next to whom there was Poseidon, sea master,
followed by Demeter herself, the reason for summoning
the council; the next seat, meant for Persephone, was empty.
Finally, Ares, the warmonger, sat beside Hephaestus,
which was humiliating to the both of them; Demeter
would not allow anyone to take Persephone's seat,
otherwise they could have been kept separate, without
risking another brawl between them, though I am sure
Zeus imposed enough respect and discipline to prevent it,
as Calliope has whispered it to this aoidos's ear just now.

The thunderous god, leaning on his right elbow, delivered
these words majestically, once everyone took their seat:
'I have summoned you all today to discuss important
business concerning Persephone, daughter of Demeter'.
Mouthing loud enough for all others to hear, the eldest
of the Thesmophoroi uttered the following statement:
'And of Zeus, lest we forget'; Hera pursed her lips
with rage, as the rest tried as much as they could
to conceal their smirk, whereas both Artemis and Athena
rolled their eyes to the Pantheon floor, not only embarrassed

for their sister, but also due to the contempt for chastity
that was implicit in their aunt's words and consequent laugh,
made worse when Aphrodite joined the males' party,
shaming all goddesses and women with her perversion.

Zeus slightly elevated his voice, so as to move on
from the provocation and silence the host, keeping
a straight face as he spoke: 'Hades raped her and is now
holding her captive in Tartarus, simultaneously refusing
to return her to her mother; Demeter, who, together
with Persephone, has the power to make the soil fecund
and keep Man alive by teaching him the secrets
of agriculture, has made it clear to me she will spread
famine and drought across the fields, if I do not take action'.

The queen of gods arrogantly intervened afterward,
looking the Mistress in the eye with hatred: 'And what
would she have you do, O mighty bearer of the aegis?
Extorting Father Zeus himself! How much further
do you dare go?', a question to which Demeter promptly
replied: 'How far would you dare go for your offspring,
sister? How far would any decent parent dare go to recover
their children? Have you any idea whatsoever of the pain
ravishing my heart every day, ever since our fiery brother
became a criminal to his own ilk, taking his own niece
for a prisoner in the world of the excommunicated?
Ah!, but of course you have not… you cast your own son
Hephaestus out of Olympus for limping and being too ugly!
What would you know about motherly love, then, sister?'.
Hera prepared to respond with fire from her eyes, but Zeus
took grasp of a lightning bolt and cast it in the center
of the Pantheon, angrily silencing the conflict: 'Quiet!
There will be no more foolish ruckus during this session.

90 I cannot persuade Demeter to change her mind; besides,
apart from Persephone, she is the only goddess among us
who maintains the humans alive and, so far, their cult
to each and every one of us has dramatically increased,
but there will come a time when all hope shall be lost,
95 and that is when we shall cease to exist as their rulers.
I did not recreate Man from those worthy of surviving
the flood so they could gratuitously perish collectively.
On the other hand, ordering Hades return Persephone
of his own accord will only provoke a conflict between
100 sky and underground, and I shall not have another war!
We have had our share of battles; let the men kill each other,
if they so desire, but we will have peace and live in harmony'.
Having finished his speech, the bearer of the aegis got up
from his seat and walked forward, to where the bolt had hit.
105 With his hands behind his back and his chin leaning
on his chest, covered by the massive beard, Zeus turned
to face the Olympians, surveying each of them with his gaze.

'Father', Athena called, dragging all eyes unto her.
The thunderous god felt relieved the most prized
110 of his children decided to speak, assured she would have
a rational plan that could be put into place without fuss.
'Ah!... my sage daughter intervenes; speak your mind, child',
Zeus said, as Demeter despised him for taking Athena only
to be the most intelligent of his children, disregarding Kore.
115 'Uncle Hades will surely resist leaving Tartarus to testify
for his crime, so, perhaps Hermes could be sent underground
to make a deal with him, offer him something in exchange'.
Hermes was getting ready to address his sister directly,
when the eldest of the Thesmophoroi added the catch:
120 'Hades has tricked my daughter into eating pomegranate
seeds, and, as you all know, anyone ingesting them

Persephone's Fall

in the Underworld has to stay there a month for each seed'.

Everyone soon began talking to each other, igniting
a small commotion among the gods, for the brilliance
125 of Hades, and the goddesses, for how cowardly he had
made sure there was no possible escape from his clutches,
except for Aphrodite, who considered the plan ingenious;
originally not an Olympian, she was the exact opposite
of Persephone, Athena, and Artemis, who had not taken
130 on their father's side, and gladly, as made clear in their mind.
Now, it was Artemis indeed, who had been with Persephone
in the dastardly moment, who put a stop to the bedlam,
outraged: 'This is your sister whose face you are laughing at!
Not all of you, obviously, but she is a sibling to the majority
135 of this council, and yet, there you are, boasting like swine.
Your manhood blinds you so that it does not matter
whether you take a woman against her will or not, as long
as you satisfy your brutish pleasures and leave no stone
unturned for a nice catch, regardless of who they are.
140 You are all repulsive and disgusting, including you,
«goddess of love»... you nurture no such thing as love.
Your son is very much unlike you, for he is the real
messenger of the heart, not you, the likes of a mistress'.
Shocked by the goddess of wilderness' insults, Aphrodite
145 prepared herself to respond, beginning with these words:
'Now just wait a minute...!', having been cut off
by Hephaestus: 'She does have a point, you know.
Your promiscuity turns everything you touch into tragedy;
it was insufficient for you to cheat your own husband,
150 so you made your lover here (meaning Ares) kill Adonis,
Persephone's greatest love, bluntly out of jealousy.
Who would have thought a lover could afford such a luxury?
No matter, the both of you paid for it dearly', he concluded.

The main subject of the council was becoming secondary;
155 so much so that Dionysos, who had been drinking nectar
the entire time, decided to randomly intervene nonsensically:
'A toast to that and evoe! We should all get stark nude
and throw a frenzy exactly the way I like it, so much fun!'.
Hera, who, as we know, was not his mother, made short
160 work of the young god's ridiculousness: 'Quiet, boy!
If you have nothing intelligent to offer, then refrain
from pathetically gagging and keep drinking silently'.
Shrugging his shoulders, the god of wine poured his cup
downward and inward, not caring at all for the matter.

165 Angrier by the minute, Demeter imposed authority herself,
without waiting for Zeus to do so, he who had never cared
for Kore in the first place and was only playing the part
of a concerned parent, in reality fearing his disappearance
among men for lack of hope, putting an end to his reign:
170 'Enough! I have heard and seen enough of this bestiality.
I want my daughter back and that is the only way Mankind
has a chance of survival, so you had better make haste,
brother, and summon the Fates; they alone can put an end
to Hades's depravity, it is their prophecy, not yours'.
175 Rubicund because of an apparent lack of authority,
Zeus was quick to reply, unhinged: 'That may be so,
O goddess of disgrace, but I still get to make the calls
in my own council, as I do not recall giving that up!'.
The queen of gods was most certainly bored with
180 the matter entirely, the reason why she begged of
her consort: 'O thunderous Father, please withhold
the tempestuous temperament of your aching pride
and send for the sisters, so we may get over and done
with all of this, for both the sake of Man and ours'.

Persephone's Fall

185 Uneasily coerced to yield, Zeus did think his wife's
words wise, and with a confirming nod directed
at Hermes, the message was conveyed to bring in
the three Moirai; the messenger of gods quickly changed
his footwear to his pair of talaria – winged sandals
190 made of gold, designed and created by Hephaestus,
and swiftly flew across the clouds to bring back with him
the three white-robed elder goddesses for their testimonial.

During the few minutes that followed, perhaps another
aoidos would have most attentively listened to the Muse
195 commanding his verse, whispering unto his ear
what might have happened during the time they waited,
the gods up above, in the Pantheon; however, nothing
worth noting took place, apart from the continued
drinking and eating, of which Demeter shared neither
200 a sip or bite, anxious as she was for the sisters' verdict.
Although Atropos could not sever Persephone's life thread,
she was indeed the most inflexible of the trio, surely
making it difficult to change the course of these events,
but maybe if Clotho and Lachesis could be empathized with,
205 they might just reach a final decision that could appease
the motherly pain of the eldest of the Thesmophoroi.
Indeed, sometimes silence does become a better companion
than the loud rumbling of the usual petty side-conferencing,
useful only to fill in the space left hollow by the heroic verse.
210 In just under three minutes, measured by Khronos,
the father of time (and not the king of Titans, or so
we are led to believe), Hermes returned to Olympus
with the elder entities, to whom the gods also subjected.
'O powerful Zeus, I bring unto your presence the Moirai',
215 the messenger of gods said, taking his seat once more,
leaving the three sisters in the center of the hemicycle.

Truth be told, they looked dreadful, in that aged format;
only the white they wore made them look immaculate,
somehow, though it was undeniably difficult to take them
seriously, when they had only one eyeball to share.
All three had sockets in their rightful place, though hollow,
similar to two wide and hairy nostrils bearing an empty gaze.

'Clotho, Lachesis, Atropos – you who sit the closest
to my throne in divine hierarchy, hearken my plea,
for Mankind's fate rests upon your shoulders, as always,
risking an overall elimination from the face of this earth,
should Demeter's will to spread chaos be carried off,
unless Kore is returned to her by the end of this council'.
As Zeus spoke, the one eye, tailed by its optic nerve,
gently floated in front of the sisters, looking sideways
at each and every one of the Olympic gods in the assembly,
studying them, making sure the thread of their immortality
did not contain any loose ends or knots as it was woven.

Once the thunderous god mentioned Persephone's name
in the presence of the council's guests, the floating eyeball
steadily gazed at the goddess of harvest, who was startled
by the bloodshot organ's sudden interruption; the ogling
was even scarier because it did not blink, as it lacked lids.
Slowly waving, the eye's optic nerve became sharp
and flew to the likes of an arrow into one of Clotho's orbits,
one-sidedly rebinding the optic tract through the chiasma.
She was the first to answer Zeus, though facing Demeter:
'O mighty father of the skies, we know only too well
why you have summoned the three of us to the light
of your heavenly horde and reason, by Phoebus illuminated
and by Pallas assisted, though much too clouded in grief
by the mother of that whom was unrightfully taken'.

Persephone's Fall

The trio kept walking toward the goddess of harvest,
and above the clouds of Olympus was formed another layer,
250 darkening the power of Apollo's natural lighting;
this was yet another understatement proving just how
powerful the Moirai were, dimming the Sun itself
to their will, toward an eerie scenery the Pantheon
was hardly ever used to, always atop the sobbing
255 pockets of tears that could either bless the grounds
with harvests, or doom them altogether in a rotting flood.

Lachesis made use of her turn to speak, retrieving the eye
with a sleight of hand, magically wielding it herself,
literally taking a closer look from her point of view,
260 pushing Demeter further into a nerve-racking tremble:
'Fear not, O goddess of nature, for not all is lost;
Persephone's thread might be endless as an immortal,
but that which she has been enduring for half a year
will find its closure soon enough – such is our prophecy'.
265 Hopefully, the goddess asked of the seers: 'Will Kore
come back to me, then? Definitely? Will Hades let go?',
a question that found its answer in the voice of Atropos,
who, in a flash, retrieved the all-seeing eye for herself,
gazing attentively at the eldest of the Thesmophoroi:
270 'A word of caution must be given before your expectations
rise higher than they should – Hades will continue to have
power over your daughter, and never in the remainder
of eternity will she return to you completely; the warden
of Inferno has been given the right to keep Persephone
275 by his side for six months precisely, whereas the other half
is for you to enjoy in her company (should have she eaten
more than six pomegranate seeds, the longer the dark lord
would have been able to hold on to her, perhaps the entirety
of Phoebus's revolution around this convicted earth).

280 Come the following equinox, your cub will have returned
from the depths of the dead and back to the living world'.
Having spoken all three at last, they simultaneously
disappeared in black smoke, though Apollo was allowed
once more to cast his rays of light across the dark mark,
285 clearing any evidence the prophetic sisters had been there,
in the parliament of gods, watched over by justice in the form
of Themis, holding the scale in the Libra constellation,
assisted in purity by the aforementioned Astraea, of Virgo.

The council remained silent until the smoke vanished,
290 giving Zeus the appropriate cue to utter his final verdict:
'Well, then, everyone here has heard them clearly –
Persephone is to spend half a year with you, Demeter,
and your turn will have finally come in a matter of days;
in the meantime, Hermes shall convey Hades his warning,
295 so as to be prepared to hand Kore over back again.
Make sure, sister, your end of the deal is honored
and feed Mankind, before my creation is brought down
to dust; it will not take long before they begin slaughtering
each other as tribute to us, and I do enjoy a good war myself,
300 but only for sheer sport, not because I wanted to strip
this earth out of all its living creatures, the most formidable
of which being those made to our very own image'.

The goddess of harvest was still petrified from the fate
the Moirai themselves had attributed her captive daughter.
305 Her palms rested on her knees, bound together as one,
while her head pended from the neck, bent to her chest.
In a tremor, she uttered these somewhat unhinged words:
'I did not expect I would have to share Kore with Hades...
never in all my eternity had I foreseen such a tragic display;
310 I cannot even bear to think about it – six full months

Persephone's Fall

forcibly out of my sight and straight into the hands
of the infernal wretch, guardian of death and pestilence.

Moved by both her aunt's speech and empty eyesight,
Athena approached Demeter and tried to enunciate
315 a few honeyed, comforting words: 'We cannot change
the prophecies, dear Mother, especially those of the Fates',
but it is possible to make the best out of what is given;
half a year is too long a time to withstand, naturally,
and yet... perhaps what we think to be Kore's doom
320 and imprisonment might just become her freedom.
It is so often we mistakenly believe our liberty is self-made,
confusing a free spirit with a soul trapped in loneliness.
There might just be, in what seems like agony and pain,
that deliverance we had always been waiting for;
325 it does not mean it is bad because it comes from a stranger...
sometimes, the best events of our lives take place and shape
from the most surprising of hearts, and maybe Hades
deserves just that, a chance to reveal his true self,
perhaps not so diabolical as some of us picture him'.
330 That was the effect Athena had over those she spoke to;
her eloquence was so definitely unquestionable that many
often stared at her, delighted by her line of thought,
put into the softest of tones and most significant wording.
She had both the charisma and persuasion required to make
335 one change one's mind and feel warmly tucked in oneself.
It was her intelligence and sensitivity that made Zeus proud,
more than any other of his children, no matter how gifted.

The goddess of bread felt like in a trance, just by looking
Pallas in the eye, softly moving her gaze toward observant
340 Zeus, finally engaging the messenger of gods, Hermes,
to depart immediately toward the Underworld, carrying

Tiago Lameiras

with him the orders of the thunderous god, father of skies.

Canto VI

    O Muse of epic tales from hearsay by the aoidos told,
    penned down by the poet to an insufferable demise bound,
    I beg of you to carry on and ladle unto my spirit the nectar
    of versified prose, so I may proceed, in a wordsmith's loom,
5 with the telling of Persephone's story, woven to the Fates'
    wishes, final and unnegotiable, though perhaps worthy
    of finding solace amid all the horror into her face inscribed,
    in the shape of wrinkly contours, aging her without ever
    having to do so, for she will never know what it is to be
10 trapped in a deathbed, struggling to speak before Hades
    welcomes us to his underground realm, still hoping
    to be sent to the Elysian Fields, after wasting an entire life
    in pursuit of glory… at the cost of wrath's good measure,
    pointing out the heir to a formidable empire, eventually split
15 between sons and comrades; but I must restrain my tongue,
    for it is not yet the time of iron, rather of bronze and heroism.

    The purity of Kore's heart disabled her from the fantasy
    she was used to witness on earth, where the greenness
    of her home, by her mother's side, kept the atrocities
20 of Humanity well concealed, until the day Hades's love
    inadvertently decided it was time to reveal the ugly truth
    about the reality of Mankind, which could only be tamed
    by the gods, regardless of being wrong or right, though
    Persephone eventually accepted the Screech Owl's task
25 as a necessity, especially after learning humans could kill
    their own children and feed them to others, including
    her poor, distraught mother, ever so wrongly deceived.
    Hekate, the goddess of moonlight, kept her company
    and, sharing Athena's wisdom, recommended she try to get

30 to know Hades better, understand his reasons, secluded
as he was from Helios, having his face constantly rubbed
in ash from the fiery doom he had agreed to look after.

Why had he chosen the path of solitude, why had he parted
from his own kind, living like a recluse he was to surveil?
35 Poseidon had the seas and oceans to rule, yet he did not
wander astray from his divine family; indeed, his dark gowns
suited him best, for, as I have sung, he was the black sheep,
but not in the commonplace sense of the phrasing, of course.
Living as the god he was did not mean everything to him,
40 if he could not fulfill his life to the likes of fullhearted men.
He had already found the purpose he so anxiously sought,
only he knew not, however, what to make of her (not «it»).
Six months had gone by and none of his dedication ever
pleased Persephone... it seems like only yesterday I spoke
45 Calliope's words, saying love can never be a transaction.
Collect as many sovereigns as one may, one will not have
acquired the other's affection; should it be so, love would
have to stand out of the formula, ceding its place to greed.
The young Mistress's heart was far too pure to give up
50 on her principles and become collected based on shallowness.
The greyish lord had seen someone much different than that,
a woman so common and dishonorable as a courtesan
and her demeaning trade, no – there was nothing as such
about Kore; Hades was used to reading people's auras,
55 and the maiden's was clear as the crystal water she had been
in front of at Pergoussa Lake, before it was parted in two
halves, ganging way for the golden chariot of Inferno to pass.
They would soon be interrupted by Hermes's convoy, though
neither was aware of it; whatever it was they wished to say
60 to each other, it had better be done quickly, no punch pulled.
Ever since that day the youngest of the Thesmophoroi

tried to help other Tartarus prisoners while seeking revenge
for having been taken herself an inadvertent recluse,
Hekate's presence had become more than welcome
in what was to be her friend's new home for half the year.
Knowing Demeter was busy enough as it was persuading
Zeus to intervene on the matter of Persephone's rape,
the goddess of moonlight's ascendance to the living world
was kept at a minimum; all she had left was order the Moon
to rise after twilight and set before rosy-fingered Dawn.
The predominant green once seen across the fields had yet
to show itself again, as mother and daughter kept apart.
Everyone who saw it found the scene desolating, but Hekate
sought comfort for herself in comforting the young Mistress;
they only had each other, and Hades eventually considered
that isolating the woman he had the most affection for
would merely continue to contribute to the decaying
of a relationship that had not even existed between them.
It had taken its toll and time, but the Screech Owl
knew he would never be loved back if he did not grant
Persephone the freedom she ever so anxiously longed for;
she was a free spirit herself, so… how could someone
like that be contained and why should another do it?
If Hades wanted to grow on Kore, her wishes should be met.

'You should go and talk to him, child', Hekate suggested,
now that Persephone was free to roam around the palace
whenever she wanted and could easily find the Underworld
Lord in one room or another, if not on the grounds,
though Hades himself discouraged approaching the inmates,
not only for her safety, but also to spare her from witnessing
their horrid, sordid fate all the time, regardless of how fairly
the sentence applied had been delivered to said convicts.
'Me…? Why should I be the one to take the first step?',

the maiden asked, mistily contracting her eyebrows.
95 'He has tried doing it himself', the goddess of moonlight
noticed, 'but you continuously deny him the chance…'.

Persephone rose from the bedstead where both deities sat,
in the room she somewhat still felt enslaved to, despite
the «Hadean Spring» the master of death had begun to show.
100 As she wandered her starry eyes across the great feast
she was always provided with, together with all the jewelry
that sat in place and had never been worn, the goddess
held both hands in front of her, as her arms leaned against
her bosom, whose contours became improvingly defined
105 by the himation covering her naturally sculptured body,
having no other garment underneath, such as the usual
chiton or peplos, a bit more customary with mortal folk.
Kore's beauty strove beyond imagination, though Calliope
keeps reminding me it is not up to me to talk about it,
110 as much as I may wish to fiddle the kithara to which I sing
these verses, uncanny to those who have never known love.

Lost in her thoughts, the maiden finally faced Hekate again,
saying: 'He was utterly vile when he snatched me from
the shore where I was painting my flowers, taking my body
115 like that of a mistress, a common courtesan flaunting
her skills with swine… if there is indeed chivalry within,
he must be the one to prove it, not I', she concluded.
'Then again', the Moon's deity replied, 'a young woman
such as yourself must not indefinitely dwell in her pride.
120 In order to wield, one must also know when to yield.
As right as you may be to feel anger toward Hades,
he has been trying to prove to you who lurks inside.
The door to his inner self has been open; hold it for him'.
Persephone was rendered disarmed, actively gazing

125 Hekate, focusing on her face's several features,
as if her sight were in a twitch, unstoppable, restless.
That is often considered to be the sign of a coherent
cognitive process, unlike the dullness of slow eyes.
In short, the youngest of the Thesmophoroi had already
130 taken that possibility into account, that she should not
give up her goodwill, seeking to reason with her uncle.
'I guess you are right, my dearest friend… I shall do
as you say and speak to Hades myself; out of the pair
of us, one must overcome the other's lack of judgment',
135 Persephone decided, as she walked out the bedroom door,
heading straight down to the entrance hall to the palace,
where she thought it was most likely for him to be, though
she was really not aware of his routine, what he did,
or the places he would wander about in that endless
140 underground realm whose limits no one has yet been told.

As she descended the grand staircase, grander at every step
from top to bottom, the maiden realized there was nobody
in sight, even though there was, of course, plenty to see.
The most intriguing of all the artful objects Persephone
145 had come across with before, when she first attempted
her escape (or a revolt from other prisoners, at least),
was still the covered statue, considering all other things
were plain visible; why anyone living on his own would
want to collect that many items was beyond comprehension.
150 Could it be that the Screech Owl was a kleptomaniac,
collecting just about everything he could find to suppress
his sentiments of loneliness, therefore defying said concept?
One may only wonder – there is no telling for certain;
one must always consider every possibility and avoid
155 being quick to judge (that is a lesson one hopes to learn
rather sooner than later, as bitterness can be unpleasant).

Besides, he had a pet, though Kore was unaware of it,
given the fact she had entered the Realm of the Dead
through an unusual passage that required no guardian.

160 Unable to restrain her curiosity, the goddess of rebirth
approached the hooded object and uncloaked it by untying
the loose knots that barely covered the sculpture's plinth.
As she pulled the piece of cloth, it came floating down
like a silk shroud, uncovering a most remarkably carved
165 figure Kore had only seen in the clear waters of Pergoussa,
her own reflection, though unaffected by the wind's ripples
on the surface – no, this was the finest marble there was,
and she had been so beautifully sculptured that she could not
hold in a gasp of surprise and amazement, though naturally
170 she did not fall in love with herself, unlike poor Narcissus,
tainting his handsome appearance with his own blood,
to Echo's eternal unhappiness and Nemesis's dark pleasure.
A golden plaque embroidered in the base of the statue read:
«Persephone, daughter of Nature, mother to Man, sunlight
175 to the King of Tartarus, unbound from darkness at last».

It was Hades himself who came in through the main doors,
determined to take a break from his duties as the warden
of the afterlife prison, halting only a few steps beyond
the entrance, after his eyes caught the splendid sight of Kore.
180 The maiden was so distracted by the enchantment
of her masterpiece portrayal, that she did not notice him.
The Screech Owl did not know what to do, exactly,
whether to step back toward the grounds he had just left,
or to make Persephone aware of his presence, but gently;
185 scaring her was the last thing he wanted, taken awkwardness
had already raddled his approach to her with enough failure.
And so it was the greyish god put his hands behind his back,

looked aside and cleared his throat, announcing himself.
The goddess of rebirth gasped, only this time she felt fright,
190 as opposed to the feeling of awe that had bewitched her
not many moments before, when revealing the sculpture.

Persephone was prepared to run away, when Hades asked:
'Please! Wait, I beg of thee, do not flee, I mean no harm…
I just thought thou shouldst know I was here, otherwise
195 it is likely thy thoughts of me would become even grimmer
for ogling thee from afar, quietly, just like the ferocious lion
carefully watches its prey, attacking it through the marsh'.
Kore stood her ground and tried not to seem petrified,
hoping to avoid relaying any possible signs of weakness,
200 categorically replying like so: 'Well, that is precisely what
one would think, considering one's history with thee…
imprisonment, isolation… seeking to buy my affections
with feasts and jewelry, none of which I ever asked for.
Then again, this artwork I had not yet seen… it was covered,
205 so I naturally did not wander about for too long, fearing
I would ignite thy wrath by prying into thy privacy'.
The Screech Owl was quick to respond to the allegation:
'No! Thou couldst never set me alight, and most certainly
not because of thy unwrapping of a gift I built for thee'.
210 The expression of surprise on Persephone's face led him
to start walking toward her, slowly dimming their distance.
Her will to step back and start running to her bedroom,
which was the only place she felt safe in within Tartarus,
also seemed to vanish; whether it was a conscious action…
215 perhaps the wisdom of the goddess of the Moon had struck,
maybe the youngest of the Thesmophoroi was beginning to
not only give Hades a chance, but more importantly, herself.

'For… for me? Thou hast sculptured this statue for me…?',

Persephone asked, astonished, a question to which the ruler
of the dead replied like so: 'Yes, it is thine… is thy face not
well portrayed? Dost thou think thou art misrepresented?'.
Hades began to worry he had done a poor job, to both
their dissatisfaction, though his was clearly at a larger scale.
Kore was quick to comfort the god who had taken her
by force, only to reveal the best she had inside her heart:
'No, no, no! Not at all! I am simply… speechless and in awe.
I can see how much thou gavest of thyself in every detail…
the amount of dedication herein is undeniably commendable.
I never imagined thou hath the delicate hand required
to produce a beautiful and noble work of art such as this'.

The Dark Lord's restlessness went as fast as it had shown,
giving Persephone the opportunity of looking at his smile
for the very first time in an equinox and a solstice combined.
There was nothing evil about it; on the contrary, the relief
he displayed across his face comforted the maiden's spirit,
progressively making her lower her guard against Hades.
'Nevertheless, it is not yet completed', he enounced,
extending both his arms and hands, as he lifted the statue
just enough to avoid friction with and dragging on the floor.
It seemed to weigh no more than an ostrich's feather,
fitting the quadrangular recess in which it was meant
to be placed, right in the center of the palace's grand hall.
All there was left to do before lodging it into the ground
was turn it to the left by ninety degrees, so it would face
the entrance, making Hades's home not only his, but Kore's,
to whoever in eternity could feel welcome to marvel
at the exquisite masterpiece, crowning Persephone
as Queen of the Underworld and Princess of Mankind.
The Screech Owl ended his inaudible incantation
and smoothly set the sculpture in stone, never to be removed

Persephone's Fall

from its rightful place, making a parallel between his home
and his heart, vesting Kore as the sole guardian of both.
'Dost thou mind I address thee in a more informal manner
of speech, Milady? With all due respect, most certainly',
255 Hades quickly added, to whom Persephone nodded lightly.
'I do not mean at all to be disrespectful toward you,
my young dove, who carries an untainted spirit within...
the day I first saw you, the same on which I brought you
here, I immediately memorized your physical features.
260 I give you my word as I have never eavesdropped by the door
to your bedroom or tried to look through it to my delight.
You simply struck me, for lack of a better word; your imprint
became distinct in my judgment, and from thereon I knew...
no other could complete my heart the way you did without
265 ever even taking a glance at me and how dark I must seem'.

Persephone felt unable to withdraw and kept listening
attentively: 'The rather pleasant summer breeze whispered
through your hair, absorbing Helios' sunrays and therefore
changing color, from a somewhat dark brunette to a fairer
270 shade, one no other woman could share, for you are unique;
its tips kept sliding on your naked shoulder, tickling it
as you tickled your flowers with a precise lick of paint
from your brush, coloring them ever so vividly in tones
I did not know, incarcerated as I am in this cave of doom...
275 I could sense the softness of your skin throughout the whole
of your body, needless to undress you in my imagination.
And then... then I saw your face, the sweetest, most candid
expression confirmed by the Oneiroi, as you already know;
a shining smile, not just with your lips and teeth – above all,
280 it was the eyes, like two emeralds retrieved from Poseidon's
domain, nurtured with the love of Nature, entrusting you
with her lifelong cycle, treasuring you for your brilliance at

taking care of every living being she created, from ladybugs
to eagles, from rivers to seas, from twigs to trees, from dirt
to mountains, amid which gods made their ethereal homes'.

His discourse was addressed to Persephone, naturally,
though he kept looking at the eyes on the statue's face,
as it was an exact copy of the original, but larger than life.
When Hades stopped weaving Kore's beauty in words,
the exact opposite plunged into the ambience, but not eerily,
no – silence simply occurred because it felt appropriate.
Regardless of how entrancing words may be, carefully select,
pauses become a necessity, filling the sonorous void with
what speech is unable to provide... spiritual completeness.
In that time (which perhaps to our fortune I cannot measure),
the maiden was incapable of withdrawing her sight from
the Screech Owl, the ruler of Tartarus, master of the dead,
her incredibly swift assailant, now blessed with inexplicable
gallantry, which either he failed to show sooner, or she
did not allow herself to see, though she cannot be at fault.
At last, their eyes met, and neither knew what to do then.
Although personally I would have liked to cut this scene
at this exact point, perhaps slowly fading to a private
sort of darkness, away from the curious, jealous eye,
one that cannot help but pry into damaged souls,
seeking their subsequent destruction from which to gain
a sordid-like sort of satisfaction, there is yet one last thing
to do before Helios can return to the skies, marking
the beginning of the equinox – sever a bond that has only
just now been tied for the very first time in six months.

Outside, the sound of flapping talaria echoed into the hall,
flagging an entrance; Persephone broke her eye contact
with Hades, bedazzled by Hermes' sudden appearance.

Persephone's Fall

It is astounding to think that all Kore had wanted for so long
315　was to be delivered from that devilish site and, when her wish
finally came true, she no longer knew how to react, despite
having imagined she would definitely jump with joy.
Even though that was not the case, a glint in her irises
did not go unnoticed by the Dark Lord, his eyes sparkling
320　as well, but because of the tears gradually cascading down
his cheekbones... he knew who it was, pacing toward them.
And because he knew, he felt happy for the young maiden,
as well as distraught, not only for him, but rather for both.
The steps in the corridor became less reverbed and flatter,
325　each of them marking the proximity of the grand finale.
Hades smirked, a sad smile warped by the conflict of two
opposite emotions: self-deprecation and altruistic happiness.

'Uncle Hades', Hermes began, when coming to a stop,
'I am here on Zeus' orders to...' – without facing him,
330　still admiring Persephone's candid expression, the ruler
of Tartarus lifted his hand to halt the divine messenger.
'I know why you are here; it is the daughter of Demeter
you must inform of the good news you have brought'.
The goddess of spring was beyond confused, frantically
335　moving her sight between the two male divinities, when
she was at last able to articulate the following words:
'What is it? What good news? Why are you here, Hermes?'.
The visiting god thus spoke directly to Kore, ignoring Hades:
'I have come to take you with me and back to your mother.
340　The Moirai have pronounced themselves, meaning the six
pomegranate seeds you ingested when you first got here
are worth a month each; because you have been underground
for half a year, now, you have the right to return to the world
above (and Olympus, if you like), granted you must come
345　back here, once you have spent the other half of the year

with Demeter – that is your new cycle of immortality,
and not even Zeus has the power to amend it, as you know.
In fact, he merely confirmed the Fates' inevitable verdict'.

Needless to say, Persephone shed tears because of the news
350 she had waited to hear for so long, reunited once more
with the goddess of fertility, curiously supported by Zeus,
though the maiden did not know what his concerns had
actually been about, as the Council of Gods revealed.
She felt like holding her brother, but the input was soon aft;
355 it would have been, perhaps, inappropriate, considering
divine incest was not exactly a reason to be worried about.
Yet again, Kore wears no masks, and shows Hades respect,
not only because she is still in his house, but also because
she would not lightly touch a male figure, whoever he was;
360 that was a condition she shared with her sisters, Pallas
and Artemis, witnesses to the surprise attack at Pergoussa,
the maiden's first contact with a man, ceding wrist and waist.
The youngest of the Thesmophoroi glanced at the culprit,
knowing not what to say to him, most likely because
365 she was unresponsive to herself, clueless as to a reaction.
However, Hades made haste in comforting her, slowly
closing his eyes, nodding and opening them back again,
as if he were stating it was all right, that the time had come.
Keeping his promise that not one finger with be laid on her,
370 the Screech Owl kept his hands crossed behind his back,
thinking whether he should confess it all and say he had
fed her the seeds deliberately, just so she would be forced
to stay in the Underworld, but, after a short internal debate,
he decided not to spoil his love's joy with further agony.

375 The messenger of gods extended his arm and showed Kore
the path that would take her back to the light of Phoebus,

and she started walking down the hall by his side, often
looking back at the Dark Lord, who made his every effort
to conceal the sadness of his weak smile, as his most
380 valuable treasure walked away, even though he knew
part of her had latched itself into his heart, never leaving,
and always coming back in the timeliest of fashions.

Before the flight of her deliverance, he called for Persephone
in one of the moments she was facing forward, making her
385 turn her head back immediately, uttering with sorrow:
'I hope one day you can forgive me', as he waved goodbye.
Unsure if she had understood his statement fully, Hades
saw his life fly in the distance, toward the upper world.
When he realized no one else was nearby, he broke down
390 at the statue's feet, unaware Hekate still stood upstairs,
bearing witness to the good there was inside his heart.

Spring

Canto VII

The waters of Pergoussa Lake, in Enna, were frozen solid.
The same surface that had once mirrored the blue sky
indefinitely was now covered with a thick layer of ice,
as if blocking an exit shut, one through which a relic
had disappeared beyond the bottom, assumed to be lost,
perhaps forever irretrievable, damning Man to a sordidly
painful death – burned alive, not by heat, but rather frost,
their bodies held in place, holding on to spread as much
warmth as possible to the entire family, starved to the bone.
Notos alone was incapable of fighting off his three brothers,
cruelly extinguishing whichever flame dared to rise and,
therefore, not even Aeolos could stop them, should Demeter
cease to interfere ever again in keeping human sustenance.

I would have to say that, considering humans' resemblance
to the Olympic deities, the cognitive process itself
was similar, which is to utter quite simply that hope
hardly ever dies, though as grim as the scenario may seem.
It is precisely that necessity to change our own fate
(regardless of what the Moirai may have already woven)
that compels us to move on, therefore creating our luck,
and just as men, women and children kept praying
the gods would continue to offer them their most treasured
gift, life itself, so did the eldest of the Thesmophoroi
manage to grow a streak of positivity, because she had
refused to give up on her daughter, who meant everything
to her, and so persistence would eventually have to pay off.

The Lady of the Golden Sword gazed at the body of ice
with an apparent emptiness in her eyes, wishing she could

tear a hole in the ground and fetch her daughter herself.
30 Alas, and despite being divine, Demeter had no such power;
the only Olympian allowed to traverse between worlds
was Hermes, as he was the messenger of gods and had
free passage, especially via his sandals, hinged with wings.
The remainder of the Pantheon was limited to two domains,
35 which were either sky and sea, earth and sky, or earth
and underground, granted Hades fit the latter category,
whereas Poseidon fit the first; the majority of gods
and goddesses fit the middle, and that is how precise
the distribution of realms had been, once the Titanomachy
40 was over, albeit they all risked overstepping the borders.
Of course, there was the volcanic direct access to Tartarus
through Mount Aitne, though it was impractical, as lava
was impenetrable; before the trespasser could dive in,
their body would have already been burned away
45 and only the ulterior self would be able to move on,
disrupting the initial purpose of trying to break in alive
and coming back out again unharmed to tell the tale.

Immortality did not make a good enough persuasive
method to risk traversing domains, confident one
50 would not be scarred, for if Hephaestus suffered physically
with his limping, unable to walk straight in a divine pose,
getting burned for eternity was not something to look
forward to, which was why Demeter, having descended
the marble stairway leading up to Olympus, yet again
55 restrained herself from plunging into the volcano's gut
and from making any rash decisions that could cost dearly.

Having turned her back on the lake, the deity of agriculture
walked into Hekate's cave, taking refuge and holding on,
waiting for her own seed to be reaped from the soil

60 the Judge of Death himself had obnoxiously sown her into.
    It is yet too early to think about what she would say,
    once Kore confessed her mother Hades had grown on her
    for some inexplicable reason beyond comprehension,
    but it is possible Khronos will indulge us when we least
65 expect it, for good news usually travels faster at a time
    no one is looking for it; trials and labors must overcome
    be, for us to acknowledge the importance of light over
    darkness, as without the latter, the first would be forgotten
    or even taken for granted, like so many of us are, to both
70 our misfortune and others', though it may take time
    for them to realize how big a loss they have suffered,
    perhaps even greater than what our perspective points out;
    depending on how attached one is to one's care for the other,
    one eventually concludes there really is not a victor.

75 Halfway into shelter from an unprecedented snowstorm
    she had created herself, blocking her nephew's golden
    crossing in the sky above from shedding warmth and light,
    Demeter heard a powerful impact outside, as if a solid
    barrier was being brought down by an army of Achaeans,
80 led by heroes such as Ithaca's king, Odysseus, Agamemnon,
    ruler of Mycenae, or Achilles, monarch to the Myrmidons.
    The thumping grew stronger, eventually leading the Mistress
    back out again, hoping her prayers had been heard at last.
    Although the eldest of the Thesmophoroi was divine
85 herself, she still felt like a much more ulterior force than
    the Zeus-led Pantheon existed, an entity to whom gods
    turned to in moments of requirement, and she was right;
    Elpis, the personification of hope, greater than divinity,
    stood by her, holding her abundance-spewing cornucopia.
90 Walking on her bare feet back to the cave's mouth,
    where snow had begun to accumulate, nearly avalanching

into Hekate's personal recess built into the rockface,
the goddess of harvest climbed the six-month elevation
like some sort of a ramp too difficult to get a grip of,
tripping every now and then to a quadrupedal position,
dragging her body with a great deal of effort, so as to
reduce the friction between her skin and the albescent
surface; she could have morphed into any snow-prepared
animal, such as the swift fox, the long-range jumping hare,
or perhaps a corporeal bear, far more resistant to a blizzard,
all of which had been naturally gifted with camouflaging
abilities, but the Lady of the Golden Sword chose not to,
for she felt as human as can be, literally pulling herself
onward, as the rhythm of the thumping grew stronger
and persistent, as much as the heart trying to burst through
her ribcage, wishing to be set free at all costs, no matter what.

Just in time, Demeter saw a crack beginning to take shape
in the center of the lake, although unclear, as she kept heavily
breathing with expectation, as though as if all her doubts,
all her anxiety, all her rage, were about to be cleared.
The goddess of human sustenance ran as much as she could,
reaching at last the border between snow and ice, where
Persephone's painted flowers had once bloomed in grace
throughout days of endless sunshine, their dirt bathed
by the clear water, like an oasis set in the very epicenter
of a Mediterranean paradise – enchanting Trinacria, no less.

Underneath the gapped surface, a tone of scarlet bubbled
through the soil, which became erect to form a boiling cone,
swiftly bursting through the ice cap, melting it like butter
to comb one's hair, glistening under Phoebus's regent.
The eldest of the Thesmophoroi was projected backward,
as a fountain of lava started spilling, sliding down toward

the base of the newborn volcano; molten rock projectiles
were thrown across the lake, whose area and depth neared
two thousand plethra and less than a hamma, respectively.
The surrounding trees, dressed in pure white, soon became
afire, resembling torches appropriately made to the size
of the Cyclopes, the giant, fabled creatures no human
had ever seen, though we know Zeus had an important
role in their freedom, which confirms their existence indeed.

Dark and intoxicating smoke started to spread, as the ashes
fell on the snowy plain, poking holes across the frozen layer.
It looked in fact as if that quiet area had become a battlefield,
where a group of concealed archers kept loosing their bows,
setting the tip of their arrows in lit petroleum, spreading
the scorching scene; such was Tartarus' self-introduction
to the earthly world, a great deal more explosive than when
Hades had ridden his chariot through, six months before.
The great balls of lava spewed from the volcano's mouth
penetrated the thick layer covering the lake, letting its waters
breathe at last, though the temperature shock eventually
solidified them, causing the underworldly debris to hit
the ground, to the likes of boulders catapulted as warfare.

Encapsulated and therefore unharmed by the fiery fluid,
Hermes came out of the mountainous structure, safely
holding Persephone against his chest, thus fulfilling
his mission to both the Pantheon and the distraught mother.
As they both safely landed by the shore, with the help
of the messenger's talaria, the pinnacle of mass destruction
immediately receded, collapsing on itself beneath the surface,
mystically pulled back to the ground like a thread attached
to the eye of a needle, one that not even the gods could see,
for Gaia, a primordial deity, mother of Ouranos (the sky),

from whose copulation she bore the Titans, the Giants,
and Pontos, the sea, was Mother Earth, capable of sewing
her own seams; part of her legacy had been passed down
to both her grand and great-granddaughter, the Mistresses.
The final residue released by the small-scale volcano was left
spilled all over the ice, which either melted or drew water
over untouched spots at the surface, making it transparent.
As for the trees that had caught fire, they looked as though
they were crying while the flames consumed them, liquifying
the flakes they were dressed in, simultaneously revealing
their true essence, sap, igniting even more their hellish fate;
luckily, on the other hand, the snow had choked the grass,
preventing the development of an even worse scenario,
had it grown and functioned just like the wick of a candle.

Demeter, apparently rendered unconscious from the impulse,
did not manage to witness the rebirth of her own daughter,
precisely what Kore was known for; perhaps it was not just
the rebirth of Nature the Moirai had predicted and woven
for Persephone, but also her rejuvenation, delivered at last
from a rather long labor, heavily scrutinized every single day,
her patience tried somewhere no one would ever call home,
or so she thought in the beginning, as there was yet too much
to clear inside her mind, especially because of a last-minute
misunderstanding, duly perceived only on the very last day,
which is not a treat at all, but rather a terrible joke played
on the situation's interlocutors, similar to a poor comedy.
Who the fool is to have such great fun at this, I cannot say.

'You may open your eyes now, Persephone; you are home',
Hermes gently said, seeking to comfort his distressed cousin.
Although the journey from the underground up had gone
in a flash, the maiden did not realize it until it was all over,

185   her last sight of Tartarus having been none other than Hades;
      as soon as he was out of visual reach, she tried to preserve
      the picture in her memory, the captor in front of a statue
      he had built of and for his captive, not so menacing at all.
      The impulse from the launch surpassed both travelers,
190   thus rupturing the same suture in the lake's ground the two
      had just burst from; as the rather small cone submerged,
      Mount Aitne, in the distance, trembled and shook most
      of its snow all the way down to its base, resembling tears
      the Screech Owl was sadly shedding for Kore's absence.
195   Though the tremor was felt in the vicinity of the volcano
      alone, it was as if the youngest of the Thesmophoroi's heart
      had been shaken just as much, making her lose her balance
      and fall on her knees, softened by the snow laid to rest.

      The messenger of gods took hold of her and hinged his words
200   with wings to the likes of those borne on his golden talaria:
      'Cousin, open your eyes! It is over now. Unveil your beyond,
      Demeter is ahead, lying on her back like an animal carcass'.
      At the sound of her mother's name, the goddess of springtime
      woke up from her trance and glanced at the snowy dunes
205   waving up front, where the unconscious goddess of harvest
      lay, getting back up on her feet instantly and leaving Hermes
      behind, who followed her running on his heels, rather than
      flying toward his aunt, allowing the daughter to approach
      the mother first, as he considered to be more appropriate.
210   'Mother! Mother, are you all right?! I am here, I am back!',
      the maiden cried, her tears streaming down her cheekbones
      like a fresh waterfall in the forest of Trinacria's smaller isle,
      Ortygia, Southeast of Syracusa, where both hunter deities,
      Artemis and Apollo, were given birth to by Leto, a Titan
215   goddess who was impregnated by Zeus before the latter
      married Hera, his lawful wife; although the event took place

prior to the union, the patroness of childbirth herself forbade
Leto from giving birth on land, hence her need to escape
to the recently formed Ortygia, not yet taken for an island.
220 Artemis was the firstborn, followed by Phoebus after nine
days of labor, receiving aid from her fast-growing daughter.
In a matter of days, the twins rose to their fullest power
and protected their mother from any threat in her way,
most of them under Hera's orders, which was the case
225 of Python, a dragon, slain by Apollo at only four-days-old;
eventually, Leto became favored once more by the bearer
of the aegis, which his wife and sister disapproved of,
leaving, nevertheless, the mother of the twins alone, as in
the future there were other women and illegitimate children
230 the goddess of marriage would have to be on the lookout for.

Kore's touch had worked its magic, awakening Demeter
from her unprovoked slumber; I would guess the bonding
between mother and daughter had been more than enough
to scare the Oneiroi away, as time was of the essence
235 and six months slide past us much too quickly, especially
when we are experiencing a wonderful time, which was
certainly not Persephone's case from the autumnal equinox
onward, the limit that had now been imposed by the Moirai.
Not so curiously anymore, the last few hours, to say the least,
240 had flown by at the speed of a shooting star in the night sky.
The eldest of the Mistresses' sight became clearer, once her
ears assimilated her cub's cries and her skin felt her touch.
There was no question now that both had been rejoined,
which made Demeter's heart warmer than ever before.
245 Sweet as honey, the now relieved mother delivered unto
Kore the following words: 'Persephone! Oh!, my child…!
At last, you are back from the clutches of Hades's pestilence.
Hold me, I beg of you, hold me tight, so I know I dream not!

Persephone's Fall

Feel the ambrosia in my veins, daughter of mine, it is afire,
it boils as much as the entrails of Gaia all around us both!'.
The young maiden could feel the heat taking over her body;
no matter how long you are stranded in an infernal domain,
nothing is as warm as love, whose power is unmistakable,
regardless of its sort, for it is the affection that truly counts.
'I feel it, Mother, I feel it!', the goddess of rebirth uttered,
as both held each other close on their knees, on the snow.
Hermes, sensitive to the sight, felt he had fulfilled his duty,
softly departing back to Olympus, like he had not been there
at all, leaving that scene of pure motherhood untouched.

Tangled like the roots of two trees in a forest side by side,
the goddesses of human sustenance and springtime began
to spread their divine power from the point where they knelt,
melting all the snow and ice from their vicinity to the whole
of Trinacria, thus reviving Nature to how it always had been,
in harmony, resetting its balance with all living creatures,
allowing Gaia to inhale again, smothered for far too long.
A green carpet of fresh grass extended in multiple directions
from the divine epicenter, similar to the rippling observed
in bodies of water, the closest of all Pergoussa Lake, which
appeared to swallow the icy surface, its euphotic zone
in plain nudity, undressing its white robes for Helios' arms
to embrace the entrapped waters of Kyane, a Naiad nymph
who had witnessed the rape of Persephone, having turned
into fresh water out of disappointment for failing to hold
the maiden from the grasp the Screech Owl had taken
on her, thus becoming a part of the great pool, even though
(depending on who we ask) some might claim she was in fact
a natural spring in Syracusa, liquified by Hades, punished
not only for witnessing the rape, but also for attempting
to halt it, regardless of her inability to do so successfully.

The reflection from Apollo's golden chariot immediately
shone on the watery mirror, which glinted back at it through
the dark skies, covered until then by solid, flaking clouds.
Needless to sing Ouranos felt mighty relieved to see Gaia
285 in all her grace and splendor, as both were again reunited.
Aeolos, the king of winds, had at last recollected his right
to overpower the stubbornness of three of his subordinates,
calling back Boreas, Euros and Zephyros, who reluctantly
stopped their chaotic blowing, allowing Notos to assist
290 Demeter and Kore in their efforts to give rebirth to Nature,
softly spreading an agreeable breeze mixed with Phoebus'
sunrays, which aided in the melting of the snow across
the fields, clearing lands where once crops had grown,
thus providing humans and other animals with their survival.

295 Shoals came back to life in the depths of the lake, where
plankton was recreated to feed the newly revived shoals
swimming all over the aquatic area; up above, trees, bushes,
and flowers bloomed and blossomed back to their old selves;
the leafless branches and trunks that had caught fire from
300 volcanic projectiles saw their wounds healed as if nothing
had happened, ornamenting their canopies like before, as
their torsos reclaimed their bark, transpiring healthy sap.

Birds of all kinds flew together in their respective flocks,
after having been forced to abandon the homes they had
305 built with a great deal of effort, which eventually collapsed
due to the snow's heavy weight and lack of protection
offered by the trees' foliage against the ravishing gusts.
Among them, there were rock partridges, long-tailed tits,
marsh tits, greater flamingoes, herons, and shorebirds, like
310 seagulls, hoopoes, and thrushes, natives to the territory;
the sparrow was, of course, the most common of them all.

Persephone's Fall

Incredible amounts of brightly colored plantations grew
across the plains, from Enna to Pánormos, all the way up
to the foothills of Eryx and the shores of Selinoûs, followed
315 in the coastline to the Southeast by Hērákleia Minoa,
Akragas, and Géla, painted with the rainbow's palette,
just like Persephone had done by her mother's suggestion.

The Potamoi, river gods, flowed freely throughout Trinacria,
bathing the newborn flora, as they also offered their bodies
320 to the several faunae living within, carrying schools to the
Mediterranean, where the sea's own nymphs, the Nereides,
were expecting them, in order to provide the fishermen
with their daily feast and trade, now that the boats were
no longer trapped in the middle of ice and could thus sail.

325 From above, where the Olympians observed the whole
of Humanity, a hidden sigh of relief came from between
the bearer of the aegis' lips, as he sat on his throne, naturally
failing to admit to anyone he feared the worst: the end
of cult to the gods, hecatombs, and inexistence on account
330 of forgetfulness, for, even though Zeus had created Man,
without any subservience left to be shown, what purpose
would all the Grecian gods and demigods bear from thereon?
In short, all entities whoever depended, relied on each other.
That was how the balance had been kept since the beginning,
335 when Ouranos found support atop Gaia, who held him up;
from that moment, having Chaos been destroyed, the world
took shape and bore a harmonic balance that required all
to be at peace, in spite of Man believing otherwise, making
his own rules, and quite seldom based on the wisest he could
340 come up with, the misfortune of Nature and her creatures.
Then again, Man had been made to the gods' own image;
whose fault was it harmony was severely unappreciated?

One would have to guess temptation surely had something
to do with it, an element beyond control, mastered by
345   neither mortals, nor immortals; just quite simply set loose.

In the middle of the sea, close to the toes of the peninsula,
order became gradually observed and dominant, as the
snow-clad island shook its white dust away, once again
turning into a green haven where Leto herself had been made
350   welcomed by locals, protected by her twins, who, sadly,
promised to protect Ortygia only, instead of all Trinacria.

Canto VIII

Afterlife in the Underworld progressed as usual, routinely,
though, naturally, there was a snag to an already abhorrent
song to listen to: the ruler of the dead was broken and bent;
he had been struck by the keen sting of love, venomous
to the purest of hearts, unable to handle the innate sadness
of being split from their better half, on account of factors
third parties alone can control, rather than themselves,
which was what hurt Hades the most, forced to retire
from his dedication to Persephone, regardless of having
failed to show it properly, keeping her so close and yet so far.

There were times when the Screech Owl would simply
stand in front of Kore's statue, staring at perfection itself,
but not necessarily as far as his work was concerned, no.
Rather, it was how Nature had constructed the maiden
so beautifully that all he had had to do was copy an ulterior
sculpture into a block of marble and chisel through to release
the embodiment of candor, intelligence, purity, sageness,
not just completing him, but more importantly, doubling
those exact qualities within, bringing the best out of him.

While it is true the king of the Underworld was irreducible
most times, making sure his inmates suffered appropriate
punishment for their actions on earth, every once in a while
there came headed to Tartarus aboard the ferryman's boat
souls who had mistakenly been sent to the eternal prison,
instead of their rightful place in Elysium; Hermes, messenger
of gods, was responsible for the task – leading the dead
to where they would spend eternity, but because he had been
busy following Zeus' orders to retrieve Kore from his uncle's

lair, there had been an inexcusable misunderstanding, mostly
because the person in question had accidentally died on a day
they should have rejoiced and remembered for years to come.

It was the guardian of the Underworld gates who sounded
the alarm, refusing to pry them open for a guest who did not
belong there in the first place and was visibly frightened
to see what lurked on the other side of the wall, invisible
to whom had not yet crossed the diamond-encrusted doors.
Now, because no mortal had ever gone to Tartarus and come
back alive to tell the story, those who deservedly perished
were clueless as to Tartarus' features; only the gods could
reveal what went on below ground, especially as far as their
direct killings were concerned, namely Ixion and Tantalus,
whose fates were simply unthinkable, to put it quite bluntly.
My guess is the shiny jewels embroidered all over the iron
structures were intended to produce a feeling of false hope,
considering no redemption whatsoever could be found there.

When Persephone was still being held a prisoner by Hades,
I sang to you about this aforementioned gatekeeper creature.
His name was indeed Kerberos, and he was undoubtedly
a fearmongering tricephalous creature, though domesticated,
funnily enough, obedient only to the Master of Death.
Aside from the three heads, the furry canine possessed
yet another particular feature – he could only see when
his eyelids were shut, whereas, when open, he was blind.
For a dog, of course, a damp nose always came in handy,
should anyone attempt to distract him from his watch duty;
it is said the only way to appease him is to give him a baked
treat made of flour and honey, which is placed by the body
in the funerary pyre, along with the ferryman's payment;
now, considering his only purpose is to cross the River Styx

60 with the convicts on board, one can only ask oneself
what it is he does with the tally of his passengers' fares.
However, I think a far more important question is begged:
it is not what Kharon does with the obols, but rather
how much alike everyone is, once they make their descent
65 from the earthly world onto the plain of the restless dead;
it does not matter how rich one is across one's lifetime,
for if Tartarus is one's final destination, then Hades cannot
be bribed to a lighter sentence because of a generous tariff.
The Judge of Death has no use for gold or silver coinage,
70 despite his taste for collecting and creating works of art.
In the end, bronze or even copper (one-sixth of a drachma)
is what everyone is reduced to, having no criminal stand out
for their wealth in life, which is what might have sent them
away from Elysium in the first place – greed and conceit.

75 Accurate as he was telling the guilty apart from the innocent,
Kerberos howled in the distance, having caught his master's
attention well beyond the gates of the infamous Underworld,
bringing him back from his daydreaming, even though it was
always dark below (except for the flames' trembling light).
80 I need not tell you which thoughts he had lost himself in,
trying to escape a rather sour reality he had not been used to
for quite some time, because, although he never saw much
of Kore until the deadline of her presence in his palace, still
he felt he had spent the best time of his eternity when she
85 was near, the closest he had been to getting rid of loneliness,
not just to please himself, but especially because Persephone
was his one true love, and no other woman or divinity
filled his heart as much as she did, without even trying to.

The King of Tartarus had his peace taken away from him,
90 ceding its place to a rather anxious spirit concealed under

his human-like complexion, ether and flesh bound forever;
immortality is the greatest gift men failed to be awarded,
and perhaps rightly so, for such is the cycle of living beings:
to carry on the powerful legacy of dignity and honor
95 of their ancestors, thus keeping their memories intact,
outliving the gods themselves, for they will always be there.
It is those whose death was beautiful, not by the bloodthirsty
blade or the hawkeyed spear and arrow, but their integrity,
who live on for millennia, immortalized by the poets' songs,
100 even when all the gods no longer have their say in the world,
run by the true deciders of fate, makers of their own luck.

It did cross the Screech Owl's mind the maiden had returned
of her own accord, swinging her back to the only family
she had, but such an idea immediately became vile, as Kore
105 would never sacrifice one sort of love for another, for both
should subsist side by side in one heart alone, the daughter
and the lover, in spite of her uncertainty regarding the latter;
Hades had tried his best to fuel the flame in the maiden's
chest, but it was also up to her to increase it with every intake
110 of breath, a deliberate arsonist setting her wilderness ablaze.

The Judge of Death bound his time toward the entrance,
holding his garments on one arm, puzzled by the unordinary
calling, as he walked over the earth's entrails and between
the living dead, criminals toyed with by the wrathful Inferi
115 for their abhorrent manners spanning most of their lifetime,
invisible to those sentenced to being both dead and alive;
as their earthly body turns to ashes on the pyre, unattached
becomes their spirit, only to reincarnate the chastised flesh,
for a soul does not bleed or hurt to beg for inexistent mercy.

120 When he finally arrived at the diamond-encrusted iron gates,

Hades was presented with a row of defendants awaiting
their entry to and subsequent trial in the ethereal tribunal.
They were all disembarking Kharon's boat, a simple yet
maneuverable single-oared barge, capable of dealing with
125 the wrath of the Styx itself, as the bronze collected from
the prospective inmates was distributed along the crossing,
tempering down the human traits of the agitated river.

The ferryman was preparing to leave, when his master
prompted him sternly: 'What goes on here, O eerie Kharon?
130 Why has Kerberos howled thrice in unison, lest his warning
be heeded? Have you lost a ghoulish character on the way?',
questions to which the rower responded assertively, though
unforgetting himself: 'No wretch has been lost to the tempest
of the waters, my Lord; on the contrary, they all stand
135 in your presence and are accounted for, though one of them,
the girl, seems to have been misplaced among the scum and,
therefore, the hound of hell does not let his guard down,
waiting for you to decide what is to be of her fate, my Lord'.

Although the situation was rare and most definitely new
140 to those who had just died, some actually hoped they had all
been mistakenly brought to dark shores, when they should
have in fact been taken to the illuminated Elysium plains.
'Who is this girl you speak of, ferryman? And what is
the reason for this unfortunate and inopportune mishap?',
145 the Screech Owl demanded to know, as Kharon maintained
his tone: 'As I understand, O mighty Hades, the messenger
failed to guide this shipment as it is customary, resulting
in this rather peculiar outcome; each and every one of them
descended on their own, prepared to pay the toll, and so
150 I did my duty by bringing them here, to your ghastly domain.
This is whom you seek', he said, forcing the young woman

to advance by pushing the upper side of his oar to her back.
She slowly stepped forward without complaining, her throat
blocking her ability to speak, and her eyes flooded in tears,
walking erroneously, as if she were about to tumble and fall.

Hades stared at the girl in an unequivocally undistracted
manner, wondering if someone as delicate as her could have
actually committed a crime so brutal in its form that she
had to be sent to his realm to pay her dues with her own life;
not only that, the fact she had had a rather premature death
also seemed to get the best of him, anxiously twisting within.
Could it be that perhaps Zeus had punished her with his bolt,
setting her afire after refusing to lie with him in disguise?
The bearer of the aegis did not accept rejection so easily.

Leaving such thoughts to the side, The Judge of Death then
moved on to questioning the girl, exactly where they stood,
in front of the other convicts, who kept their fingers crossed,
still hoping they had been mistakenly taken underground,
to the very guts of the earth, where the scum from above
reeked a festering stench, worsened by the asphyxiating fires.

'What were you called on earth?', the Screech Owl asked.
Sobbing just slightly, fearing to upset the mighty Dark Lord
with involuntary squeaks, the girl moved her head down,
looking only at her feet, whispering her reply like so:
'I am Eurydike, daughter of the Sun-God Phoebus Apollo,
and an oak nymph, in spite of apparently being mortal…'.
All the more puzzled, Hades moved forward with his query:
'And how was it you died? Did you commit such serious
a crime that the Olympians should hither discard you?'.
The nymph explained, holding her gown with both hands,
which appeared to be some sort of white, wedding robes;

on her head, she wore an oaken crown, ornamented
with fresh flowers the likes of which Kore and Demeter
had conjointly revived: 'No, my Lord, unless... we should
by crime infer the right to fall in love with the man I could
solely dream of, for so long unaware he was indeed real,
and wed him on the rebirth of spring, only to perish
on that day precisely... I have kept my honor up to this day,
my Lord; never have I lain with my widowed husband,
for I am pure and take pride in it, knowing he was the one
man to ever lay a finger on me, but all we did was hold
hands and exchange the taste of our tongues, massaging
one another, hoping we could survive the blizzard together,
sharing the warmth of our bodies...' – Eurydike was unable
to proceed, hiding her face in the palms of her hands,
forming a shell in which she concealed her embarrassment.

The entire panel of spirits listened closely to the nymph's
story, generating the most assorted reactions in both men
and women; the first were mostly excited for having a virgin
in their presence, unleashing their lecherous side and proving
Tartarus was undoubtedly the right place for them to be in,
whereas the latter, though guilty for one reason or the other,
felt sorry for Eurydike, asking themselves for Zeus's beard
how it was the Moirai could have allowed the girl's thread
to break so soon, without even letting her enjoy adult life
by her husband's side, severing it on such a special occasion.

Because the murmuring was beginning to develop into quite
the stir, the ruler of the Underworld turned to his pet beast
and sternly gave him these orders: 'Round all the criminals
up and take them inside, Kerberos; enough commotion!'.
The canine barked his three heads all at once and displayed
terrifying muzzles, threatening to devour the wretched souls

like Kronos had done with his children, though with another
purpose, of course; frightened, they all scarpered, away from
the tripled dentures' range, piling on each other at the gates,
waiting for the overture to become a bit wider and clear
some room, although many were bitten and dismembered,
summarily serving their sentence without even being tried.

Kharon assumed he was no longer needed and began rowing
away from the shore; it was not a question of feeling grossed,
on the contrary – he was far too used to that sort of display
and decided to go back, as the Styx turned red with blood.
I dare say it was a scene far more gruesome than any battle
I had ever witnessed, read about or heard of, and there are
plenty of stomach-churning killings I have had the chance
to see across my time, though I must add they were rather
unpleasant, naturally; what kind of barbaric behavior is ever
agreeable to watch, I ask myself, for both Music and Poetry
are my best weapons against all kinds of suppressing tyrants,
and it is only through the art of composing the feats of men
are duly immortalized, as were it not for the power of words,
where would their glory go, but forgotten in the eons of time?

Hades had obviously been insensitive to Eurydike, though
it was his intention to spare her from all that attention.
The problem was, whenever the Screech Owl intended
to do good, he would always fail to do it in the most proper
of fashions, something only Persephone seemed to be able
to teach him through confrontation, for the scenery was
affecting the nymph far too much, especially when the blood,
still warm, reached her bare feet, bathing them as it spilled
into the thirsty river, cresting on the shore, claiming more.
Only when she looked like she was going to be sick did he
warp themselves back inside, instead of just walking back in.

The Dark Lord took her directly into the palace, avoiding
other potentially horrifying episodes Kore had come across
with during her temporary rebellion against imprisonment.
Eurydike was not too keen on opening her eyes, trembling
still from the shocking, barbaric savagery of a bloody beast.

Hades took blame and tried to comfort the nymph with these
wing-hinged words: 'I apologize for what has just happened,
child... it was not my wish to further darken your grief.
But come, now, hold your peace and spare your candid tears;
one of my duties here is to read the soul of every person
standing before me, especially when their bloodshot eyes
cloud the truth about their arrival to these shores, instead
of Elysium, which is where you should have been sent to,
free to run across the plains and prairies, for I do not sense
the presence of any sort of evil whatsoever inside of you.
We must clear up this rather unfortunate misunderstanding
and send you to where you belong, but... for the time being,
I would like you to make yourself comfortable in my home.
You need only ask, and you can eat and drink as much
as you wish; I will get a few of the Danaids to care for you,
starting with a soothing bath to wash the blood off your...'.
It was then he noticed, withholding his tongue from any
further ado – the nymph had been bitten on one of her feet
by what he supposed would have been a venomous snake.
That is why the Judge of Death could not detect maleficent
forces in Eurydike's heart; she had not committed any crime,
she had merely been the victim of a stupid, disgraceful death.
And though she was dead, Hades had no desire of making
the nymph carry those marks for eternity, wherever she went.
Soaring across the great hall, a handful of Danaus' daughters
were summoned to fulfill their duty and clean the wound
using the same water they could not purify themselves with,

but were destined to forever move in jugs to their bathtub.

Eurydike meant to thank the Screech Owl for his kindness,
though she was still too frightened to utter any word at all
for the time being; Hades did not consider it to be rude,
as he understood how hard it must have been for the nymph
to adapt to death so abruptly, without preparation such as
living to an old age and embracing eternal peace and quiet,
or knowingly engaging in hubris, regardless of the number
of springs she had seen while walking on the world above,
hoping to find happiness and live by its side, together with
her mourning husband, of whom she knew nothing about,
once her spirit was erroneously called upon to descend into
the afterlife funerary pyre, in spite of not being burned in it.
As the Danaids escorted the nymph to one of the lavatories
in Hades's abode, she wondered what was it the former
bridegroom would do with her corpse, for no obol had been
put in her mouth, though there she was, about to dine in hell.

The group of women charged with the murder of their men,
in turn, had their own plans in mind, other than tending
to Eurydike's needs, deliberately disobeying their master.
Bearing in mind they were preparing a purification bath
for someone who actually deserved it, innocent as she was,
the water spilled from the jugs into the tub did not leak,
and so the daughters of Danaus saw fit to use the nymph
to achieve their own deviant goal, which was to redeem
themselves in a murderous manner – an uncanny paradox.
If they kept Eurydike underwater long enough, the whole
forty-nine of the Danaids could finally escape Tartarus
and, if not come back to life, then at least move to Elysium,
thus avoiding eternal damnation, even though their sentence
was definitely not the worst to withstand among the dead.

Now, as I have sung to you in the near past, physical death
comprises the spirit's abandonment of the earthly body, left
to decay underground or, more commonly, burn to ashes;
310 in the afterlife, however, the soul takes a different form
very much similar to a physique, only it does not decompose
or burn away – on the contrary, it is preserved to sustain
the exact, same conditions of a flesh and bone complexion
without shutting down on account of excruciating pain
315 or irreparable damage, like blood loss or excessive charring.
This means that, should Eurydike be forced to remain below
water, she would agonizingly drown over and over again;
one can only imagine what it is like to flood the lungs once,
but to lose the ability to breathe and burst one's chest…!
320 Of course, when a killing spree runs through the veins
of murderous swine, increasing the number of casualties
does not seem to be that insurmountable, but rather normal.

Two of the Danaids initially accompanying the oak nymph
made haste from the lavatory she had been taken to and
325 found the remainder of their kin, who were busy performing
regular domestic tasks in several locations within the palace.
The word that Eurydike could be their ticket out of Hades'
clutches immediately spread like wildfire, proving none
of them had learned nothing from their previous crime,
330 apparently willing to worsen their punishment even further.
What they failed to realize was that they were all under
surveillance, regardless of the Screech Owl not being present.

As the women poured into the tub their jugs of water,
filling it up without any leakages or any other mishaps
335 in need of acknowledgement, they mischievously tried
to offer the nymph some rather comforting, honeyed words,
pretending to understand what she was going through,

as they simultaneously undressed her and removed her crown
of flowers from the top of her head: 'Come, now, darling,
do not fret... such a beautiful face you have got, and you are
mucking it all up with your tears... everything is going to be
all right, you need not worry', one of them said in somewhat
of a condescending tone; a second Danaid spoke followingly:
'We all know what it is like to die so suddenly and abruptly
in our prime. Can you imagine an entire offspring eradicated
in a single, brutal attack? Our father was devastated, but not
for long, as he too quickly met his demise, pierced by a blade.
Naturally, we felt confused as soon as we walked down
the plain of the restless, having the ferryman in front of us,
prepared to collect his toll... the messenger of gods failed
to guide us to where we should be now, in sacred Elysium.
Master Hades promised us he would sort it out for us all,
after we claimed our coming here had been a mistake...
alas, none of us was ever lucky to see his promise fulfilled'.

The mariticidal creatures knew perfectly well what they were
doing, successfully inducing innocent Eurydike into thinking
the Screech Owl had fooled her, unintending whatsoever
to set her free or at least spare her from slavery, which was
what had seemed to happen to the daughters of king Danaus,
according to the viewpoint inflated into the nymph's mind.

Of course, her curiosity was aroused, and she therefore asked
for the women's confirmation of those purported events:
'Did he honestly do as you say? Did he promise to deliver
you from this vile place, even though he has kept you here?'.
Those gullible words were like music to the women's ears,
devilishly smirking inside while struggling to keep a straight
face in front of Eurydike, to whom they replied like so as
they helped her into the tub: 'Indeed! Treacherous scum,

we dare say... of course, we cannot overpower the greyish
370 Dark Lord, and that is the only reason why we have not
yet left; I think I can speak for us all when I say we would
rather be repeatedly in agony than being the housemaids
to this swine', one of them concluded – quite convincingly.

A peculiar ambience filled with expectation hung ominously
375 in the air, setting somewhat of a dark tone in the silence that
had suddenly taken place in the lavatory, as the remainder
of the Danaids lined up on the other side of the door, fighting
their way to put one of their ears against the only barrier
left between eternal slavery and the purification of their sins.

380 Eurydike already sat in the tub, stripped of her white gown,
as well as of the crown of flowers she had been wearing atop;
being a daughter of Apollo, she was a wondrous work of art
to behold, though the descendants of Danaus had their focus
on how exquisitely the clear water looked, contained to the
385 very last drop, for they could not afford to spill any, despite
the nervousness crawling under their skin, one they were able
to conceal quite brilliantly, as honesty was not their nature.

Sadly, such is the foulness those of us who prize ourselves
with values to the likes of honesty and dignity must face
390 when stepping on solid ground, mandatorily fraternizing
with all sorts of creatures for the gods' pleasure, as both
the bearer of the aegis and his queen make their moves
across the board; Zeus intrepidly slides the pawn he wishes
to test, whereas Hera, depending on her mood, either sends
395 her venomous vipers as punishment, or acquits the poor devil
by instructing them on how to escape or defeat the menace.

In my (perhaps) not so humble opinion, their perverted idea

of fun is cornering humans, so they may kneel and request
their help, asking for forgiveness without precisely realizing
400 what it was they did to begin with, thus keeping both faith
and Man himself alive; it begs the ghastly question yet again:
what would the gods do without us, but more importantly,
what would we do without them watching us, blackmailing
us into showing how bold we are by testing our own thread,
405 wondering just how long it will hold before Atropos slices it?

I cannot tell you how convinced I still am Eurydike's death
could have been prevented, if that satyr had not been sicked
on the nymph, happily dancing at the sound of the kithara…
what I am yet to confirm is who teased the beast against her.

410 Lost in her thoughts, she closed her eyes and submerged to
the bottom of the bathtub, reassuring herself she could stay
below, hoping to set herself free from a place she should
never have seen, wrongly taken or not, which was the case.
Her hearing became temporarily impaired, filled with sounds
415 from the depths, as if the ocean were slowly swallowing her.
The sharp intake of breath she had taken was going fast,
there was not much time left to give up on her fatal intent,
but as she prepared to come back up, incapable of selling
herself gratuitously after what she had already been through,
420 she felt four pairs of hands thrusting her down, grabbing her
arms and legs; it was the spike of anxiety bursting across
her chest that made her exhale the last remnants of air in
her lungs with a cry of horror, silently sparkling the surface,
as her ripple-twisted vision saw the terrifying grins of the
425 murderous women, clenching the white blades they had in
each finger into her afterlife flesh, turning the water crimson.

Without waiting any longer, one by one the Danaids bathed

in Eurydike's pure, innocent blood, immediately shattering
to pieces dissolving in the water like salt; once the others
430 realized what was happening to their sisters, they tried to
run away, but all forty-nine had already filled the room and
the door was suddenly shut, unyielding to their cowardice.
The water then arose in the shape of an eddy and suctioned
all the foul women into it, turning them to oceanic grains
435 piling underneath the oak nymph, purified at last by the
destruction of those attempting her second assassination.

Dazed and confused, Eurydike saw a cloaked figure looking
down at her, but failed to realize who it was or where they
had come from, losing her senses, taken by the Oneiroi to
440 a calm and resting place where no one would disturb her.

Canto IX

'My friend, I am ever so sorry for your loss... no one saw it
coming, you could not have prevented it; Zeus's beard,
no one could!', Jason exclaimed, seeking support from his
Argonaut companions on his attempt to comfort Orpheus,
the kithara player who had taken part in the expedition to
Colchis, where the Golden Fleece (made from a winged ram's
skin) lay, a gift the gods themselves had presented the locals
with, marking the authority and kingship of Aetes, the ruler.

The son of Apollo (also depicted as the possible offspring
of Oeagrus, a Thracian king) and Calliope, the muse who
has been inflating my spirit so far, was down on his knees,
next to the marking on the ground where his wife had fallen.
He held his face in his hands, as tears of anger, frustration,
and rage dripped between his fingers, grasping his traits
with the intention of inflicting pain, thus chastising himself.
Once Jason spoke, then he let go, unveiling an underlying
layer of blood pressed against his flesh, as if he had ripped
it out, just like he had pulled his hair and torn his gowns.

'The truth of the matter is I could have foreseen it, Jason,
I could! The gods bestowed me with the gift of clairvoyance,
do you not remember anymore? All sorts of magic within me
and I was simply not here to protect my newlywedded wife
from that monster! If only I had slain him in time, Eurydike
would not have come this way and the viper would have slid
by, unprovoked, instead of lying beheaded in front of us!',
Orpheus shouted back at Jason, pointing to the dead snake
the entertainer of the Argonauts had sliced himself, after
puncturing the satyr with the assistance of his companions.

'I have been deliberately distracted! Both my judgment and awareness were tampered with so I would remain clouded as to the presence of the creature in the vicinity of our event', Orpheus added, positive that his gift had been subjected to a case of the gods giving and taking away; the question was: why had they done it? Also, which one was the perpetrator? And finally, what had happened to the oak nymph's body?

Aethalides, renowned for his imperishable memory, recalled Mopsus's similar death; he too was a son of Phoebus Apollo, which made him a brother to Orpheus, not only in-arms, but also in blood: 'He had the ability to augur from birds' flights, and yet, we lost him in Lybia to the very same venomous fate. It is quite possible the gods may be conjuring against us right now, as we speak', Aethalides said, looking up to the orange sky, as the Sun-God's chariot returned to its stable, clearing the path for Hekate's darkness and cratered pearl, possibly the main attraction of the dome where the Olympians rested.

The men bickered a while about how imprudent Aethalides may had been in his accusing of malfeasance on behalf of the gods, yet again toying with their destiny, even though their mission had been successfully completed, safe for a few losses along the way, though not all had resulted in death. It was Lynceus's intervention that made the Argonauts rest their tongue, as he sided with Aethalides concerning his hunch: 'I too look into the skies and see nothing but clouds. Herakles still is visible to me in Libya, but from the gods… there seems to be nothing in sight, in spite of it being far by their own desire, which is why it must have been meddled with', he added; the former crew of the Argo began to feel restless, fearing that, perhaps, their expedition had not been enough of a trial already; the son of Zeus and Alcmena was

60 busy with his twelve labors to secure his immortality, but
the others... well, they would not be roaming on earth
indefinitely, which made them ask themselves whether
there might be some sort of a compensation for their
new efforts, or if it was all just for divine fun, as the gods
65 expected to feast on the hecatombs made in their honor.

Medea, daughter of Aetes and Jason's spouse, having come
aboard the Argo with the latter once the Golden Fleece was
in his possession, was also a priestess of Hekate, and by the
goddess advised in secrecy, she mystically uttered a few
70 words, flowing through the air like the winds of the night,
carrying dandelion seeds across the land to further spread
the wisest of messages: 'Blame not the gods, son of Apollo,
lest you eager for a wantonly, untimely death; there is yet
a chance you may be able to recover Eurydike's lost body,
75 either to give her a proper burial, or to bring her back to life.
Trust Hekate and myself, being one of her priestesses, and
the Olympians shall entrust you with a brand-new mission,
as epic as Jason and his companions', in which you took part.
Pay the goddess your respects, all of you, beginning tonight,
80 and you will soon know what to do, Orpheus, under her
guidance, one you must never, ever question', she concluded.

The Colchian priestess seemed to have really been possessed
by the goddess of magic, speaking like an oracle in a trance.
The moment she was done with her foreseeing, apparently
85 not as crippled as the widower's, a draft trespassed the men
and they all went to their rest; Orpheus was the only one
who stared at Medea for a moment before turning around
on the grounds of Tempe, the foothills of Mount Olympus.

Earlier that day, the son of both the god of Music and the

90   muse of Epic Poetry had convinced himself he would walk
    through the door of his new home carrying his brilliant wife.
    When he crossed the entrance, however, it was like pure void
    had taken over, not just Orpheus, but also the house, empty
    of the joys meant to be lived by a newlywedded couple;
95 his woe was as strong as if he had just come from a burial
    ceremony, making it worse, the more he thought about it.
    Eurydike's body was simply gone and there was no possible
    explanation for the fact, apart from Gaia swallowing her
    corpse, perhaps preventing its profanation by ill-intended
100 entities before the widower could even place an obol in her
    mouth, enshrining her divinity afterward in gusts of wind,
    once the flames had consumed her flesh and razed her bones.

    The abode was barely lit, relying only on star and moonlight;
    it was enough to guide Orpheus to the terrace in the back,
105 where he saw his glooming golden lyre, resting on a stone
    bench, looking simultaneously abandoned and placed there
    on purpose, which was strange, considering the bard had
    spent nearly all day with it and did not remember at all
    bringing it back home, where he had not been since morning.
110 Confused by the unordinary misplacement of the instrument,
    he took hold of it and approached the balcony, overlooking
    the shores of the Aegean, whose cresting was rather peaceful.
    Orpheus took a deep breath and felt compelled into playing
    a tune on the kithara, just like his parents had taught him;
115 its powers had proven useful before, for it could charm all
    living and non-living creatures into doing as he well pleased.
    Unaware of what he had begun to play, the former Argonaut
    fiddled himself to sleep, even though he did not realize his
    mind was absent from his body, by Morpheus induced into
120 dreaming under Hekate's orders, sat by his side as he played,
    observing him underneath her dark cloak, transparent inside.

Persephone's Fall

The goddess of magic then averted her sight to the far sea
and spoke calmly, mimicking Orpheus's inner voice, as if
the sound of his consciousness was reverbing on its own,
instead of being enunciated from a third-party, although
hinged with wings: 'I know of your grievance, son of Apollo.
I have seen inside your heart and I know how it became
shattered not many moments ago by the loss of your loved
one, the only person on this earth you cared for the most.
It would seem to you the gods have purposefully meddled
with your desire to be happy, taking the very source of said
happiness away from you, leaving no traces behind, leaving
you incapable of even performing the proper burial rites,
for the body has disappeared, which is rather unusual…
but fear not, as there is a reason for both Eurydike's flesh
and bones to have been concealed from the living world –
she lives still, and can be recovered from where she has gone
to, though it is up to you to pay the toll to retrieve her;
your talents and wisdom have proved themselves critical
aboard the Argo, and now you must rely on them again
for your own cause, one no man could ever think of in his
right mind: entering the Underworld alive, and leaving in
the same manner, notwithstanding the fulfilment of a highly
important condition – always trust your instinct, and never
doubt it for a moment, otherwise the penalty shall be severe'.

Hekate went on telling the foreseer (as he charmed himself)
that he should request the advice of a goddess he would find
by the banks of Pergoussa, in Trinacria, who would proceed
to helping Orpheus bring Eurydike back, showing him
one of the many ways into Tartarus, descending with his
heart still pumping warm blood across his body's vessels;
the son and apprentice of Calliope should also keep his lyre
with him at all times, as he would be sentenced to damnation

if he forgot it, unable to avoid his own demise, when facing
the many obstacles that lay throughout his journey across
the Mediterranean and its subsidiaries, as he would not be
traveling on horseback, let alone on foot – the adventure
was bound to be entirely maritime, apart from the required
resupplying, of course, with many isles on the way to port at.

The goddess of darkness wished Orpheus Godspeed and left,
disappearing in mid-air, like shadows and dust scattered to
the wind; the Apollonian, back to himself once more, halted
his playing the kithara, hardening the muscles on his face, his
mouth half open, shielding his teeth, staring at the horizon
with bloodshot eyes in need of lubrication, due to the lack of
blinking while spellbound by Hekate, who aimed to take
Eros's place and reunite two couples who were simply meant
to be, ultimately proving that love is much too powerful to
meddle with, whether it be the gods' will or mere misfortune.

The former Argonaut finally blinked, overcome with visions
of the same ilk he had had need of earlier that same evening.
He knew he had a job to do, and the ribcage inside his chest
grew like that of a swan, suddenly recovering all the hope he
thought had become irrecuperable, once the satyr spilled
innocent blood, that of his beautiful and brilliant spouse.
Planning the voyage was of the utmost importance, but the
Apollonian had to rest, nevertheless, in order to maintain his
wits about him, never yielding to doubt, just like he had been
told in his strange dream, by a feminine voice pertaining to
his consciousness, one he did not recollect hearing before.

Meanwhile, Jason and Medea lay next to each other, talking
of the unfortunate events they had sadly witnessed that day,
camping outside, under Nyx's nightly portrayal of Ouranos.

The entirety of the Argo's former crew (or those who had
185 survived the expedition against King Pelias, to say the least)
was staying outdoors, for Orpheus's home was too small
to receive such a plethora of guests, and because he did not
wish to assume any preferences, they agreed all of the invited
on the Apollonian's side would bring their campaign tents
190 with them; Eurydike's guests already lived in Tempe, which
meant they could sleep in their own abode, after the feast.
They had showed their hospitality by offering the Argonauts
a spot under their roof, but the latter kindly declined, stating,
as warriors, they were used to spending the night in the wild.

195 'Dwell in neither blame, nor sorrow, Jason – Hekate will
not allow Eurydike's death to have been in vain; Orpheus
must prove himself worthy of his love for the oak nymph.
Trust me, I am the goddess' priestess, I know these things',
Medea said, seeking Jason's comfort based on the knowledge
200 the goddess of the Moon had passed unto her, without,
however, revealing too many details, thus withholding
the prophecy intact and avoiding any dire consequences.
The commander quickly rested his wife, intending to show
her he bore no doubts whatsoever regarding her foreseeing:
205 'I would not dare put your word into question, my love,
but I do feel sorry for my man Orpheus... I cannot imagine
what it would be like to lose you to such an eerie, dreadful
fate; what if the satyr had chased after you, gifting your life
to the viper's venom?', he thought, looking Medea in the eye.
210 The priestess matched his sight as he spoke, having averted
it to the tent's top once she detected an ominous tone in her
husband's question: 'Does it... does it please you the beast
charged for Eurydike instead of myself, Jason? If the satyr
had come toward me, would you have swapped me for the
215 nymph, if you had the ability to do so?', she eerily asked him.

Jason gulped, averting his sight just as well, once the priestess completed her questions; quiet hung mid-air for an indefinite amount of time, as the leader of the Argo carefully thought of the words he was preparing to enounce, hoping to provide at least a satisfactory answer that did not challenge any of his principles, morals, or integrity, all of which combined.

'Death does not please me in any way, no matter whose it is. The only agreeable outcome of this evening's event would either have been the immediate slashing of the satyr before he could lay eyes on Eurydike, or his complete absence, so no one would have been at risk in the first place – that is how it should have all happened; Orpheus would be rejoicing right now, instead of shedding tears, pulling his hair, and pinching himself all over his body to a dreadful display of bruises in the most assorted locations – his spirit is scarred enough as it is, he does not require his flesh to go with it', Jason said, elevating the valor of his words as he kept talking, adding afterward: 'Also, and more importantly, an innocent life would not have been taken; Eurydike still had much to live for, and the son of Apollo would have made her happy. He loved the nymph more than anyone or anything on earth; she became his life, the moment we returned from Colchis. Not even the sirens could win him over with their charms... it was always the other way around; a true master of the lyre, he is, regardless of how bad the situation at hand may seem. He would have lain down his own life, just to spare her'.

Though she was listening to her man's every word, Medea looked back at him, appearing to concentrate only on her question: 'But if you had to choose, Jason? If you could replace one woman's death for another's, would you do it? Would you give up your own happiness for Orpheus's?'.

The repetition of the priestess' first question was already
a strong blow to sustain, but to endure it divided by three,
it creepily sounded like a deliberate piercing of the entrails,
strategically bleeding out from vital key points, to the likes
of Talos, the giant guardian of Crete, who Medea herself
hypnotized, forcing him to dislodge the bronze nail he had
in his left ankle, from where his only vein went all the way
up to his neck; powerful as she was in sorcery as Hekate's
apprentice, Medea confused Talos' senses and thus he pried
the hatch open, releasing the ichor that made him immortal,
which flowed, indeed, like molten lead, rendering the statue
exsanguinated, a kind of death thought to be possible to Man
and animals alone, but never to an apparently indestructible
creation attributed to Hephaestus, in warmongering skilled.
Lest I forget, Hera took part in the plan by exposing Talos's
weak spot, one he shared with yet an infant warrior whose
name generations to come would permanently remember.

Jason slowly turned his head to face his inquisitive spouse.
For a moment, he thought she was trying to enter his brain
just by looking at him in the center of the irises, focusing
on the other side of his eyes, but the leader of the Argonauts
was cunning himself and broke visual contact with Medea,
swerving his sight to her hand, which he held firm, unwilling,
however, to inflict pain, enouncing these honorable words:
'I shall not discuss who it is I would have rather seen killed,
for it is not my job, as a mere mortal, to make decisions with
respect to the work of the gods; nevertheless, I will tell you
that, should the gods decide to take you away from the earth,
then I would ask Zeus himself to strike me with a lightning
bolt and accompany you across the Styx in the ferryman's
barge, for taking the woman I love away from me would be
the same as taking my life, leaving behind just flesh and bone,

a soulless body in penance, a walking corpse still breathing.
There is no greater dishonor than failing to share the same
fate as the other half, outliving them like a faint memory'.

The Colchian sorceress did not insist in her pursuit for more
answers, satisfied as she seemed with the wits her spouse had
about him; she lifted the hand Jason was holding and laid it
on his chest, intertwining their fingers, while resting her head
on his heart and shutting her eyes, preparing to go to sleep,
about the same time the Thessalian kissed her hair, laying
down completely, heading into their dreams, respectfully.
Judging by Jason's profound breathing, he was sound asleep;
Medea, however, was wide awake, opening her eyes in the
darkness (like those of a lioness), feeling betrayed by how
untrue she knew her husband's words to be, she, who had
left her people for him, she, who had saved his life, slaying
her own dragon to help him retrieve the Golden Fleece, she,
who in the end was merely a barbarian, compared to true,
Greek royalty, but the time will come for that tale to be told.
Someone wiser and word savvier than this bard of yours
will let you know all about it, though there are those who
might say he was somehow influenced by another's gift
for Poetry, but only the gods can state it as a fact, not I;
it would be far too imprudent to pretentiously behave godly,
whether or not we are their descendants (or even children).

Now, may I sing once again, O endless source of inspiration,
of the Apollonian who had had a dream under the guidance
of the goddess of the Moon, Hekate, none other than, just
before she ordered the nightly pearl to retreat and make way
for rosy-fingered Dawn, who, as we know, laid down a clear
path in the sky for Phoebus to cross every day, riding his
golden chariot, by his four horses driven and with improved

310 eyesight, now that spring was back from its rather long rest;
whenever balance is broken, everyone must pay their dues.

Judging from the progressive luminosity, the god of the Sun
should be somewhere over the Hellespont and would soon
be arriving in Tempe, which meant it was time for Orpheus
315 to rise from his slumber and make haste for his expedition.
He had barely slept, of course, once he realized something
could still be done to retrieve Eurydike from Tartarus.
Quickly hopping off his bedstead, he left his sandals behind,
but did not forget to take his kithara with him, as instructed;
320 the Apollonian climbed on top of what appeared to be some
sort of a dais and harmoniously began to fiddle the strings
on the musical instrument, calling out of their homes all
villagers, along with his former companions, who were
leaving their tents one by one, entranced by the melody
325 Orpheus had learned from his divine father, arriving just
in time to listen to it and carry the notation along the way,
across the whole of Greece (including Trinacria, naturally).

As he played, everyone gathered in a circumference, making
him the center of all attention; up front were the Argonauts,
330 including Jason and Medea, standing next to each other.
A mistress in sorcery, the daughter of Aetes was impervious
to the melody's effect, for she knew where to place her focus,
and, therefore, did not easily become enchanted, like most
men and women, the aforementioned pawns of the godly
335 board upon which the game of humanity was gambled;
but because she was also a priestess of Hekate, she knew
what it was that Orpheus was doing, by playing and singing
– he was recruiting people experienced in both naval affairs
and perishable goods, in order to have them build him a ship
340 and supply her with food and drink for his first leg asea.

Medea joined the Apollonian and started giving the locals
instructions on what to do, eloquently speaking these words:
'People of Tempe! Heed the calling as you are summoned
by the power of golden lyre, upon Orpheus bestowed, who,
seeking to indulge the will of the goddess of darkness Hekate,
must fulfill a new quest, now that the Argonautic expedition
has seen its end – a perhaps even greater quest than the latter,
more honorable and glorifying, for the son of Apollo seeks
not power, nor royalty; his kingdom is not of this world, as
it was taken from him to the house of Hades, lodged inside
his newlywedded wife's heart, Eurydike, the oak nymph.
And because Orpheus remains a vassal to the latter's love,
even though he could mourn her death and find shelter
elsewhere, assisted by Khronos, the father of all-healing time,
the goddess Hekate, whom I serve, has made the decision
of giving the grieving husband a chance to go look for his
wife and bring her back from the world of the dead, for she
has not perished, but rather tumbles on the limbo, falling
into eternal damnation soon enough, if nothing is to be done.
We therefore require from you that you put your hands to
your respective jobs and assist us in any way you can, so we
may all ready Orpheus to set sail sooner, rather than later,
for it is the will of Hekate and all other gods watching over
us from their home on top of Olympus, one we are far too
privileged to catch a glimpse of right from where we stand'.

Apparently experienced in rhetoric as much as in witchcraft,
the priestess grouped the people according to their livelihood
and other secluded skills, and sent each partition off to their
duty – all of this as Orpheus kept playing and singing, thus
combining two of the most precious gifts the gods could have
ever offered Mankind, apart from life: Music and Poetry;
one cannot live without the other, as they share one essence.

Lumberjacks and wood collectors were sent out to the forest, so as to collect as much raw material as they could, afterward passing it on to the carpenters, who were both supervised and assisted by experienced Argonauts, such as Ancaeus, son of Lycurgus, who had rowed in the middle of the Argo, by Herakles' side; his homonym, son of Poseidon, who became the ship's captain after Tiphys's death and, of course, the main builder of the Argo herself, Argus, Athena's helper; Jason had been the one to choose the vessel's name after him, who, along with Orpheus, pushed the men into giving their best in all sorts of situations across the journey's many legs, including the strait between the Symplegades (also known as Clashing Rocks), which seconded the Hellespont as the narrowest maritime passage of the Propontis, which connects the Aegean to the Black Sea, bordering Europe and Asia.

Orpheus himself seemed to be in a state of subconsciousness, as he wept for the premature loss of Eurydike to the Screech Owl... his tears had begun to spread like wildfire, touching not only the people's hearts, but also the gods', who watched from above; Hekate had already told him how he could still retrieve the oak nymph from the flames of hell, so now he could count on Hera, the goddess of matrimony, to assist him, and not even Zeus felt like stopping her from lending a hand – the Apollonian was far too distraught and broken. His voice, combined with the saddest of tunes reverbing from the lyre, were simultaneously magical enough to reach out to the sternest, like the bearer of the aegis, ever insensitive.

The construction of the vessel went smoothly, and it still is uncertain how long it took to build, though I suppose it must have been quick, as it was meant to transport no more than two people – Orpheus and Eurydike, once he had found her;

the remaining compartments were meant for the musician's
resting quarters and food storage, which mostly comprised
the few reserves of bread and wine the inhabitants of Tempe
had kept throughout the unexpected, never before seen cold.
It would have been hard to preserve great amounts of meat
at sea, and should Orpheus feel the need to eat fish, he would
have to catch it himself from the water, as there could not be
any fresher, wherever he went; also, great portions of fruit
were donated bearing in mind the final objective of keeping
him alive to bring back Eurydike exactly in the same manner.

They gave him as well a bow and a quiver with arrows, as a
special greeting to Phoebus Apollo and his sister, Artemis,
the Olympian hunters hecatombs were dedicated to on the
night before the departure, including all other gods above,
so that they might be compassionate for Orpheus and keep
him from harm's way, thus honoring his promise to Hekate;
where there were tears of grief, there were also tears of hope.

After having played a tune for entertainment purposes only,
with no magic involved, the bard lifted his wooden cup, filled
with nectar, and proposed a toast: 'If I may briefly have your
attention, please', he asked, seconded by the enthusiastic
Jason: 'Let Orpheus speak, that his eloquence and rhetoric
may draw the attention of the gods, as we bid him farewell,
and that the son of Apollo may return in one piece from
a glorious voyage no man has ever undertaken before, for
a much more valuable treasure than gold – the love of his
life!', he concluded, as he took a gulp from his cup, nearly
choking under Medea's meddling, though a general laughter
was sparked, attributed to the inebriating powers the sweet
nectar had over those who drank it without watering it.
'Hear, hear!', the Argonauts replied in unison, hitting their

435 fists on the feast's tables, laid out in a quadrangular shape,
as if preparing for battle, joined by the equally joyous locals.

'Thank you, Jason, my friend, Medea, Argonauts, neighbors,
in short… family – indeed, the enterprise I am about to take
forward will not be easy; danger and peril are undoubtedly
440 expecting me along the way, even though the jeopardy they
pose is probably nothing, compared to what lurks in the end.
No man has ever set foot in the house of Hades alive before,
that we know to be true… what we fail to realize is whether
it will be possible to come back out again and bring Eurydike
445 with me… excuse me…', Orpheus pleaded, trying to recover
his composure, something the people understood perfectly.
He then carried on, wiping his salty tears with his free hand:
'Again, I would like to thank you all for the undeniable input
you delivered into building Euro, which is the name I have
450 given her, in honor of Eurydike and the location of her yard,
as well as the farmers and collectors of my food and beverage
supply, who have also shared their husbandry with us this
evening, as we ingest the greased offerings we make the gods,
so that this tale may be told to generations to come, inspiring
455 them to never give up on their convictions, particularly love.
Evoe!', he cried, calling upon Dionysos's blessing, although
the god was not that much impressed by the bard's speech.
Everyone else echoed Orpheus, raising their cups in a cheer.

In the meantime, they would eat and rejoice; come dawn, the
460 departure would be swift, for there was no time to waste.

Canto X

Allow me, my sacred Muse, to pick up the song of reunion
between Persephone and Demeter from where I left off, prior
to the dark tale of blood-covered Eurydike, half-alive down
under, in the kingdom where death and pestilence reign
supreme, though under the stern, but fair watch of Hades.
Indeed, I must plead guilty with respect to my wandering
about, for there is yet plenty to tell and summertime keeps
getting closer, marking the end of a new cycle bestowed
upon Kore – she, who was so happily minding her own
and ended up violently taken away, involuntarily putting
Mankind at risk, for Demeter would not yield to conformity.

I believe by now you, my dear rhapsode, can hear yourself
citing that part of the story in your mind, over and over.
Fear not, however, as now has finally come the part during
which the goddess of rebirth opens her heart, not only to us,
but far more importantly the Lady of the Golden Sword,
her beloved mother, who, perhaps not so surprisingly, failed
to comprehend (judging from a first glance, at least) how her
daughter could have felt a connection between her and the
Screech Owl, other than the natural bond of uncle and niece.

Needless to sing (despite my doing so) deities had the power
of metamorphosis, which means they could turn into anyone
or anything they wished (being the bearer of the aegis one
of the most experienced in the field, due to his illegitimate
encounters, as you may remember), and so both Mistresses
did not bear their usual appearance, blending in like farmers,
who were back on the fields, sowing to hopefully reap before
any unpredictable weather came back to starve them all.

They were walking next to each other, overseeing all the hard
work the people were going through across the newly bred
fields of Katane, whose only remainder of white was on top
of the Aitne, as if it were mirroring some sort of tranquility
in Tartarus, though the youngest of the Thesmophoroi knew
it not to be true, after having witnessed such horrid displays,
which was what the goddess of agriculture was clinging on
to make Persephone realize how absurd it was for Hades
to feel any sort of love whatsoever, no matter how charming
and extraordinarily bright and beautiful her daughter was.

'What could possibly make you consider, even for a moment,
that your uncle from hell loves you that passionately, after
taking you away from me, making you his prisoner, and
deliberately feeding you pomegranate seeds to force you
to stay with him, child of mine?! It is simply unimaginable!
Do you have any idea whatsoever the lengths I went through
just to convince your neglecting father to order that Hades
returned you to where you belong…? I restlessly sought you,
I searched everywhere, and there was no way you showed!
It broke my heart, Kore, it did… I abandoned the mother
goddess for you, I nearly left all these people to die of freeze,
perhaps starvation, because you were the only one I could
focus on… were it not for Zeus's need to be adored, he would
have left you underground; he abandoned the both of us
before, why should he care for an estranged daughter now?
Hades took the liberty of sentencing you to imprisonment,
mark my words, child… how will I spend the rest of eternity
dividing you with him? And worse – how did he get to you?
That ash-covered maniac has enchanted my baby to fulfill
his own desires… and she does not object to the sordidness
of it all! I am shaken…', Demeter cried, as they reached
the top of a hill overlooking the Ionian Sea, turning her back

on Aitne, disgusted with what her brother had done to Kore. Across the insurmountable body of water there lay Greece, a nation whose name was owed to Hellen, father of Greeks, the Hellenes, as they call themselves, and not a woman for whom all of the Achaeans would come together, as described by the glorious Homer, by Orpheus gifted with heroism.

The maiden had a dry mouth, rendered absolutely speechless; she knew having said conversation with her mother would resemble a trial, but it is one thing to imagine, and another to live through it, which is somewhat philosophically scant, even though it is true and there is no way of denying it.

Persephone was confused on her own, and was therefore not sure what it was she really felt for the Dark Lord, connected to her by blood, but a perfect stranger as far as her heart was concerned, so abruptly meddled with without having the proper amount of time to think, though I must add that, when singing of love, pondering upon it for too long will eventually lead to a rather unhappy ending, and two souls that are meant to be together simply vanish into thin air, for they cannot live on without the other, immortal or not. We do know the Screech Owl has been vaguely staring into eternity ever since the youngest of the Thesmophoroi left Tartarus, and he might have even become resentful toward his new inmates, despite their not having anything to do with his issues, but... what of Persephone and her feelings?

She averted her sight from the horizon and turned her visage to Aitne, observing the top of the mount, breathing deeply. Then, after undressing the white coat off the stratovolcano with her sight, toward the foothills, she took hold of her hands and turned back at Demeter, who was silently crying:

'Mother, the burden I carry in my chest is too heavy to bear, for I know not what it is I feel... at least, right now, I do not, because... when Hades grabbed me by my wrist and waist, all I could experience was horror – the sudden fracturing of the lake, the parting of the water, and an eerie death odor coming from the entrails of the earth, as he took me down in his chariot... golden, like Apollo's, indeed, but... those sable-black horses looked phantasmagoric, it was some sort of nightmare I could not wake up from, and the more I tried to release myself from him, the tighter his grasp, unwilling to let go of me, as he took me deeper into the fires of hell, a scorching environment of putrefaction and darkness...'.

Seeking to take advantage of Persephone's tale of misfortune for her own good, Demeter tried to reason with her child, as she turned away from the Ionian as well to face her, driving her hands to her cheek bones, in despair: 'Well, there it is! There you have it! He took hold of you like a butcher's piece of meat and would not let you come back! Had it not been for Hekate, I know not whether you would be here with me, right now. Wait! Did that scoundrel dishonor you? Did he abuse you at all?! Hold nothing back, child, and I will sever his head, even if he cannot be killed!', she said, waving her right index finger in front of Kore's face, who was somewhat horrified to see her mother threaten to be violently bloody.

'No, Mother, no...!', the maiden replied, unconsciously shielding the ruler of the Underworld from Demeter's wrath. Then again, she was not lying – Hades had not laid a finger on her for six full months, which is what Persephone tried to explain: 'Once we landed, he had a group of murderous women lead me to a bedroom they had prepared for me, and during the time I stayed there, I was fed with the best food and drink, even though I never ate much', she ended.

Demeter's mouth was half-open and the eyes were half-shut: 'Murderous women...? Taking care of you? Who were those creatures and why did Hades make them his slaves? How did he know they could be trusted?', the divinity of Humanity's sustenance asked in shock; Kore was not aware of the full story, but she attempted to answer her mother either way: 'As far as I know, they were daughters of Danaus, ruler of Argos; their father told them all to kill their male cousins, the sons of his twin Aegyptus, from Egypt, on their wedding night, and so they did, apart from one of them, who refused to kill her husband, allowing him to avenge his brothers by killing his uncle, and because Hades needed someone to take care of his palace, he made them service him in every need'.

The goddess of agriculture sternly asked, based on the last part of her daughter's statement: 'Including carnal needs? Did he make them his whores because you refused him, partying every night separately with each of them, or maybe all of them simultaneously, in a Dyonisic orgy, perhaps?!'.

Persephone had at first felt shock concerning her uncle's behavior toward her, but Demeter seemed to display a sort of mannerisms and language her daughter did not recognize, which was even more cringing to behold than the sentences the dead had to fulfill for eternity, so long as Man kept these gods alive by offering them cults of praises and sacrifices. 'Mother, I...', Kore began, apparently unable to acquire proper words to explain how it was she felt: 'You seem to have changed... I can barely tell you apart from the angers of the world, anymore...', she concluded, obviously shaken, if not scared of who the eldest of the Mistresses had become.

'Well, what did you expect? Ever since you were born, not
for a moment I have let you out of my sight; then, suddenly,
one of our own family bursts through the soil and takes you.
All these fields you see before you became useless to those
who rely on them to live, as they were rendered frozen solid.
No matter how much they pleaded, I never obliged until
the day you came back and gave birth to Nature once more.
Your place is by my side, and not amid burning pestilence!',
the Lady of the Golden Sword exclaimed, turning her back
on Persephone to face the horizon again, contracting her face
and crossing her arms under her chest, as if in a tantrum.

The maiden, in spite of her purity and innocence, was now
progressively learning to stand up for herself, even if it meant
clashing with her own mother, like the Titans before them,
which was why she was now shielding Hades to the full
extent of her consciousness, unsparing of a rather harsh tone
in her words: 'My place is where I determine it to be, Mother!
I am not a small child anymore, and I am definitely not
planning on lingering around for the rest of my eternity.
I may be immortal, but ichor runs through my veins as blood
would inside a human female; my belligerent father made
men and women to the likes of us, and we therefore share
with them a heart in which the most assorted feelings are
stored, being that love reigns supreme, when compared to
those of a much different ilk, such as arrogance, superiority.
Hades showed me that side of his, and because of it, he fell
foul of me, nevertheless displaying remorse for his demeanor.
We all make mistakes, Mother; it is not just humans, it is us
alongside them, and in his eyes I saw tears different in nature.
He was sorry, distraught, confused, lonely, and disturbed;
do you reckon it is easy for someone living in the Underworld
to know what it is like to deal with someone who has not

been sentenced to a sour eternity, someone you care for?
He has lost his touch around other people, indeed, but I
intend to help him get it back; even if I did not, the Moirai
have already made that decision for me, which means there
is no turning back now', she concluded, staring at a shocked
Demeter right in the eyes, bloodshot from lack of blinking.

The goddess of harvest found it hard for a moment to pace
her arrhythmic heart and articulate a good enough discourse
to throw back at her offspring; once she collected a few
words in her mind, the Lady of the Golden Sword moved on
to putting them in a sentence, still unsure about what she
was prepared to enunciate: 'How... dare you?! I am your
Mother! You do not get to talk to me in that tone, ever!
I have revolved the whole of Olympus to bring you back
from the devil's teeth, and this is how you repay me, girl?!
I raised you to become who you are today! It is not like
you were born an adult, like Pallas, through your father's
skull, or grew up in just a matter of days, like Artemis!
I bore you in my womb, similarly to a mortal woman, left
by the magnificent bearer of the aegis to my own fate,
with a child in my arms!', she said, breathing heavily, fast.
There was still one final remark to add, after which their
mother-daughter relationship would have undoubtedly been
bashed (though I cannot say how much): 'You know...
maybe it really is best that you are forced to go underground
every six months, so that you may learn to cherish the taste
of freedom and eager for it, once you grow tired of being
a prisoner to that usurper – a maid, like the other women'.

Persephone just felt knocked off her trail like never before;
she did not know what to say, how to feel... her eyes were
wide open, together with her nostrils, completely deranged.

215 Demeter, of course, realized she had gone too far in her
reprimand, and was about to open her mouth and apologize,
when Kore quickly lifted her right index finger, looking away
into the fields, in which both men and women were working
without noticing there was an argument going on nearby.
220 The maiden then laid down her finger and faced her mother
once more, uttering the following words: 'I have never put
into question your motherhood, nor have I ever renounced
you as my only family, regardless of my half-siblings on my
father's side; all I wanted during my entire stay in Tartarus
225 was to be set free and come back to you, relying on Hekate
to keep me company and help me maintain my strength, as
the day was bound to come, sooner or later, but – Hades
never touched, dishonored, or disrespected me, and neither
has he ever taken advantage of women as foul as mariticides.
230 Again, what he did was wrong, but he always wanted what
was best for me, which is why he agreed to let me go when
Hermes went down to bring me back, because he loves me,
and I love him for that; he may be Zeus's brother, but they
do not share a trait of adultery – he offered me his heart,
235 and now I want to look after it, make sure it is protected.
There is nothing to be ashamed of in a male who relies on
a female's care, protection, and understanding; I will always
be your daughter, Mother, but I too deserve to be happy
the way I feel is right to me, and not to you or anyone else'.

240 Having enunciated that discourse in a fit of controlled rage,
Persephone turned her back on the goddess of agriculture
and moved in parallel with the coastline, heading South.
Demeter tried to call her repeatedly, but the maiden never
yielded to the cries of a once again distraught mother, left
245 alone this time by her own daughter, and willingly so.
Because the reverbing of the crying was becoming intrusive

to Kore's eardrums, she traveled at divine speed, instantly
disappearing to a point somewhere between Katane and
Syracusa, still close to the sea, from which a more relaxing
sound came, the soft cresting of the waves over the wet sand.
She decided that it was a good spot to walk from, though she
would not move straight away, as she definitely needed
to wind down from all the fuss she had just been through.

The youngest of the Thesmophoroi had said it herself, that
she respected her mother and had never doubted her good
intent for a moment, but it was also time for the innocent
child to grow up and make some decisions of her own,
which is what the rebirth of Nature was all about, in the end.
Even though it is a cycle, as much as sleep (which we need to
restore our energy and place all new information properly),
personality keeps growing on, like deciduous trees, shedding
their foliage when the time comes, dressing back up again.
That was flora's fate from now on, and the goddess of its
renewal would accompany that same pace, growing stronger
each day, with an all the more impervious gown to display.

Walking toward the Ionian, Persephone took her sandals off
and let her feet submerge the grains composing the shore,
step by step, without rushing her pace, for there was no need
to make haste anywhere else; besides, cooling off her anger
against her mother took not only its toll, but also its time.
One of the factors that helped her in her ordeal was to feel
the breeze delicately blown to her face by Euros, the East
wind god, along with the agreeable temperature of the water,
which bathed not only her feet, but also her ankles and,
at times, her shins, pasting her tunic to her silk-like skin,
the kind salt could not dehydrate or erode, as the goddess
had been so perfectly created that it would take a lot more

to significantly alter her physiognomy to something it was
never meant to bear – Khronos's wear and tear of the flesh.

Poseidon watched her from afar, holding his golden trident,
as the bearer of the aegis would hold one of his lightning
bolts, though defensively, instead of pointing it out like a
javelin, ready to be thrown as far as possible for an athlete
competing in the games at Olympia, made in honor of Zeus
himself every olympiad, which is to say roughly four years.
The god of seas could understand why Hades had done
his deed – Kore was absolutely remarkable, and, as opposed
to the common courtesan, she was not one to be discarded.

His showing up had been entirely random; he could have
been watching her from Katane, but it had not been the case.
With such an insurmountable domain to rule, there were
plenty of places he could be at, though he had made it
a decision not to wander too far from Hellen's courtyard.
Having closed her eyes as the Eastern sibling of the Anemoi
kept flying toward her, Persephone failed to realize her other
uncle could be seen about two stadia away into the water.

Out of the three brothers who had split the sky, the sea, and
the Underworld between them, Zeus and Poseidon looked
very much alike, as opposed to Hades, who bore a slightly
different poise and appearance, as I have sung not long ago,
thy faithful bard, no less, permanently at thy disposal.
The Dolphin never wore any clothes, apart from when his
presence was requested elsewhere that not in the sea, such
as the Pantheon, in Olympus, in which case he would bear
a cloth over his male parts, unlike now, with his bare torso
in sight, using the waters as a drape from the waist down.
Leaving his niece to her thoughts, without engaging in any

conversation at all, he too left the area, accompanied by
a series of aquatic creatures whose allegiance lay with him.

310 Of course, one might wonder the reason why I should even
care to mention the presence of Poseidon, especially when
he did not even actively contribute to the telling of the tale,
but mind you that the gods are everywhere, at all times,
prying into affairs they ought not meddle with, although
315 there is no one who could possibly keep them away, for they
are indeed the gods, and to them we owe our very existence,
which can be made either longer or shorter, depending not
only on us, but mostly their temperament, which is why
we keep humoring them to live through yet another day
320 of our personal mortal coil, for if an obol must be paid
in death, trials must be dealt with daily as the necessary
fee to stay alive (and not always comfortably enough).

The Lady of the Golden Sword, alas, did not feel as relaxed
as her daughter, bearing within a feeling of guilt that was
325 suppressing her lungs and forcing her to breathe irregularly.
If she had a strong enough reason to blame the Screech Owl
before for Persephone's new lifecycle, bound to go up and
down for eternity because of those damned pomegranate
seeds, shrewdly fed to her under Hades' clear and specific
330 orders, now she really would have liked to kill her brother,
for it was still his fault that Kore had yet again disappeared,
and what was even worse – of her own rancorous accord.
If the Judge of Death had never met the young maiden, all
the suffering both mother and daughter had to withstand
335 would never have taken place, and most assuredly they
would not have had this latest argument, bringing them apart
once more, even though neither gods, nor Fates had anything
to do with the events in question – hence the reason for

the goddess of agriculture's newly brewed, burning wrath,
instead of the cold, eerie sadness which had generated winter
for the first time in the history of the descendants of Hellen.
The spring the latter were getting used to after a long break,
blessed with the blooming and blossoming of greenery all
over Greece and her adjacent territories, bringing in delicate
breezes from Poseidon's surrounding realms and domains,
depicting landscapes with the most vivid of colors and tones,
was about to become an actual, scorching hell on earth –
not that mortals would now burn alive or become charred;
perhaps they could die of thirst, should the cisterns and rivers
dry out due to a lack of precipitation every now and then.
The most important concern, however, was the rupture of
balance – at this rate, peace will never be achieved among
the gods, let alone men, who will stop at nothing to fulfill
their greed, which, deep down, is the gods' greed, mirrored
by their own creation, one intended to have been cleansed of
evil by a great flood, bound to withstand a great drought
as of this exact moment, to Gaia's repeated disappointment.

Canto XI

    Meanwhile, spirit-inflating Muse, what say you with respect
to the oak nymph we last saw lying atop a pile of purifying
salt, beneath her sown from the Danaids' evil proclivities?
Ah!, but of course… the cloaked figure she had last seen
before losing her senses from the inexorable commotion:
who were they, after all, for neither male, nor female traits
had been ascertained by Eurydike's eyes, fading to slumber?
The answer to that query remains yet to be sung, indeed,
but it will only take a matter of moments, as voices can be
heard in the distance, though gradually sounding closer.

    The plethora of indistinct echoing belongs in fact to Hades
and Hekate, who was talking to the ruler of the Underworld
just before her departure to the overground, where she would
telepathically meet with her priestess, Medea, who would
then leave a mystical impression in the air circulating above
Tempe, found by Olympus' foothills, facing the Aegean Sea.
The rest you have naturally already heard, concerning
Orpheus's trance, which would afterward make him collect
the best locals he could find to execute some tasks for him,
in the name of Eurydike, himself, but most importantly,
the goddess of darkness and the remainder of the Pantheon.
Without this inflation of inspiration, the Euro would have
never been built and supplied by the finest men and women
available, if the Apollonian was to surpass the first phase
of the expedition he had adopted as his very own enterprise,
moving from Argonaut to Euronaut, may Hera bless him.

    If the Muse will allow me to versify my personal opinion,
I find a great deal more honor in this sort of trial, rather than

going to battle for the sake of glory; after all, the price to pay
is the kind I would not want to stain my hands with – blood
from fathers' sons (if not daughters, once they have been
repeatedly ravaged by an entire army... tears are brought to
my eyes when I think about it, a fate much worse than death).
Let us just leave it there and fill this melody with a different
kind of harmony; we shall catch up with Orpheus later on.

Because she was still in shock from nearly having died
for good, Eurydike remained unaware of her whereabouts,
though the Muse has just now whispered unto my ear
the oak nymph had been taken to one of the many bedrooms
inside Hades's palace, where Kore had also strolled about
and realized it was surrounded by a cascade of molten rock,
apparently falling into infinity (it is impossible to know
for sure, as there are neither living, nor undead witnesses
to share the story with Calliope and, consequently, myself).

On the other side of the door, in the hallway, the ruler
of Tartarus was bickering with the goddess of magic about
what had happened to his forty-nine maids, the descendants
of Danaus, granted Hekate did not hold back concerning
her reply: 'I turned them into salt, O majestic Dark Lord.
They were trying to drown Eurydike in one of the bathtubs
they were sentenced to try to fill with water ever since they
were sent here, and because they kept failing at purifying
themselves from their murders, the only way they came up
with to ditch your domain and head for Elysium was to force
the nymph to stay underwater while they lay down in turns
on top of her, but their nemesis was the fact that water
is sacred and cannot be used to cleanse the wretched from
eternal damnation, if that is their fate, which was the case.
Of course, once the ones queueing realized the first two

60   or three had met their demise by touching the water, they tried to escape, but I would not let them, and so a bit of witchcraft was enough to flood the entire room, thus dissolving the remaining Danaids into the salt that cleansed both Eurydike's foot wound and the latent poison within'.

65   One could easily gather Hekate's presence in the Underworld palace made Hades feel split in two, making him slightly nervous, but also confident, probably because he knew that keeping in contact with the goddess of the Moon meant he was somehow closer to Persephone, granted both deities
70   had become friends during the maiden's involuntary stay, and they likely spoke to each other above ground, though something told him his sister Demeter's interference could harm Kore's thoughts as far as he was concerned, deterring her heart from her true feelings by clouding her mind.

75   However, and before he moved on to talking about his love, Hades bade Hekate to give him more details concerning the nymph lying in bed next door, namely what was it he should do with her, considering she was not dead after all: 'I cannot keep someone alive down here, it is unprecedented!
80   If word were to spread, every poor soul brought to Tartarus would want to go back to the world of the living; either that, or stay dead and be transferred to Elysium, acquitted of all charges – my prisoners would want to riot their way out. What would I do then? Feed them all to the dog? What of
85   their sentencing? I would just be doing them a favor, ending their misery once and for all, and I can think of a few who would definitely not think twice about the offer in question'.

The goddess of darkness, impatiently shaking her head in disapproval, sought to lay her plans out for the Screech Owl:

90 'My Lord, this is not a question of jurisprudence we are
    discussing; it is the unfair taking of a life that is at stake!
    The girl has told you herself, she died on her wedding day,
    having her whole life ahead of her by her husband's side…
    while it is true the will of one god cannot be reverted
95 by another (if indeed one of the immortals is the culprit),
    then at least we are allowed to make a few modifications
    and accommodate the needs of the mortals, which has taken
    place before – do you not remember the way Tiresias was
    toyed with by both Zeus and Hera? There is your precedent.
100 Others need not know about this, except perhaps for Kore,
    who would at last realize you do have a sensitive heart'.

    Speaking cunningly honeyed words, Hekate had managed
    to get Hades's attention, namely via the last sentence of her
    speech: 'And why, pray, would this become Persephone's
105 concern? What has she got to do with the nymph?', he asked.
    He seemed rattled at a first glance, though it was curiosity
    that was truly responsible for the contortion on his visage.
    The sorceress continued her explaining: 'For the time being,
    the one thing Persephone and Eurydike have in common
110 is distance – from the men who managed to win their heart.
    The problem is… neither of them want it to be that way'.

    The Screech Owl's face moved from a bedazzled expression
    of contortionism to one of latency (except for the eyes, which
    were wide open): 'Do you mean to say…?! Have I just heard
115 this correctly?! Persephone… loves… me…?', he faintly
    asked and exclaimed, turning halfway to the opposite end
    of the hallway, stunned by the best news he had ever heard
    in his long eternity, waiting for this sort of revelation since
    the beginning of time, by Father Khronos set into motion
120 in the early days both Gaia and Okeanos engendered him.

Persephone's Fall

I realize this moment may resemble one of those situations
you can foresee a backstabbing taking place somewhere
in time, but there really is no need for mystery, as Hekate
only wanted to bring together two couples by having them
125 interact with and help each other with respect to their needs,
which is to say, if Hades gained Eurydike's trust, then maybe
Persephone would be even more convinced of the cleanliness
of his heart; Orpheus would beseech Kore to lead him
to Tartarus, so that he could bring the oak nymph back
130 overground and resume their joint life, which had barely
even started, thanks to that perverted beast's intrusion.
The Apollonian had yet to find out why the satyr had shown,
though he knew it had had no intention of messing about
with Eurydike – otherwise, it would not have trodden
135 in her direction as violently as it did, hoping to kill her.

May I just interrupt the course of the narrative for a brief
moment to thank the ever-glorious Calliope for her teachings
as far as the ellipsis technique is concerned; it is undeniably
appropriate for the stylization of an epic composed by one
140 whose head has been lost, both literally and figuratively.

The goddess of magic placed her right hand on the Screech
Owl's left shoulder, delivering unto his ear the inexorable
truth by means of words hinged with wings: 'My Lord,
I believe it is rather obvious by now she has nurtured such
145 feelings for you for quite some time, now; however, and this
might actually be something new to you, not all women
are willing to part with their best kept secrets straight away,
for those are stored in their heart, whose depth is unknown
– even to themselves, most of the time... I too am a woman,
150 I too know these things, and as much as I try to understand
them plainly, I often fail in said task, which can turn into

a trial for men', she said, candidly answering Hades' queries.

She then continued to speak in the same, non-abrasive tone,
bringing her hands together as she stepped in front of him,
155 facing the unfairly Dark Lord again: 'Alas, such is women's
delicateness, for love, which may seem far too simple to some
males, is always a matter begging careful thought from our
side, though I will admit that, at times, putting our mind
to too much pondering may result in disruption, incoherence.
160 Persephone shall not return only because you tricked her
into it, my Lord… she is coming back because your abode
has already started to feel like home, to her, and that is key
to convincing a woman (Kore, in this case) her home is where
her love lingers about, and I do not mean your great palace,
165 but rather… your own heart, O majestic Lord of Shadows',
the goddess of the Moon concluded, bowing to Hades with
her left arm gently pressed against her womb, as she unfolded
the right one upward, assuring her allegiance was to him.

Before returning to earth, there was still one final detail
170 to add to the conversation, which is what Hekate quickly
moved on to: 'This girl indeed does not belong down here,
my Lord; nevertheless, it is my advice you should keep her
accommodated for the following three months to the best
of your ability, so you may show Persephone how much
175 you cared for the nymph while she stayed here, waiting
for her own pass to go back, should her husband trust
his instincts, and I very well hope he does, for if he does not,
then you will be entitled to use your powers in full to unite
them again, one way or another', the divine sorceress said,
180 dissolving into dust, leaving a trail of smoke behind, without
even clarifying Hades on whatever it was she meant, making
him look quizzical (with a far more rested face than before).

Having come round to her senses, the very nymph they had
both been talking about sat up on the bed, gently tapping
her head, as if she were involuntarily checking her status,
trying to figure out whether all those scenes riddled with
violence she had witnessed had been in fact tricks played
on herself by her wicked subconscious, which seemed to be
into a rather sordid sort of humor, much worse than a shade
of dark – even though it is mainly eerie, it can also be fun,
but... judging from Eurydike's look on her face, she likely
did not see it that way, as she was undoubtedly disturbed.

The moment her vision was restored back to normal, leaving
no traces of blurriness behind whatsoever, her attention got
caught on her feet (the right one of the pair, to be precise).
The oak nymph definitely remembered something had
happened to her foot; a viper had taken hold of her flesh,
releasing poison into her bloodstream as it bit through.
The orifices, however, engraved by the snake's sharp fangs,
were no longer there, making her all the more credulous
it had all been a nasty nightmare (if there ever have been
any of those worth remembering for their oneiric kindness).

There was still, of course, a minor detail to be sorted out:
the bedroom she was in did not look familiar in any way,
which naturally made her wonder where she could be.
Glancing to her right, a bench held a resting oaken crown,
ornamented with fresh flowers – it was the same she had
worn on her wedding day; that memory was excellently
preserved, for it was the most beautiful event she had ever
lived, regardless of not having lived that long, even for
a mortal, considering some demigods and their female
counterparts are not eligible for immortality, though it was
also true they could work toward it, just like Herakles.

Once he was separated from the other Argonauts even before
they arrived in Colchis, therefore fulfilling the gods' design
(which is to say Hera's, mostly), the greatest Greek hero
of all time (whom others would look up to) hailed to Thebes
and married Megara, the daughter of King Creon, who bore
him a son and a daughter; in a fit of vicious rage and insanity
by Hera induced, Herakles not only slew his family, but went
mad, having been tended to by Antikyreus, who eventually
healed him after resorting to a herb by the name of hellebore.

Having realized his crime, the hero fled Thebes to consult
the Oracle of Delphi, who was also being entranced by Hera.
Pythia, the high priestess to the Temple of Apollo, forwarded
Herakles to Eurystheus, the king of Mycenae and Hera's
favorite candidate to remain enthroned, forcing the hero
to become his servant for twelve full years, during the course
of which twelve labors (though originally ten, had it not been
for Eurystheus's disapproval regarding two of them) would
be performed; as of this moment, I cannot be precise as to
the exact number of tasks executed so far, but there still
is a long way before Herakles can complete the entire list,
orchestrated in the background by his stepmother, Hera,
who had nurtured hatred for him ever since he was an infant.

What I still have not sung to you is that, yet again, this was
a game like any other, played by both the king and queen
of Olympus, considering Zeus's advocate was the son he
shared with Alcmene, Herakles's actual mother, which
is why he was a demigod in the first place and was able
to strangle the snakes that had come out of Hera's statue's
eyes, in the house of Amphitryon, the hero's foster father,
albeit his human side, which made him mortal to the likes
of the common man; it was up to him to use both his brains

245 and brawn wisely, if he was to survive over a decade filled with unimaginable tasks and achieve the purpose of it all.

All drifting aside, Eurydike had not yet thoroughly examined the room and, holding the oaken crown ornamented with fresh flowers in her hands, she spun halfway and glanced
250 over at the left-hand side of the bedstead, only to realize the horrible truth – it had not been a nightmare, after all. It was there, lying on the back of a chair, her wedding gown; there were blood spats all over it, and the silk had been pierced in several places, turning what had once been a lovely
255 dress into no more than a rag, completely and utterly useless.

The young oak nymph was unable to hold back her tears… in the end, who could blame her for carrying the pieces of a broken heart and not being able to mend it properly, unknowing of her husband's whereabouts (or even hers,
260 come to that), along with the realization it would now become rather difficult for her to trust anyone else, except for herself, which is the part it all gets tricky to the Screech Owl, who must earn her trust, as foretold by the sorceress. There was also a table to the far side of the bedroom, covered
265 with food and drink, either cooked by promoted-to-servant inmates, or simply engendered by magic, which was surely the case (at least, it was a lot easier to prepare it all like so, if I am entitled to express my opinion regarding laziness…).

Suddenly, there was a knock on the door; it had been gentle,
270 but abrupt enough to turn Eurydike's visage dead-white, were she not alive in fact, with her blood flowing where it belonged, instead of coagulated from the viper's venom. Surprisingly, the nymph had not yet taken a look at herself to check what it was she was wearing, now the wedding

gown had been stained on and ripped to pieces, though she was obviously not going to just leave it there, as perhaps there still might be a chance of mending and purifying it.

Someone had changed her to an also white but slightly transparent tunic, albeit the opacity of some areas meant to be seen by Orpheus alone, if only he were by her side (preferably somewhere else, back in Tempe, resuming their lives before the tempest that had eerily come to haunt them). Having realized she was decent, Eurydike cautiously walked to the door and placed her right hand on the knob, though before opening it, she timidly asked: 'Who is it...? What do you want...?', gulping afterward due to a rather dry mouth.

The Judge of Death was nervous himself, bearing in mind what the goddess of magic had told him; still, he spoke as clearly as he could, trying not to sound threatening or any other tone of the kind: 'Eurydike, are you all right? I was wondering whether we could converse for a while, should you feel fine by now', Hades softly enounced, doing his best. Given one of her hands was already busy, she drove the other to her heart, allowing a somewhat afflictive expression to show on her face, crimsoned with an augmented flowrate of her blood (something she could tell from the sudden warmth of her cheeks, as well as the skyrocketing drumming of her internal tambourine, resounding behind her breast). Her mouth was half-open, exhaling a fresh breath, albeit tremored by fear and preoccupation for what was to come. The bench where she had found the oaken crown was close enough for her to drop said head ornament, along with the slashed gown, carefully placing both objects on the seat.

Clearing her throat, the oak nymph pushed down the knob

Persephone's Fall

305 on the door and opened it, facing the Dark Lord for the first
time after he had brought her to that very palace, his abode.
'My Lord', Eurydike uttered, bowing slightly before Hades.
The Screech Owl looked apprehensive, though he tried
to hide it; he too cleared his throat as an excuse to move on
310 and said, after having balanced on his toes: 'Please, there is
no need for formalities. This may be my home, but you are
no subject of mine – at least, not for the time being, anyway.
Let us hope you will only come back once you have lived
the whole of your life still ahead of you, instead of being gone
315 much too soon from the earth above... after all, your spouse
would like to know what it is like to enjoy sharing his own
life with you (that is how I would feel, if I were in his place)'.

Needless to sing (though I shall fiddle it all the same, as you
may have already guessed) that the oak nymph was rendered
320 speechless; it is rather sad to admit everyone does indeed
picture Hades as an unmerciful lord, and a dark one, at that.
After all, what else could people think of a deity whose realm
is the hellish Underworld, where criminals are sent to serve
timeless, brutal penalties, chastised, burned, starved, as if
325 they were still alive (just to mention some examples Kore
saw herself during her own imprisonment in Tartarus)?

Looking to extract even if only the slightest amount of reason
from the Judge of Death's words, Eurydike blinked thrice,
moved her hands toward each other, concealing her belly,
330 and switched her weight from one leg to the other, making
eye contact with Hades again: 'I beg your pardon, my Lord,
but I am afraid I do not understand what it is you mean'.
The Screech Owl felt embarrassed for apparently failing
to convey the message appropriately, involuntarily unveiling
335 a somewhat forced smile, contributing only to his further

embarrassment, for he could tell the grinning must have looked fake, without moving the muscles around his eyes (and that is one of the techniques any of us can make use of to make sure whoever it is that is smiling at us actually means it, instead of standing there, doing us a favor by smirking).

Moving to and fro once more, Hades yet again cleared his throat and sought to be a bit clearer, this time, commendably losing neither his temper, nor his delicate touch toward the nymph: 'Eurydike…', he said, bringing his hands together as well, 'to put it quite bluntly, you are not dead – so much so, that I am not even looking at a soul sentenced to prison. The moment you were «killed», your body disappeared from where it lay on the ground, and burial ceremonies were never performed, because… there simply was no one to be burned. If you will allow me to confide in you, I am quite surprised the ferryman brought you with him without receiving his payment… that is usually one of his reasons to turn down passengers (along with other criteria he decided to set of his own accord, although I never gave him permission to do so)'.

It may not have looked like it (because of her stunned visage), but the nymph was carefully listening to the Screech Owl's every word, and the more she listened, the more confused she felt, which is why she innocently asked the following questions: 'So… when those women who were meant to take care of me said my taking a bath would cleanse me from my venomous wound, they were right? Did they resurrect me?'.

Before answering, Hades tried to make Eurydike feel at home and asked her to walk with him, intending to move from the hallway to the hall itself, where they could lounge and maybe have a bite or sip a bit of nectar, instead of standing there.

Persephone's Fall

Feeling somewhat entranced because of all the revelations (even though no sorcery had been performed on her), the oak nymph obliged Hades and walked by his side, without ever touching each other, for mutual respect reigned supreme.

370 Shortly after, the Dark Lord in turn obliged Eurydike, providing her with this explanatory speech: 'The Danaids, as they were called, did save you indeed, though it was not their intention; as I have said, even though you were in the verge of death because of the poison, that was never the case,
375 and although the bath they give you was intended to purify your wound and rid you from the toxicity streaming through your body, they took advantage of it and tried to cleanse themselves instead. The only way they could do so would be to keep you inside the water, otherwise it would simply
380 flow away, for the crime they committed, mariticide, is far too loathsome to be forgiven; there was, nevertheless, a cost, and the price to pay would be murder – by drowning you. Only then would you have in fact died, if Hekate had not intervened, transforming them all into salt with her sorcery.
385 Salt is purifying, which means that, in the end, they managed to achieve what they desired the most, but not necessarily in the way they would have wanted it to happen', he ended.

There was still much to discuss regarding Eurydike's future in Tartarus, but Hades decided she had heard enough for
390 the time being, inviting her to relax by eating and drinking – this time without throwing any pomegranates in the way.

Canto XII

    Whisper unto my ear, O Muse of epic voyages and unsung
heroes, what has become of the Apollonian, after yet again
my having fiddled the lyre elliptically, defying the Father
of Time himself and the rules he so thoroughly laid down
5 long before any of us knew what it was to inhabit this world.
I shall try to give my best as I couple your harmonious voice
with Phoebus's melody through my fingers deciphered,
spanning thousands of stadia not only across the Aegean,
the Ionian, or the Mediterranean, but also the Propontis,
10 inexhaustibly bathing the fields in Phrygia, fertilizing them
toward prosperity, so help them the goddess of agriculture
and her daughter, now that the soaring blizzard has passed.

    May the birds in the skies listen to these prayers as well,
keeping the harpies away from both Orpheus' supplies
15 and himself, for the spirit of vengeance does not lie within.
Rather, the goddess Hekate has inflated him with Pandora's
only gift – hope, hope that he may find his away aboard
the Euro toward the shores of Trinacria, where he will be
expected and led to his everlasting love, magically gone
20 from the surface of the earth, though unknowingly alive.
It would therefore be prudent to beg Hera, the matrimonial
matriarch, to cast the Erinyes' abhorrent couriers out of
his way, allowing him to shout «evoe!» at the sight of land,
in this by Apollo guided as well, heir to the power of Helios.

25 As of this moment, pray, whither does the Euronaut head,
O formidable daughter of Zeus, the first of the square root
in Olympus's backyard sown and reaped in all splendor?
Ah!, but of course... he is currently port-rounding mainland

Greece, now situated between Kythira and Crete, Southeast of Attica, the tip of the Peloponnese Peninsula, being the first island another home of Aphrodite's, hopefully aiding in the success of this intrepid enterprise whose goal, after all, was love, and the goddess' son, Eros, was its main advocate.

As the Euro cradled itself in the Northeastern current, driven further asea with yet an unclear destination point (practically speaking, that is), the ship's only crewmember and captain – consequently – gazed around, inexorably reminiscing about the episodes he had lived through after taking part in Jason's own expedition, whose target had nothing to do at all with Orpheus' intentions, fully supported by Colchian sorceress Medea, and not just because she was under the goddess of darkness' instructions, but especially due to resentment. Even though she would one day experience a fit of madness herself, very much alike Herakles's tantrum, right now she found comfort in trying to make someone else happy, a man who truly deserved to spend the rest of his life by his wife's side – preferably overground, skipping eternity for a few good years still, as the lingering of the soul is always granted; whether it departs to Tartarus or the Elysian Fields is unclear (even to those directly involved in the process, including Hermes to begin with, Kharon, and the Dark Lord, no less).

Even though the night before his departure Orpheus and all other people involved in the process of building the ship had offered hecatombs to appease the Pantheon watching from the sky, not all gods were convinced the Apollonian really had it in him to sail through the most assorted obstacles to retrieve Eurydike, which is why a divine wager was placed on the table, dividing the deities into two factions – one that sought the Euronaut's success, and another that would try

60   their best to test his boldness, making him meet his demise
much earlier than expected, should it become necessary.
We must constantly remind ourselves how disposable
we are to our creators, something that, in a distant future,
may yet prove how alike we are, pretending to possess
65   the godly right to rule over our kinsmen and offer the crowds
the deadliest of spectacles, regardless of how merciless
historians may define us, as everlasting memory is everything
in our time; may I just add that some of us prefer to be
remembered by all the good deeds we did, instead of murder,
70   whose responsibility ultimately rests upon only one person's
shoulders, no matter who thrusts the sharpened blade across
another man's torso in the end, all the way to his back,
dripping blood all over the arena, not to crudely mention
the sand-covered entrails spread on the sand, fed to felines
75   after disembowelment, a putrid, disgusting scene to behold.
Yet, I foresee it will attract a great deal of followers to whom
such displays will become perfectly normal in the pursuit
for their cultural enrollment, may their souls be timely saved.

   As Orpheus leaves behind Crete to portside and Kythira
80   to starboard, a threat he had once faced before lurks under
the surface, and it is precisely because he is minding his own
and is unprepared that the time is just right to engage in an
attack, one whose weapons are similar in talent to those
entrusted to the Euronaut by both his mother and father,
85   though the perpetrators of the ambush need not any sort
of musical instrument to perform their magic, for they are
neither human, nor fish; they are, to be precise, hybrid.
From the waist up, they are some of the most beautiful
women a man could only ever dream of taking as his wife,
90   but from the womb down, no legs can be found, as they are
likely conjoined and covered by a scaly tail similar to that

of a swordfish, even though they did not carry piercing noses;
their teeth looked sharp enough, whenever they felt enraged.
So that I may satisfy the mystery at last, these sea creatures
are known as sirens or mermaids, depending on who we ask.
Personally, the first sounds a bit more poetically appropriate,
so I will henceforth continue referring to them by that noun.

If there is anyone or anything to go by as the personification
of temptation, then sirens are indeed a chaotic piece of work.
This does not mean, however, they are constantly heartless,
for their emotions can too wrestle with the power of love.
What most of us do not know is that the goddess of grain,
none other than Demeter, not only tried searching for Kore
all by herself (even though Hekate contributed a great deal,
of course), she also had these precise creatures help in her
daughter's rescue mission, offering some of them wings
to widen both the search area and their limited capabilities.

However, and considering Hades took hold of Persephone
by traveling through the entrails of Pergoussa, the Lady
of the Golden Sword cursed the sirens all the same for not
having intervened in the process of the maiden's abduction.
May I return to the beginning, when I sang the youngest
of the Thesmophoroi was not alone at the time, as she had
been joined by half-sisters (Pallas and Artemis), together
with a group of Oceanids, which means the sirens were not
necessarily restricted to their home in the seas, but what is
important here is that, if two Olympian goddesses failed
to stop Hades, what were these creatures supposed to do?
They could not possibly mount a wall of resistance against
the Dark Lord's sable-black horses and his golden chariot,
had they been present at the lake or not (which was the case).
Besides, the moment Hades ripped Gaia's seams, so were

the waters parted in half, which would have drifted away
any aquatic living being from the edge of each partition;
125 either that, or those caught in the middle of the scene would
have just fallen into the earth's entrails, perishing instantly.

In spite of all these simulated scenarios, a distraught mother
is always right, as one may generally assume, so not everyone
would dare risk a confrontation, especially with a goddess.
130 Demeter did not require the bearer of the aegis's permission
to handle minor magical creatures, so she did indeed curse
their existence, sentencing them to the capital penalty, should
a mortal survive their enchantments, not only by enduring
their melodic songs, but also by avoiding the crash of the
135 ship they boarded against rocks, which was the sirens'
ultimate objective; our man Orpheus had already duped
them before, aboard the Argo, saving the crew from jumping
into the water and the ship from colliding and sinking.

Naturally, not everyone can be saved, at times, which is
140 precisely what happened to Hylas, Herakles' personal squire.
He was abducted by water nymphs on the way to Colchis,
and his master stayed behind to look for him, though he was
deliberately unsuccessful by will of the gods, bearing in mind
other plans for him, as I have sung to you not long ago.

145 The sirens did not always swim together, and that is why
those who were outsmarted by mortals died, whereas others
were safe, as long as they kept away from these outcomes,
turned entirely disastrous to them by an enraged goddess.
Even if they went to Poseidon, the curse could not be undone
150 by their king – those were the rules affecting everyone
and everything, and they were simply impossible to override
(there was nothing he could do to atone their fate, either…).

Keeping his gaze static in that focal point where the sea
caresses the sky, apparently trying to disguise the void
in his soul, mirrored in his darkened irises, the Apollonian
was still unaware of the imminent ambush, one the sirens
wanted to be brutal enough to turn it into an example to
future sailors who dared defy their power; they did not know
Persephone had returned from the Underworld and, even
if they did, it would have been risky to ask Demeter to uncast
the curse, for the maiden was back indeed, but not forever.
They trusted their dark abilities, they knew they were good
at what they did, and this seaman in particular had been
the cause of their sisters' demise, who needed to be avenged.

By the power of metamorphosis, one of the sea creatures
volunteered to transform herself into the Euronaut's lost
love, none other than Eurydike, with the intent of making
an entranced Orpheus follow her wherever she told him
to go, even if it meant having to jump into the sea, where
all the others were impatiently waiting to tear him to pieces
and paint the water with his blood, leaving only the bones
behind to dissolve and become a part of the seabed, like all
the other countless grains of sand sustaining the weight
of the Mediterranean and its localized maritime brothers.
Even though they were half-human (or a third, minding
the wings), they supposedly still had some humanity left
in them, which is why the concept of killing another human,
tearing his flesh off with their bare, naturally bladed hands,
and eating it as if the foreseer were no more than a roasted
lamb basted with grease as a hecatomb offered to the gods
was eerily disturbing – especially when the victim in question
was none other than a man who had taught cannibals to live
on fruit, rather than each other's pieces, thus civilizing them.
Then again... the sirens were far too savage to look up to

185 rationality as a means of blending with Hellen's descendants;
their ability to communicate in the tongue of Man seemed
to be quite satisfying, for it served their barbaric purpose.

Having assumed both the body and voice of the oak nymph,
the selected siren was flown aboard by two of her sisters
190 hinged with wings (only, in this case, it was not something
to be proud of, unlike honeyed words also gifted with them).
The false Eurydike was silently placed aft, right by the ship's
stern, completely dried off, as if she had not touched a single
drop of water, which was easy to fake, given the sea was calm
195 and had not yet shown intention of swiping the Euro's deck;
the operation had gone smoothly, unnoticed to Orpheus.

The bard was so in touch with his inner self that he could
not hear the siren turning the helm hard to port (the fact
the bearings were brand-new aided the deception), which
200 would make the ship head straight for the rocky coast,
shattering it to pieces just off Pylos, still in the Peloponnese.
All the other sirens in the water kept following the ship,
progressively changing their formation into an escort,
so as to make sure the vessel would definitely founder.

205 As soon as the deed was done, the morphed half-breed
called upon the Euronaut, speaking as innocently as
Eurydike herself would have: 'My love...! At last, we are
united once more!', she cried, convincingly ecstatic.
Orpheus, who had been sitting on a small barrel filled
210 with fresh water, turned around abruptly, eventually falling
over by tumbling the improvised seat, hitting his head
so hard on the edge of the table placed on deck, that his
kithara took a tumble as well, sliding off the surface and
into the middle of a stack of baskets and boxes containing

perishable goods, on which he would feed before docking
again, and only the gods know where that would be,
for what seems to be a clear course with land practically
in sight may completely transform into a living nightmare
of ripped sails, masts sliced in half, leakages, in short –
a tremendous, thundering storm, which is why it is always
wise to keep the bearer of the aegis in a good mood.

The Apollonian's sight was blurred for a while, not only
crippling his sense of orientation, but also making him forget
about his lyre entirely; having introduced what was about
to happen, I believe I speak for all of us when I say he had
his luck about him, as a knockout would have made it too
easy for the bloodthirsty sea harpies, which is, quite bluntly,
what they actually were, aside from the beautiful visages,
the fish tails, and their magical voices (the common harpy
would never make anyone want to throw themselves into
the water, with all the typical rattling and cooing of a raven).

Once his senses came back, Orpheus took a good look
at the first thing he saw, which was not a thing, come to that;
it was his wife, exactly as he remembered her – floating hair
absorbing the sunlight, turning fairer by the second, crowned
with the same oaken wreath ornamented with fresh flowers
she had worn on her head on their wedding day, sparkling
eyes to the likes of precious emeralds collected by Gaia from
the mines of Mount Smaragdus, in Egypt, making the Moon
jealous of such brightness, one Hekate cannot hope to match
with her cratered pearl… they were so powerful that they
ensnared the whole of his senses, and, naturally, the magical
smile, the first feature he had seen her display, making him
fall for it on the spot, at the very beginning of their spiritual
bond, eventually growing beyond the border of metaphysics.

Now, though he became dazed and confused for a short
while, the Euronaut was aware he had hit his head, for it
was still badly sore in the back, where a small bump had
grown, yet much too sensitive to touch with bare hands
and no ice, though it was to the incident he attributed
his vision, because it was simply much too farfetched to go
on a voyage specifically to find Eurydike and have her
right there, in front of him, aboard, all shiny and new...
so many resources used, so much time invested building
the Euro, all of Tempe's inhabitants involved in the process,
together with the Argonauts' supervision, and that was it.

Hekate had warned him to always yield to both his instincts
and feelings, for there was no one he could trust, apart from
his own consciousness, but the situation imperatively begged
the question: how could Orpheus possibly yield to suspicion
after having fallen over, nearly knocking himself out, only to
face his wife in front of the helm, as if she were piloting him?
That was it – Eurydike had shown herself beyond a physical
dimension; she had merely returned from the house of Hades
to keep her husband company and provide him with advice
on how to quickly approach his destination by avoiding
any storm that may lie ahead, a manifestation of both Zeus
and Poseidon's wrath is how one may describe it, like a clash.

Even though the gods could intervene at any moment, they
often enjoyed letting the plot unfold before taking action,
for whatever happened on earth was a spectacle that needed
to be enjoyed, and that is where the bearer of the aegis's
authority over all other deities usually came in, preventing
them from changing the outcome of a determined situation
much too rapidly; only at the last minute would he allow
his or another's side to either save or kill off a character.

Obviously, because Hera had taken Orpheus' side, Zeus, the thundering master, was not on his wife's team (in fact, he rarely supported her, regardless of the matter in question). However, he did not exactly wish the Apollonian an ill fate, either, considering he was his grandson, though not Hera's… which is why it would be perfectly understandable (but only according to divine logic) for her to try and kill him as soon as the right opportunity arose; the question was the foreseer's hope of finding his wife to resume their reduced marriage was a moving enough story for the queen of gods to change and give a mortal man a chance Zeus himself could not be bothered to take, with his constant journeys down to earth, in search of another woman with whom to engage his virility. As much as I would love to pronounce myself on the hybrid creature resulting from the crossing between a man and a pig, it is obligatory I maintain my composure and, thusly, restrain my tongue, or it is the end for me (redundantly speaking).

And so, yielding in fact to his gut (despite being delusional), Orpheus took hold of one of the table's corner and pulled himself to an upright position with the aid of his arms, while feasting his visual sense on who he thought to be Eurydike. The Apollonian stepped forward, nearly tripping again on another rolling barrel, but nothing of the kind took place. He looked the vision in the eyes and faintly whispered words of love with frustration, a concoction known to be the recipe for despair: 'Eurydike… my lovely wedded wife, you have come for me… I was on my way to finding you myself…! I am so, so sorry I allowed that beast to take you away from me… someone deliberately clouded my mind, I am sure of it! Otherwise, I could have anticipated the attack and, maybe… died in your place – but never gratuitously, never without fighting that perverted, promiscuous half-breed!', he said.

Persephone's Fall

As he spoke, the distance between them both was shortening,
for they both walked toward each other, finding themselves
in the center of the Euro, the ungoverned vessel that seemed
to be already doomed, after having just been named, laid
down, and launched on her maiden voyage, without anyone
on it to batten down the hatches and row away from danger.

'It was not your fault, my darling husband... I would feel
much worse, should the satyr have taken your life, instead
of mine. I cannot cogitate a world you are not a part of...
I believe... I believe I would have severed my wrists, just
to join you in the Underworld, and I see no shame in making
such a daring claim. We are not supposed to let death do us
part – if you die, I die with you, that is the principle of love',
the sea snake told the Euronaut, purposely forcing him
to look at that same equation from a different perspective:
'But... then I have failed you... you are dead, whereas I am
still breathing, unworthy of life for not having joined you...
I am a coward! A pedantic, pathetic coward!', Orpheus cried,
holding the false nymph with all his strength, as he hid
his face behind her left shoulder and into her hair, blown
by the gentle breeze of a calm day at sea, heavily exhaling
on her neck, which he also kissed repeatedly, warming it up.

The siren was beginning to ache from all the pressure put
into that profound holding of Orpheus, and her visage was
really not that of someone who found that intimacy pleasing;
on the contrary, her facial expression was turning darker
by the second, though, fortunately for her, one of the winged
sirens came hovering by the ship's railing to check up on her
sister and she too displayed a threatening expression to keep
the guised one calm and not give the game away for nothing.
The tripartite creature also pushed her to quickly wrap it up,

340 descending back to water level to join the others and avoid
getting caught by frail sailor, whose foreseeing abilities were
apparently crippled still, clueless as to what was going on.

Being a sunny day as it was, Phoebus had his airways clear
to watch everything that was going on, but Zeus had ordered
345 him to stay put and continue to drive his golden chariot,
which was naturally revolting to a father who loved his child,
but there was really nothing Apollo could do about it…
the bearer of the aegis's will is always above any other god's
desires and must, therefore, be done, however reluctantly.

350 It was now time to put an end to the sirens' little game,
and so the fake oak nymph softly released herself from
the Euronaut, looked him in his teary eyes and begged him,
suddenly beginning to cry: 'I forgive you, Orpheus, I do…!
My love, we promised each other we would never move on
355 without the other, for better or worse, which is why there is
still time to be reunited, if…', she said, suspending her speech
where the Apollonian's curiosity had been most aroused:
'What? If what? I will do whatever it takes to atone this,
make it right for good…!', he said, overwhelmingly excited.

360 'If you throw yourself with me in the water', the siren said,
in a rather cold tone, though Orpheus overlooked that part.
In a fragment of time Khronos himself could not count,
even with the help of an hourglass pouring sand before him,
the bard clearly responded, without blinking not even once:
365 'Then what are we waiting for…? If that is the toll to pay
to spend the rest of eternity with you in the house of Hades,
so be it – I am ready', he concluded, offering his right hand
to the siren's, as he turned to face starboard, prepared to
step onto the Euro's railing and take a leap of faith in love.

370 With the help of the boxes stored on that side of the ship,
Orpheus positioned himself atop and helped the half-breed
to stand next to him, so as to jump together, hand-in-hand.
Pallas Athena would not stand it anymore, and ordered
an immediate and sudden blow from Euros, the East wind,
375 strong enough to tilt the vessel portside and push them both
back onto deck, which resulted in an endless tumbling
and rolling of boxes, barrels and baskets, among which
the golden kithara had become momentarily hidden and lost.

Because Orpheus broke eye contact with the siren, he became
380 fully aware of himself once more, drawing his attention to
the lyre, nearly falling into the sea, had he not swiftly held it.
It was then he discovered the horrible truth – a group of
savage-looking sirens had been hit in the head by the Euro,
and they were furious about it, looking at him with sharp
385 teeth and penetrating eyes, ready to finish him on the spot.

As for the sea creature on board, let us just say she did not
look like Eurydike anymore, for her loss of concentration
had made her forget about her morphed appearance, both
physical and emotional, uttering the worst words coming
390 to her mouth, something the real nymph would never do.
Once she saw the lyre in Orpheus' hands, she projected
herself unto him with all her weight, in an attempt to drag
him down with her, but it was too late... Apollo cast his
daylight over his son's head, inflating him with musical
395 inspiration, which made him fiddle one of his best tunes.
All sirens instantly screamed, as they bled out through
every orifice in their body, turning into floating carcasses
other fish would gladly have for an unexpected, yet satisfying
meal; the sea looked like an insurmountable red-tainted pool.
400 The bard got back on his feet and kicked the duping siren

into the water, joining the others, already submerging.

As the Peloponnese began to extend its rocky legs, Orpheus ran to the helm and turned it hard a-starboard as quickly as he could, avoiding what would have been a fatal collision. When he confirmed he was out of harm's way, the Euronaut lay on his back and looked up to the sky, thanking the gods for ridding him of an unimaginable fate he dared not wish on his enemies, as it was just beyond stomach-churning.

The Sicilian Flag[***]

[***] Although it was first adopted in 1282, following the revolt of the Sicilian Vespers against King Charles I of Sicily ([1226/7-1285], commonly known as Charles d'Anjou), the flag of this Italian island contains elements from Antiquity, influenced by its Greek colonization, namely: the *triskelion* (a three-legged spiral) in the center, the head of Medusa, the Gorgon, adorned with wings, and three ears of wheat.

The *triskelion* is representative of Sicily's triangular shape (hence the "Trinacria" designation), whereas the duality of colors diagonally disposed in right triangles represent two modern-day municipalities: Palermo (Pánormos), in red (dark area, in the image), and, in yellow (light area), Corleone, part of the first's metropolitan area, bearing extraordinary significance in the Middle Ages for its agricultural properties.

Summer

Canto XIII

As the Muse has whispered unto my ears thus far, guiding
the quill in my hand into inscribing this poem on the piece
of parchment lying before me, the island of Trinacria,
the largest in the whole of the Mediterranean Sea (the center
of the known world), stretched out by its permanently active
stratovolcano, Mount Aitne, bears a lot more tales than one
could ever imagine, for it is not only a portion of land
enriched with the most beautiful and astounding sights of all
Greece, but also a home to creatures thought to be no more
than folklore to the majority of Hellen's descendants.

The Titanomachy was not the only battle the Olympians
had to engage in to establish themselves as sole rulers of all
domains comprised between Ouranos and Tartarus, where
the Titans were eventually and perpetually imprisoned;
no, there was yet another epic episode before peace could be
achieved among deities, although the three major realms
attributed to Zeus, Poseidon, and Hades, who already had
control over them, were once again threatened by the Giants,
thus unleashing the Gigantomachy, whose outcome was too
favorable to the Pantheon, who found their rest at last,
having decided to force war on Man, rather than themselves.

This way, they could prove they were worthy, indeed,
of their seat as supreme rulers, keeping their playful battles
under control, favoring one side over another, depending
on how compassionate they were for certain individuals
or city-states completely, which could either come together
as one nation for a cause (the case of Paris and Helen's
eloping to Ilion, yet to be razed to the ground under

the leadership of Agamemnon and Menelaus, the Atreidai),
or fight against each other and, obviously, weaken their
respective hegemony and status, which was to be the fate
of Athens in quite a distant future, bringing Sparta forward.
Curiously enough, though the conflict is to be known as
the Peloponnese War, Trinacria will too become involved,
specifically from Syracusa, where there live Dorians, mostly,
all the way inland to Athenians by origin, of Ionian descent.

Recollecting Ouranos's castration by the hand of Kronos
(father to the Olympians), who was given an adamant sickle
to perform the task, under Gaia's instructions (his mother),
Aphrodite was not the only deity engendered as a result;
the primordial god of the skies did not care for his children,
whether it be Titans, Cyclopes, or the Hundred-Handers,
so they were all locked in Gaia's entrails, who, as payback,
had the hidden Kronos cut off Ouranos' genitals, and as
he did, drops of blood gushed onto Gaia, impregnating her
with the Giants and the deities of vengeance, the Erinyes.

Of the several conflicts between Olympians and Giants,
there is one in particular worth mentioning in this song,
involving Enkelados and Pallas Athena, responsible for
the first's entrapment precisely under the island of Trinacria.
Although Mount Aitne is a passage to and from Tartarus,
its constant eruptions are not a product of Hades's anger
after all, but of Enkelados's fiery breathing, for the goddess
could not kill him – it takes human intervention to do so,
which is rather odd, as it somewhat severs divine autonomy;
nevertheless, and making sure he would never rise again,
Zeus decreed that his daughter threw Trinacria on top
of the giant, burying him deep inside his mother's entrails
once more, defying Gaia's own rebellion against her partner.

60   Out of all the creatures engendered via the union of the two
     primordial gods (voluntary or not), the Cyclopes, who
     fashioned Zeus' lightning bolts, as you may recall, were
     the native inhabitants of the famed triangular-shaped island.

     With the Muse's permission, I shall now sing to you, having
65   my chest inflated with both the necessary inspiration and air
     to hold my tune, about Polyphemos, one of these single-eyed
     specimens; Gaia had not carried this particular cyclops in her
     womb, as he was the son of Poseidon and Thoosa, a Nereid,
     which made him the goddess of the earth's great-grandson,
70   a fourth-generation cyclops who, albeit conceived by sea
     deities, did not belong at all in his parents' maritime abode,
     though such a detail did not stop him from nurturing his love
     for one of Thoosa's sisters – Galateia, she was called, thought
     to be the fairest of all fifty Nereids, the maritime nymphs
75   (again, the incestual question does not pose itself in divinity).

     The beautiful Galateia, however, did not share Polyphemos'
     feelings, having offered her heart to someone else who had
     taken it without even thinking twice, the splendorous Akis,
     a mortal young man whose built made him look godlike,
80   perfectly toned and chiseled, the ideal, athletic Grecian,
     easily mistaken for a deity like Ares, for instance, though
     his intentions clearly had nothing to do with warmongering.

     The youth had long locks in his hair, which was pitch black,
     and atop his head he wore a kotinos, an olive wreath, given
85   to the victors of the Olympiads, crowning them champions.
     His visage was as handsome as his entire physiognomy,
     with dark eyes matching the hue of his locks, a proportional
     nose, and delicate lips; presuming a description of this ilk
     is somewhat shallow, he was also gifted with shrewdness

90 and was able to take care of himself, spending most days
with Galateia, both freely displaying affection for each other.

As for the Nereid, I can firmly attest she was indeed a joy
to behold and, without prejudice to the guardian of my heart,
her beauty was much superior to that of Aphrodite (it is not
95 the first time a claim of this sort is quilled down, for Psyche,
the wife of Eros, had already stolen a great deal of attention
from the goddess a long time ago, infuriating her deeply).
Galateia was a blonde, bearing on her head the very same
daylight Apollo carried every day across the skies of Greece;
100 her eyes too mirrored that exact shine on her irises' surface.
The white tunic she wore slid neatly whenever she undressed,
revealing an hourglass-shaped body, contoured by skin as
smooth as silk, destined to never look a day over twenty.

Polyphemos, whose violent outbursts were frequent, could
105 not withstand losing the most brilliant of the sea nymphs
to a rival, especially one he could easily grab and devour
with a single mouthful, though perhaps Akis was not worthy
of being consumed by the cyclops, fearing hatred would
make him regurgitate his decayed face, one he did not bear
110 to look at, regardless of how it looked after indigestion.
Both lovers would usually bide their time between Katane
and Tauroménion, with a direct view over the Ionian Sea,
whereas Polyphemos, crazed with jealousy, would lurk
behind Mount Aitne, witnessing their seamless connection.

115 One day, when the nymph finally decided she would lie with
Akis, the cyclops, in a fit of rage, grabbed a boulder from
the Northern side of the volcano, aimed it at the young man
and released it, allowing it to roll downhill, skipping every
now and then, menacingly approaching the eloping couple.

120 In a final act of heroism, having realized only one of them
had a chance of escaping the fastly approaching boulder,
and even though Galateia was immortal (which did not
matter to Akis at all), the youth sacrificed himself out of love
for the nymph, pushing her out of the way, and was instantly
125 crushed, spattering blood all over the green plains, by the
foothills of the incandescent mountain, where Polyphemos
had stayed to watch his love rival meet his untimely death.
The youth's entire skeleton was imprinted into the ground,
making it hard to tell which bones were which, because of
130 their ashy appearance, as if they had once belonged to a long
dead body recently unearthed and in risk of being scattered
by the winds, who were also inhabiting deities of Trinacria,
ruled by their aforementioned king, Aeolos, who obeyed
the will of the Olympians, traveling wherever they were told.

135 Galateia, who was still lying on the ground, confused by
her lover's apparently aggressive behavior (which, sadly,
is usually the first thought that comes to mind, when
someone who loves another is only trying to protect them
from harm's way, regardless of their proven dedication),
140 lifted her head (though the fall had made her face another
way), and saw a great deal of blood spatter right beside her;
part of it had inclusively showered her right forearm with
a few drops, warm and thick because of their volume.
She had already loosened her tunic slightly, and by rising
145 in horror, the nymph became nude from the waist up,
uncovering her bosom; regardless of such an exposure,
her privacy was the least of her concerns at that moment.

Carefully analyzing her tainted forearm, bending her elbow
as much as she could, the Nereid saw her reflection on
150 the blood that had begun to stream down, staining her

somewhat transparent, pure-white tunic as it kept dripping.
She obviously knew that blood, as much as ichor, its divine
counterpart, was meant to run through the veins of men
without ever gushing out, so, clearly, something was off.

155 As Galateia turned around, slowly assuming a lounging
position on the grass, the inhuman truth revealed itself:
not only had Akis' skeleton been turned to dust (bursting
his blood from his body), his entrails had also grossly blown;
there was wedged brain matter split into several portions,
160 a pair of burst lungs that sounded like they were wheezing,
a crushed heart – and not in a figurative manner of speech,
a pocket (the stomach) that was disconnected from a pair
of snake-like tubes (the esophagus and the small bowel),
a thick piece of flesh that had been squeezed with enough
165 force to literally expel a green juice of some sort (the liver,
the gallbladder and its bile), together with other indistinct,
misplaced systems that had once upon a time given shape
to the mortal young man, whose eyes no one could look at
anymore, given they too had exploded and were somewhere
170 amid the foremostly mentioned distorted brain matter.

The sea nymph, having gone through the churning display
with her own eyes (which, despite being still in place, seemed
like they were going to burst out of their sockets at any
moment), silently opened her mouth as much as she could,
175 drove both hands to her head and began to uncontrollably
scream in terror, plucking handfuls of hair from her head,
then moving toward her naked chest, striking it with
the white blades she carried in her fingers, cutting it open,
covering herself with both her lover's blood and ambrosia.

180 Galateia gave her best to stand on her feet, but her legs would

not let her, trembling nervously from an unimaginable shock
that would have driven anyone mad, no matter where they
stood on mortality grounds; after all, humans are a godly
creation, and there are similarities no one can possibly deny,
185 as I have sung myself repeatedly throughout this epic tale.
And so, considering her legs were strengthless, she dragged
herself closer to the remains of her lover, who, from one
of the most handsome descendants of Hellen, moved on to
unrecognizable pieces of flesh – the exact same pieces taken
190 hold of by Galateia, who desperately wanted to put them
back together and revive them, bringing the youth to life.

Polyphemos, who had kept watching from behind Aitne,
accidentally put too much weight on one of his feet, releasing
a sizeable rock from the mountain's cone, rolling all the way
195 down to where the previous boulder had crushed Akis.
The echo produced from the clashing between the rock
and the volcano's body did not pass Galateia unnoticed,
making her look up as she held the young man's visceral
remains in agony, burning her wounded chest with the salty
200 tears that streamed down her face (though she was far more
hurt inside than on the surface of her loving, delicate body).

Before the rock got her full attention, however, the nymph
met the cyclops' stare, as he was cowardly hiding the rest
of his insurmountable body; realizing her lover's death
205 had been no accident whatsoever and that the culprit was
right there, she could have experienced a fit of enraging
madness, but that was not the case, nor did she feel angry
at all, as she knew exactly what to do to punish the enormous
son of Poseidon, whose domain she had lived in until then.

210 As soon as the rolling rock was about to hit her, Galateia

used her powers to stop it, leaving it still, where it lay, preventing it from rolling away down to the sea, as opposed to the fatal boulder; underneath it, there was a pool of Akis's blood, which she magically transformed into a spring of fresh water, spreading the course of the newborn river Akis to the scattered remains of the man whose name it had just taken, thus creating a fork of distributaries that flowed from the main riverbed by the foothills of Aitne to the Ionian Sea in the shape of a river delta, bathing the newly created banks of several locations from Náxos to Katane, also named after Akis by the will of Galateia, who, being an aquatic nymph, let go of her human form for the rest of eternity, and joined her lover's spirit, perpetually unifying both their essences.

Realizing what the woman he loved had done, Polyphemos repeatedly stomped the ground in a fit of fury, though it was Enkelados who was beginning to feel rather wrathful, as not only he supported the weight of the island, his face was also feeling the pressure of the cyclops's jumping, which made him heavily wheeze and expel molten rock from the top of Aitne, forcing the son of Poseidon to go away and leave him alone, for the giant was already far too uncomfortable to withstand the outbursts of his weird, one-eyed relative.

Fortunately for Enkelados, his burning exhaling did indeed scare Polyphemos away, driving him off to the Ionian coast, instead of having him return to his cave to the North, in front of the Tyrrhenian, where he kept his flock and would often eat any invaders daring enough to try to steal his supplies. His father, in the end, had been generous to the cyclops, settling him on a landmass surrounded by the god's realm, spanning over an area no man had ever dreamed of sailing, leaking beyond the Pillars of Herakles, uncharted territory.

Persephone's Fall

When the Muse last spoke to me regarding Persephone's location, she had me sing the maiden was somewhere to be found in the Eastern coast of Trinacria, between Katane
245 and Syracusa, which was still a long way; the quarrel she she had had with her mother, Demeter, was the main cause for her wanting to leave, as the Lady of the Golden Sword could not accept the fact Kore had fallen in love with the god who had done them part for half a revolution of the Sun,
250 deliberately tricking the youngest of the Thesmophoroi into making her return to Tartarus, eternally repeating the cycle.

Now, Persephone knew better than turning her back on her mother, who was her only family (with respect to caring about her, at least); besides, it was not in her nature to grow
255 rancor in her heart, not the everlasting kind, most assuredly. For that reason, the goddess of rebirth decided atonement was in order, and so she traveled from her whereabouts back to Katane, where they had last been together; however, and for some unknown motive, the maiden overshot the city,
260 ending up further North, where the newborn river Akis now flowed, together with the immortality of Galateia.

Not only there was no sign of Demeter nearby, Kore also realized the surroundings were slightly different, beginning by how much closer Aitne seemed when looked upon from
265 that point of view, and the new river Akis delta was simply unrecognizable to the goddess of springtime, who was supposed to, precisely, be aware of all fresh water springs flowing across the island, but that mysterious one had to be new; how it had come to exist, however, she did not know.

270 Not much further away, Polyphemos was down on both knees, cratering the soft sand with his weight, looking into

the horizon with his single eye aligned with his nose,
in the center of his forehead, ornamented by only one brow.
He was mouthing something inaudible to Persephone,
who was not at all scared by the creature's size once she saw
him, which does not beg much of a surprise, considering
both the Olympians and the Cyclopes were contemporary
of each other, and even though the maiden was a second-
-generation goddess, she knew all about them (regardless
of how difficult it was to actually come across one of them,
as these were specimens who liked to keep to themselves,
socializing only between them while living a simple life,
such as sowing and reaping crops or performing husbandry,
which was Polyphemos's area of expertise – sheep grazing,
to be exact), and that is why she did not intend to startle
the son of Poseidon, otherwise he could get much too angry
and, thus, become dangerous, something the maiden was not
looking forward to from an unpredictable creature like that.

Having noticed there was a boulder nearby, Persephone
moved swiftly and took cover behind it, realizing it was
oddly tainted all over with dark stains that did not seem
to form any sort of pattern at all; whatever it was that
had covered the boulder was no longer fresh or even
malodourous, come to that, as it could definitely still
bear a stench of putrefaction, but that was not the case.
Kore could not make out what the markings were or meant,
but it was only a little while ago that we witnessed the actual
ordeal provoked by the intentionally loosened block of stone,
a kind of death one should never wish upon one's enemies.

Observations aside, the maiden concentrated on listening
to what the cyclops had been mouthing, hopefully making
sense of his words, now she was closer to him than before:

Persephone's Fall

'Father, please, I beg of you, ease the wrath you hold against
me, intercede for me to calm Mother's pain for the loss of
her sister, and do not let the bearer of the aegis discharge my
people's lightning bolts on top of my head, for I was blinded
with jealousy…! I could not prevent it, it was far stronger
than the whole of my strength combined… I will do anything
to appease you and the other gods, just halt any attempt
intended to punish me… I shall concentrate on my flock only
and avoid temptation, for I know I do not deserve the gift
of love, misshapen since birth, disproportional, relying on
one sight alone… forgive me – I kneel before you, forgive me,
O powerful Poseidon, O delicate Thoosa, O supreme Zeus,
lord and lady of the seas, ultimate ruler of the skies…!
My heart is broken for the atrocity I have committed and,
therefore, requires its pain be dimmed, soothed with your
divine pardon, so I may move on from this misled life
of a monster', Polyphemos concluded, eloquently developing
an extraordinarily rational rhetoric, much too clever
for the common beast, which the cyclops decidedly did not
appear to be, to the eyes of an astute (yet gullible) Kore.

The goddess of rebirth was convinced this cyclops could be
reasoned with, and so, she decided to reveal herself, but not
before Poseidon answered his son's prayers, engendering
a wave whose height could cover Polyphemos completely,
as a sign of the purification he had been craving ever since
the outcome of his outburst had figuratively crushed him too.

Besides, there was nothing else Poseidon, Thoosa, or Zeus
(ultimately) could do to perpetuate his punishment, for his
uncontrollable desire of revenge, sponsored by the Erinyes,
had lost him any chance whatsoever of winning Galateia's
affections, especially once she realized he was her lover's

murderer, because... it is not always about what we look
like, or what we are (a Cyclops, a deity, a Titan, a Giant...),
but rather who we are within; if someone's love for another
is real, any apparent faults can undoubtedly be overlooked.
Everyone had their own idea regarding the so-called
Dark Lord of the Underworld, the Screech Owl, the Judge
of Death, and yet... Persephone eventually came to realize
Hades had simply been misunderstood for far too long,
and the fact he understood his approach to people in general
was inappropriate, to the likes of his first contact with Kore,
was the much needed first step toward his own cleansing.

We admittedly need to learn to love ourselves for who we are
and perform any necessary changes that may jeopardize
our essence, but the gods definitely did not create Humanity
only to jest with men and women – they are supposed
to generate their own bonds, and the power of love is
the very first path, regardless of how difficult the thunderous
god has made it for humans to find their other half, putting
an end to the search, gathering all the missing pieces at last.

In spite of his size, Polyphemos was thrown on his back by
the tidal wave sent by Poseidon and Thoosa (Zeus had not
taken interest in the cyclops' pleas, leaving it to his parents
to deal with him), having lost his balance, causing a slight
earth tremor, though, this time, it had nothing to do with
Enkelados's anger – it was Gaia's doing, seeking to soften
her great-grandson's collapse on the shores of Trinacria.

Persephone, who was on her way to conversing with him,
was forced to throw herself further back, though she was
eventually caught in the wave, rendered unconscious after
hitting her head on the rock wall – she was bleeding slightly,

but it was nothing too serious that could not be repaired with a few stitches, if tended to both quickly and properly.

Polyphemos started to breathe heavily as soon as the water rushed back; he was gazing the sky in utter concentration, thanking the entire Pantheon for his acquittance, although the gods in general felt confused, as they did not know what he was talking about, but Poseidon was there, happy for him. The king of seas then abandoned the scene, having missed Persephone's presence; it was the cyclops himself who, looking around while still lying on the sand, saw the maiden, soaking wet as much as him, vividly bleeding out, or so he thought (it had not occurred to him it was ambrosia).

Putting his strength to the task, he turned around on his belly to observe her from the correct angle; it was clearly a woman. Polyphemos thus rushed to stand on his feet and get closer. He gave his best to poke her softly, but his idea of softness was somewhat beyond the tact of either gods or humans. Of course, he did not hurt her, and even if he had, she could not feel a thing; had he damaged her, though, then the pain would definitely arise, but he had only just been purified, which means he would not be so stupid as to kill again.

Holding that thought, the cyclops put his hand under Kore, excavating her off the sand, and held her fully aware of his strength (so as to avoid squishing her), tearing but a fraction of the cloth he wore to cover his manhood; it was stained, but it would have to do for the time being, as he measured the diameter of the youngest of the Mistresses' head by sight, seeking to prevent her crippling or death by exsanguination. The wound needed to be cleaned and dressed with something that could sterilize it and avoid its consequent infection;

it would not take long for the improvised bandage to soak.

395 Moving as fast as he could, Polyphemos took Persephone
back to his cave, on the other side of Aitna, just a few stadia
away from Messine, where he would take good care of her.
As he ran parallel to the Ionian, he wheezed slightly, facing
the sea and thanking his parents for their offer, promising
400 this time he would not be made a fool of and that she was
his to keep, and nobody else's – even if he had to kill again.
Both Poseidon and Thoosa listened their son's words,
but knew not what to make of them; they simply hoped
he would not do anything rash, calling his death upon him.

Canto XIV

'I humbly request thou bestowest on me, guiding Muse,
the ability to apply thy wisdom to this enterprise of mine,
so I may split it in two halves and fuel both heart and mind,
for one cannot proceed its task without the other's influence,
strongly bound by my will and honor, along with thy bidding
to never abandon ship and steer to the heavenliest of ports,
mooring my vessel in the arms of my forlorn Mistress, whose
tears I intend to wipe with my bare thumbs, keeping her safe
for all eternity, so help me Zeus almighty, by which time no
more than stardust we will have become, watching over each
other from a privileged seat in the night sky, immortalized.

'Hear me, sacred entities… heed my calling and bless me with
good fortune, that I may carry out that which I have been
entrusted with, from darkness toward the light, for my life
depends on death, which, in being cheated, shall see nothing
more than a crave to take vengeance, for it will not accept
humiliation so easily, standing its guard, seeking to distract
me from my only purpose, doing whatever it must to smite
this man down, casting the bait into the water so he may bite
firmly and be reeled in, still dangling at the end of the fishing
pole, struggling for an intake of breath he cannot achieve.

'Should he let go and embrace his fate quicker by giving in?
The goddess could not have been any clearer, and still he
yielded – momentarily, of course, but his vision was far too
clouded, just as it had been when he should have been
the most alert; confronting the decoy, however, was useful
all the same, forcing him to understand that desisting would
only pleasure the scythe-armed figure, continuously claiming

pure souls, ravishing their bodies to keep its bloodstream
flowing, but not through its veins, no… across the entrails
of the earth, rather – it has no veins, no flesh… it is but bare
bone, rejoicing from its reaping with the eeriest of smirks,
albeit the impossibility of conjuring any other expression
because of the absence of muscle; an emissary of Hades,
I reckon, throwing me off balance, openheartedly shedding
light over an easy path, a simple way, a road more traveled.

'No more shall I indulge you to your crooked laughter,
O cloaked Rhamnousia, hooded Nemesis, daughter of Nyx!
I do not dare defy the gods; in hubris I have not engaged,
for they do not want me dead – the bearer of the aegis would
have already struck me, the king of seas would have let his
daughters fulfill their malice, twisted beyond imagination,
the stern judge himself would have ordered the ferryman
to collect me… but neither of them will have it, it is too easy
to strip down a spirit of its incarnation without a fair trial!

'However, if your presence is nothing more than a warning,
then (and only then) will I allow you to collect me, should I
fail my mission and, consequently, my better half, the one
gatekeeper to my heart, as no one else possesses the strength
to bear such a burden, to carry the key that rips this padlock,
just like she did the first moment my sight drove me to her.
Indeed, it is living for another that is costly, not perishing in
ostentatious glory, remembered in the future for cowardice.

'That is how I wish forthcoming generations to recall me,
a legend who pushed on, thrusted by a gift only a selected
few happen to wield, a blessing many of us never live up to,
no matter how much effort we put into it – the power to love.
It requires skill, in order to care for another; even though

it is a part of our nature, learning to love and be loved back is essential to generate balance – otherwise, it will become our downfall, not only if we fail to tame it, but also if we do not set it loose, back into the wilderness, for it cannot be raised in captivity, especially when it comes to crippling the inexorable connection made between two souls, and not at random, no… there is always purpose in what seems to be no more than chance, a happy coincidence, a streak of luck.

'The Moirai know what they are doing, they always do… they may share an eye between all three, but these sisters need not see through their eyesight where to place a thread in the loom of life; they were engendered to be masterful at it, and not even the gods possess the autonomy to overrule their decisions – I am the first to bow to their will, whichever it may be, and as long as I survive my own labors, with no intent to achieve immortality, my heart shall be the compass to my reward, the revival of my lawfully wedded wife, who, in turn, trusted me to guard her from the menaces of any ilk.

'The Pantheon does not rekindle Man's opportunity to excel at their job a second time so lightly, and there are always certain conditions that must be fulfilled in exchange for such generosity from the masters of the cosmos, a sort of tribute to be paid, if a human is to rise from the ashes and prosper. There is a great deal of risk involved in the completion of this enterprise – I may be refused my rightful reward, even after having sworn allegiance to the sovereign and his divine kin. Nevertheless, I am ready, I am prepared, by Zeus's beard!

'I must never surrender to the kind of deal the common man would willingly sign with his blood without thinking twice. She lives, and by putting an end to my very existence, so does

she perish a second time, only not at the horns of a beast...
her death would then be spread all over my hands, and as
I tried to wipe the redness off, all the more it would scatter
across my body, tainting me with the color of dishonor.

'I am the son of Phoebus Apollo, the Sun-God, and Calliope,
the leader of the nine Muses, and both have taught me well,
not just in the art of Music and Poetry (that is but the starting
point), but especially in what to do when combining the two.
There is delicateness, sensitivity that men should also learn,
instead of wasting their time severing each other's heads.
By the power of the lyre I have defeated an enemy, for magic
is a part of me; used wisely, it brings order to where there is
chaos, light to where darkness has left its mark, and peace
to where war was once a criminal lackey of the house of Nyx.

'I am not interested in becoming an acclaimed hero like my
brother Jason; there is no Golden Fleece to retrieve and liven
my kingship up; I do not covet a throne other than my home,
with its queen by my side, hand-in-hand as we lose ourselves
in the vastity of the landscape, with nothing but the Aegean
ahead, all the way to the coast of Ilion, under Priam's rule.

'My other half, a living-dead, is on the verge of falling into
the river of souls, sentenced to the perpetual whirlpool
of the Inferi, unaware of who she is now, soon to have been.
I call upon thee, Aeolos, royalty of the winds, to set them
loose and blow my sail as swiftly as they can, pointing me
straight to the woman who my consciousness had me know
would help me, to the best of her knowledge, find the path
to the house of Hades, and return accompanied by Eurydike.

'To Pallas Athena I kneel and bow, in the hope the goddess

of knowledge will assist me in overcoming the obstacles that
lay ahead, not necessarily geographic, but especially as far as
120 mind jogging is concerned, for I need my wits about me
to avert yet another distraction that may gratuitously hand
my soul over to Nemesis and, consequently, Kharon's barge.
O goddess of undeniable wisdom, I beg of thee, protect my
brains from diverting into the darkness of confusion and
125 error, block all fits of madness the heat is bound to make
me go through under this scorching weather, which has never
been as moody as it has been for a little over a month, now.

'From my father's twin, the goddess Artemis, I request,
showing no disregard whatsoever for my inferiority in
130 comparison to the might of the gods, that the living beings
rooted deep into the earth may offer me shelter from wild
beasts, if for any reason at all they do not respond to
the charms played by my golden kithara, which I promise
not to forget again, for if I do, my head shall be the price
135 for defying the gods' trust in me, after asking for their help.
Also, if I end up stranded at sea for too long, having no more
water to drink or food to eat, I ask to be pointed to animals
a mere mortal is allowed to hunt down and baste in grease
for a hecatomb, and not the sacred species that cannot be
140 wounded, let alone killed, for fear of their divine proprietor's
wrath – the Cattle of Helios, guarded by his two daughters,
Phaëthusa and Lampetië, as the god will take the Sun away
from the skies and rise the dead from obscurity, by which
time I shall have paid the fatal toll myself for my hubris,
145 satisfying at last the cravings of the lurking Rhamnousia.

'And may Poseidon, king of the sea, bearer of the trident,
keep these waters still, permitting the Euro to fare well,
untouched, unharmed, unhailed by the fiery bolts of Zeus

in the unpredictable storms, the ambushes of thunderous
150 lightning that mirror the supreme leader's ire when defied.
Eternal brothers, I thee implore, keep me safe in my journey,
join thy strengths and cast the light of Phoebus Apollo
over me, for I sail in the name of love and love alone, not
pride, arrogance, boast, or vanity for fooling the gods into
155 making me their chosen one; ease your senses, my lords,
be compassionate, my ladies – I do not forget myself, no!
I know my place in the chain of command, I am but a bard
crying out to the stars joining the bright pearlescent Moon
of the goddess Hekate to take me where my fate lies, next to
160 the oak nymph; I am a one-woman man and my allegiance
shall never change, regardless of the wilderness' attempts
to make me obliterate the undying memories of my soulmate.
Forward we surf, my vessel and I, headed toward the wonder
that is Trinacria, the fairest jewel of Hellen's great domain!

165 'Wherever this world may lead, held on the back of Atlas,
sentenced to said punishment after the Titanomachy ended,
I shall not lose my faith and push on until my objective
has been duly fulfilled – let this be decreed in the name
of Dionysos: sever me from the neck down, but keep my head
170 as a personal offering to thee, that it may mournfully sing
my failure before the gods, if unsuccessful I come to be'.

Never in several millennia had one man spoken so eloquently
when addressing the gods, promising them his devotion
and respect for their might, their power, their rightful place
175 in the skies, in short… their kindness for having created
human life to be enjoyed by Man himself, not once blaming
them for their playful ways of controlling people's lives,
often leading them to their death, depending on the kind
of day they had, often quarreling among themselves, while

180 sacrificing a man, a woman, or even a child as a manner
of settling a disagreement over matters of no importance.

There was no doubt, Orpheus bore the spirit of a warrior
without the need for weapons and armor, as his words
were capable of inflicting damage to any obstacle that dared
185 present itself in front of him; together with his compositions,
he was indestructible, and no more than the truth he spoke:
the power of love did indeed illuminate his desire to find
Eurydike, assuming she had been imprisoned by the Screech
Owl, even though, of course, that was not the occurrence.
190 His foreseeing ability was still handicapped, but he kept on
with his manifestations of devotion and dedication to
the illustrious Pantheon, hoping the persistent clouds
in his mind would cease and desist once and for all,
restituting his magical gift to what it used to be, prior to
195 the oak nymph's tragic accident, still labeled as deliberate
in the Apollonian's mind, which was something he tried
to seclude at all costs – if the gods read his true thoughts,
they would not have started to weep, like many of them did
in Olympus, from where they listened to his every word,
200 following his every note on the golden kithara Phoebus
felt prouder than ever to have offered his talented offspring,
looking into his eyes without questioning the sadness
transpiring from the inside of their sockets, cascading down
his cheekbones and into his mouth, salting the wounded
205 verses he sang, breaking the gods' hearts in ardent pain.

Naturally, Orpheus prayed to the gods mostly out of respect,
for no other entities were above them, as the whole of Greece
was well aware; however, it was not only the Olympians
the bard had convinced of the sorrow his ordeal was making
210 him traverse at sea by himself in an unprecedented journey.

The foreseer (incredibly enough) had also been able to tear
the Erinyes apart, the deities of revenge, maleficent creatures
who no one would ever even think there was a heart inside
each of them, bloodthirsty as they were for those who craved
their rivals' blood just as much, counting on the horrifying
harpies to do their work, too demonic to describe yet again.

The nymphs of all assorted natures were sorry for him, too...
although I have frequently sung to you about principles
such as honor, glory, and morals (which can be achieved
without shedding a single drop of blood in a violent context),
and though a man's word is as worthy as a fellowship pact,
proving he can be trusted, the Apollonian did not embark
on this adventure to satisfy anyone – not the Olympians,
not the nymphs, not spirits, not fellow humans, absolutely
nobody, apart from Eurydike; once a couple is prepared
to tie the knot before Hera, who gives the ultimate blessing
when two people wed and their essences become singular,
they swear an oath of love, a binding contract keeping them
together, even in the afterlife, but such a concept is beyond
maintaining our word, for that is implicit and needs not
be brought back up, after both souls have reached out.

A true lover remembers what they swore – they do not run
away, they do not abandon the other because something
has gone seriously wrong, they do not evade responsibility;
no god is perfect, let alone a simple human being like us...
I have no reason to fear their wrath for a statement like this,
for my fate was laid down long ago, and I have always been
prepared to face and accept it, whichever ending it is I meet.
Life is but emptiness, if there is no one by our side to make
it worth our while – there is a void to be plenished, and it is
not just anybody who can do that; it has to be the one person,

Persephone's Fall

the one we would gladly die for, if they perished firstly,
the one we would force our body to live on for, even when
a fatal illness pulls us out of the light and into the realm
245 of the dead, where there is nothing but fire to remind us
of our new statute as Hades' prisoners, we, who should
have been sent to the Elysium prairies for our kindness,
and yet end up in a disgraceful domain, a stain to our name.

As for Orpheus, the son of Apollo (heir to Helios' Sun),
250 bearing in mind his own words, it is much more difficult
to live for someone thought to be dead by many, though
their thread has not yet been cut by the Moirai, unable
to sever it completely, though scarring it to its stress point,
than throwing oneself into the sea to be torn to pieces
255 and become fish fodder, if not the sirens', still displeased
about the loss of another sisterly group – by the same man.

His life was Eurydike's, and if there was a chance to retrieve
her in mint condition, he would endure every single trial,
that much the gods were aware of – now, it was time to put
260 him up to the test, one of Zeus' ideas, fiercely enraging
his queen: 'Have you no compassion for your grandson?!
Must everything be a game, to you? Orpheus's word should
have been enough for you to let him be on his way, why
keep moving the pieces on the board to make this enterprise
265 even harder than it already is?! You know, your lordship,
considering he is not even your legitimate family, I would
happily let him die without having a row with you, but he
cherishes the woman he wedded, which is something in your
flamboyant life you never actually cared about, turning me
270 into a satyr over and over again! All I am missing from the
waist down is a lower goat half; the horns, funnily enough,
are closer than ever to the stars, some of which increased

the length of these shameful ornaments!', Hera said, lashing
out at her husband for his untamable adulterous behavior,
while pointing to her forehead, in which overgrown horns
flourished, making them vanish again due to embarrassment.

The bearer of the aegis, on the other hand, felt amused and
did not care much for the goddess of family's impulsiveness
(he had not even looked at how tall her cheating marks had
become, focusing on the board displaying the Euro's present
location in the Hellenic world, spanning between the Pillars
of Herakles and the Propontis, engulfing the Mediterranean).
'Hold your peace, my darling wife', Zeus provocatively said,
without looking her in the eye, 'I do not intend to get my kin
killed, whether hit in the head by a mast, drowned at sea and
eaten by the creatures of Poseidon's domain, or any other
means of putting an end to Phoebus and Calliope's son', he
added, referring to death like a rather normal, day-to-day
activity he was used to; for a god, it was obviously not so
eerie to speak of fatality, granted his existence was eternal
(until the day Man forgot about him and all other deities,
at least, perhaps adopting one or several gods who did not
take pleasure in turning humans into torn, raggedy dolls...
the question was: what kind of god would be that merciful?).

For the time being, his plan regarding Orpheus begged solely
confirmation as far as the Apollonian's leap of faith was
concerned, which is to say that Zeus wanted to see how far
the bard would actually go for his love of Eurydike, counting
on her husband's arrival any time soon, though the wait was
not bound to end just yet; one thing was certain, however –
if the weather decided to change again without expectation
while still asea, the sorcerer would only be further delayed,
forced to moor the ship and befriend any locals on the way.

If the different tribes scattered across the Grecian nation
305 all shared the same basics of a Hellene's education, then
hospitality would have to be a tribute deemed essential.

At present, the Euronaut was sailing West, smoothly taken away by the joint breeze of Notos and Euros, leading him straight to the Eastern coast of Trinacria, exactly where he
310 was supposed to land, but handing him over his objective without presenting any sort of difficulty would have been too much goodwill on the gods' behalf, which is why Zeus gave Aeolos the order for him to, in turn, command Notos to blow harder than Euros, pointing the vessel Northwest,
315 where in a narrow passage, similar to the Clashing Rocks (though slightly wider), there lurked a double menace, just waiting for the right moment to reveal itself to the sailor.

Canto XV

And lo, did the weather become hotter each day, drying up
the cisterns one by one, reducing the streams' beds, given
the Lady of the Golden Sword was still aching from the fight
she had had with Persephone, goddess of rebirth and spring,
5 her darling daughter, the one she had gone through so much
trouble to bring back overground, where she belonged.

Alas, the youngest of the Thesmophoroi was gone yet again,
not because of another rape, but rather of her own accord,
which disturbed Demeter a lot more, knowing she had done
10 it conscientiously because of the goddess of agriculture's
outburst, unwilling to accept that Kore might had grown
and could, therefore, make her own decisions without
the need for maternal guidance; she too was a goddess,
which means she was perfectly capable of consulting her
15 feelings, her heart, her spirit, in short – her internal compass,
leading her straight to her North, and not someone else's,
her own oracle, without the need for an intermediate to
interpret her dreams in her place (one of the advantages
of becoming responsible adults, mature enough to take
20 care of themselves, setting a proper example for humans).

Of course, some parents always find it hard to let go of their
cubs, not because they are selfish, not at all… but rather
because they always fear for them, wishing they could help,
even though they tumble and fall; however, they must stand
25 by themselves, or perhaps entrust a better half to assist them.
After all, in the sage words of Orpheus, one cannot stand
by the other's side only when it is all good, only when one
is in trouble and must wind down, without ever retributing.

It is not fair for one to hold all rights and privileges, whereas the other constantly plays the role of a cornerstone, a pillar. One too must offer support – that is sharing made real, and the Apollonian is an excellent example of chivalry, willing to be tried until he finally fulfills his new purpose on earth, to become a literal rescuer, and even if the rescue were only figurative, as in a manner of speech, it would count as well.

May I just inform the gods, if they are listening to this at all, that the people, the descendants of Hellen, are not happy about another abrupt change in their ways of life, and they were just beginning to readapt to the smoothness of spring… now, it is too much – droughts are unbearable just as much as frozen solid water, slowly and painfully maiming humans with its cold sores, whose only solution is but to amputate. Still, should the icing be successfully picked, it is possible to melt it by the fire (granted the people had time to acquire enough firewood provisions before the white coating set).

None of these changes are deliberate – although Demeter's confused feelings about her daughter's double disappearance had never been a part of her agricultural teachings, holding Mankind's very survival in the palm of her hand, granaries could not be filled up forever through magic and mysticism; humans needed to learn to sow their lands on their own, in case the gods forsook them, which was not so surprising. They would either do it on purpose, to force Man to worship and ask them to be saved, or they would simply tune them off, busy as they were focusing on real-life games, using actual pawns like the former Argonauts, for instance, like Herakles or, for the moment, Orpheus; as long as they were human, they would stress their thread to nearly a point of no return, as the Moirai do not sew back strings already in use.

60   They either loom a new one, or cut it in half, marking
the end of a life; luckily enough for Eurydike, Atropos could
not tear hers in half, not even with a two-man (woman, in
this case) felling saw on a springboard; all three sisters felt
the gods had duped them somehow, and they were not at all
65   satisfied, for everyone living being, celestial or not, must bow
to their will – no matter how Zeus may be thunderous about
giving in to someone else, that is what he too is sentenced to.

Now, although deities of all sorts had magical powers,
whether they were demigods or gods to their full extent,
70   some of them were specialized in witchcraft and sorcery.
Hekate is not only the goddess of the Moon, spirits, but also
magic and, most important of all, necromancy, considered
by some as a dark kind of magic, one to stay away from,
for fear of being cursed in both the earthly life and afterlife.
75   The patroness of the arts of the dead (hence her Tartarus
abode and consequent connection to Hades) had made it
possible for the oak nymph to stay alive, meddling indeed
with her life thread, infuriating the Moirai in general and
Atropos in particular, for never in eternity had she failed
80   a single, swift, and painless cut, throwing her pair of scissors
against a rocky wall, leaving it hanging there like the tip
of a blade across a man's ribcage in times of belligerence.

Hekate was not an Olympian, and neither was the Screech
Owl; they were outcasts, ostracized by the bearer of the aegis
85   and the rest of the Pantheon, apart from Demeter and Kore,
naturally, whom she had befriended because of this episode
of epic proportions, still some good iambic pentameters
away from its end (a finger's length is not enough to count
them, believe it or not – it is the true definition of a paradox);
90   nevertheless, the current circumstances required correction.

Hekate's intentions had stuck to plan so far, but the fact that
the Mistresses had had a row and, thusly, become separated,
was threatening to the success of the entire operation, not to
mention the Olympians' intervention in Orpheus's journey,
which she was still unaware of, as the bard had not yet made
his oath to the gods and the inner voice of his consciousness,
the goddess of necromancy, no less; songs can be confusing,
at times, I understand that perfectly, but prior to getting to
the chorus, different parts must be sung to contextualize aft
the rhythm, otherwise the poetic composition is pointless.

The goddess of the Moon was back in her overground lair,
the cave in Enna, just a short walk from Pergoussa, cooling
her thoughts in the shade, which was predominant over
the dim sunlight dragging its way in, despite the depth
of the rocky recess; as the divine wielder of magical powers,
she sensed something had gone terribly wrong, attracting
chaos into what was supposed to be going smoothly, in an
orderly fashion, to be precise – alas, there seemed to be
remnants of the primordial god who favored imbalance
above all in the air, disturbing Hekate's candid planning.

As she prepared to leave the center of the island and speak
to the Mistresses about their steamy argument in Katane,
by the Ionian coast, the heat taking over her human body
while exiting the cave became unbearable, especially because
of her characteristic garments, featuring a hooded cloak.
Mysterious entities to the likes of the sorceress rarely enjoy
displaying their face, let alone their full head; discarded
by the majority, Hekate had never been too keen on breaking
the canon, for which reason she could not remember having
ever lowered her dark hood, concealing a great deal of her
visage, though she possessed no scars whatsoever to hide it.

Persephone's Fall

Ugliness was not a motive either, as the few priestesses
paying her homage did not believe their goddess bore
a crooked look in her eyes, which resembled beacons
125 in the night, mainly when the Moon revealed itself fully;
Medea, bless her soul, was one of them, never misjudging
her patroness' decisions (after all, had it not been for her
assistance, Orpheus's departure could have been delayed).

Sensing the Lady of the Sword's ire smothering the world's
130 source of breath, Hekate vanished, leaving a trail of smoke
behind, the white kind of fume, reappearing at the same
belvedere where both Thesmophoroi had turned their backs
on each other, a moment followed by Kore's walking away
parallel to the shore, disappearing at last, headed South;
135 however, neither of them could be found near Aitne's feet.
The sorceress then recurred to her insight ability, so she
could at least feel a presence somewhere on the island's
surface, focusing on the Eastern side of the triangle-shaped
portion of land in the middle of the Mediterranean Sea.
140 Two sources came up, though one was slightly closer than
the other – they were clearly not together, which did not
sound good; judging from the very first event that had led
to this entire misadventure in the first place, one would think
mother and daughter would want to spend the second half
145 of Persephone's earthly term with each other, but it was not
so, forcing Hekate to decide and pursue the strongest signal,
for which reason she combed the shore Southbound, moving
at god-speed while paying attention to every single detail
as she roamed toward the spring of Arethusa in Ortygia.

150 The Muse has already had me sing that it was not only
the birthplace of the divine archer twins, Artemis and Apollo,
bore by Leto, but also the result of her sister Asteria's

metamorphosis, once she threw herself into the Ionian Sea,
turning herself into the quail-shaped mass of land just off
the coast of Syracusa, to the East-Southeast, to be precise.
As for Arethusa, originally a nymph from Arcadia, in the
Peloponnese Peninsula, she was the provider of water for the
Hellenic settlement based off Corinth, having fled from home
once Alpheios, a river god, began chasing her across the sea.
Protecting the chaste nymph from Alpheios's lust, however,
Artemis transformed the latter into a spring, in spite of
the merging of their waters underneath the island, spared
from maritime contamination, remaining permanently fresh.

And right by the fountain, having a dialogue with Arethusa,
Hekate saw Demeter, gently sitting down by her side, so as
to avoid startling her; there, the breeze was much more
agreeable, softly blowing the papyrus reeds, which also grew
in Katane (where else would I find an endless source of paper
to inscribe my verses into, thus registering these legends
for posterity, as there are no other sources in all of Greece?).

'Welcome, Hekate', the spirit of Arethusa said from among
the flowing water, 'I have been expecting you', she added.
In a tone of surprise, the goddess of magic replied in the form
of a couple of questions: 'Were you? Why is that?', to which
the fountain answered, clarifying her statement: 'It just so
happens the Lady of the Golden Sword has had a row with
Persephone, becoming apart once more, and what is worse
is that Demeter came here looking for her – unsuccessfully.
Now, humans are yet again in trouble, risking not just
famine, but thirst also, granted our friend perspires her
preoccupation for Kore, blaming herself for pushing her
away, just a few weeks' time from the return of the cycle.
That is why, instead of freezing everyone to their death,

she is now slowly asphyxiating Mankind', Arethusa uttered, concluding her line of thought, whose every word Demeter had held on to, despite her inability to face the water spirit.

Realizing the eldest of the Thesmophoroi was turning red with shame, heating the small portion of air that was still respirable, the sorceress goddess kindly addressed Demeter through the use of words hinged with wings: 'My dearest friend, cornerstone of Man, what has driven you into this again? Persephone was so happy to have returned to your side, and now you are once more broken apart because of an argument? What was it that upset you both so much?', Hekate asked, beseeching her friend into telling her what she desperately desired to know, although strategically remaining calm (otherwise, her intentions would founder).

Before Demeter could put herself together, though, Arethusa intervened, diverting the conversation to a shortcut: 'Please, do try to convince her she can still make this right in advance to Persephone's fall if she listens to both sense and reason, or we will suffer the consequences, one way or another. Demeter must accept the fact that Kore is a fully grown goddess and, therefore, has the right to use her sensibility and cognition to feel and think for herself', the aquatic spirit concluded, giving the eldest Mistress a chance to speak.

'It is... so hard for me to accept this, I... I just cannot behold what is to become of my daughter this lightheartedly... she is going to be so unhappy, and there is no way of making the prophecy undone... the Moirai are even more stubborn than Zeus himself, that hog! Children everywhere, all his, and I was foolish enough to fall for his unresisting advances. I find solace in Persephone, my treasured little girl, who I

failed to protect from her own family… it is one thing
for a father to abandon a woman and her child (one
of the most common events in the discrepancy between men
and women), but another for an uncle to tear the seams
of the earth and rape his own niece, shackling her in chains,
treated like the common whore', the Lady of the Golden
Sword said, weeping after winding down and confiding
in her friend goddesses, who were listening in disbelief,
with Hekate in particular repudiating Demeter's attitude.

'Lady of harvests, you are lying through your teeth, and you
know it, as I know that you know I know', Hekate retorted,
making Demeter look her in the eye as if she were about
to turn her to stone, to the likes of Medusa, the Gorgon,
beheaded by yet another son of Zeus, Perseus, a hero long
before Herakles's time, savior of Andromeda after killing
a sea monster known as Ketos, just off the shores of Argos,
whose hand he afterward asked for in marriage, becoming
king of Argos, having also founded the city of Mycenae.

The goddess of human sustenance swiftly rose, attempting
to pierce the divine sorceress with words of hatred: 'How
dare you address me in such a manner?! Do you forget
yourself, witch? It is not only Zeus or Hera you bow to,
Mankind owes me their existence just as much! Were it not
for myself and my daughter, humans would have starved
and thirsted by now! I may not be a queen, but I too hold
the fate of Man in my hands', she said, frantically spewing
droplets of saliva because of the aggressivity of her speech.

'I have never forgotten myself, Demeter…', Hekate promptly
argued in a tone of disappointment, instead of anger or rage,
'it is you who have turned to a path all the others accuse me

of having founded, the path of darkness, mistrust, witchcraft,
in short – the eeriest of damnations, the worst of which, ego.
You, O mighty lady of crops and harvests, have become what
you hate the most about other gods, selfish, exactly what you
considered Hades to be, for raping Persephone; the bearer
of the aegis, not only for abandoning you and your child,
but also for only having intervened once you threatened
him with the annihilation of Man, freezing them all to death.
Allow me to remind you it is not only Zeus or Hera who feed
on humans' prayers – we all do, you included, and by now
they must be yet again terrified, for the same goddess of land
fertility and prosperity, the one who taught them to eat
without constantly moving from place to place once they
exhausted their locale's natural resources, the same deity
who brought order to the earth by giving its inhabitants
a bloody good reason to pay eternal homage to the gods,
is now chewing on their misery, not once delivering what
they so anxiously ask for', the goddess of magic concluded,
shaming Demeter on the spot, rendering her speechless.

Arethusa, marveled by Hekate's sageness, transpired through
words of absolute wisdom (undoubtedly hinged with golden
wings), gave her a nod of approval, as the deity of the Moon
had ended up doing what the spring's spirit had asked for.
Both were convinced they had finally talked sense into
the eldest of the Thesmophoroi, who slowly sat down again,
this time covering her face with both hands in the shape
of a conch, letting loose the tears she had building inside
her ever since she had last been with Persephone, in Katane;
she also began to sob incredibly loud, but there was no one
around and the other goddesses would rather have her cry
out than curse them or, worse, an already frail Humanity,
as Hellenes had begun dropping one by one all over Greece.

Hekate sought to comfort the Lady of the Golden Sword
by sitting next to her on the cistern's marble railing, without
completely turning her back on Arethusa, thus including her
in the conversation: 'It is all right, Milady… everything is
just fine… we do need, nevertheless, to find Persephone prior
to her earthly term limit, or the both of you will have thrown
away an important chance of spending your time together.
Not only that, I would… like to apologize for myself
for calling you a liar, but… you know you were distorting
the name of Hades. I concur that his approach toward Kore
was naturally not the best, but remember he is an outcast,
just like me… why do you think we both live underground?
I do not even care much about it, but the Screech Owl…
you know Zeus tricked him when the three brothers split
these realms between them; the bearer of the aegis wanted
the skies to rule from above, Poseidon took the seas and…
what of Hades? The Underworld, the house of pestilence,
the abode of the dead, possibly even more feared than Zeus
or Poseidon, roaming wherever they please, leaving their
seed in the most random of wombs, abandoning the women
bearing their children… they can kill whenever they want,
but once it is done, it is over for humans' earthly bodies.
The afterlife is what scares them the most, beginning with
Kharon, that horrid creature – he certainly bears a visage
to the likes of Nemesis; believe me, gazing at him is rather
unpleasant, and I am being euphemistic about it', she said,
making both Demeter and Arethusa laugh at her description.

Now that the eldest of the Mistresses seemed considerably
more relaxed, the goddess of the Moon moved on with her
rhetoric to tell the lady of the grain about the not so Dark
Lord: 'You see, my dearest friend, I do not mean to upset
you or dare provoke your wrath, but I am sure Persephone

told you who the real Hades was... I was there, always
by her side, lending her my shoulder for her to cry on
whenever she felt like it, but that was only in the beginning,
while she still felt ill of him for his rudeness, taking her away
by the wrist and waist; he has been dealing with the dead
for so long, now, that he has forgotten what it is like
to approach someone else who has not been sentenced
to eternal suffering... I showed her around, acquainted her
with a few examples (one of which the man who fed you
a piece of his own son), and she understood why he was
so stern, why he had lost his touch, duped by his own brother
into guarding the dead in Gaia's entrails, missing out
on the light of Phoebus, the forests of Artemis, the watery
bodies where the nymphs dwell and, on that day, where
your daughter was, too... the exact same day the cosmos
conspired for Hades to find Kore, eventually realizing
who he was and developing the same ilk of feelings that
had already invaded his heart the moment he set eyes on her.
She was never an actual prisoner, you know... her bedroom
door was always unlocked – she simply assumed
she was trapped; Hades entreated her with everything
he could come up with to make her happy, by feeding her,
serving her ambrosia, offering her jewels no man has ever
seen, let alone created... but she would have none of that,
because, deep down, she was being purchased, though her
heart had never been for sale, and when Hades finally
understood what the path to her love was, he agreed to let
Persephone go, giving her the freedom she had been craving
for about six months; what is interesting, however, is that,
when Hermes was prepared to bring her back to the surface,
her eyes were gleaming with tears, and why, you may ask?
Because she had seen through him, his heart and his soul,
and did not want to leave anymore', the sorceress concluded.

Arethusa, despite revealing herself to her fellow divinities
in the shape of an aquatic human body, was clearly crying,
and so was the Lady of the Golden Sword, but not because
she felt ashamed of herself, let alone irate; no, Demeter
355 had water in her eyes because of how unfair she had been
to both Hades and Persephone, who loved each other and,
yet, she was the one standing in their way, making them both
unhappy for having to long for each other, considering
their first opportunity to be together had been missed or,
360 rather (and in my personal opinion), had served its purpose:
getting to know each other, clarifying all doubts, so they
were now prepared to be rejoined in the fullest of harmonies.

Taking Hekate's hand, Demeter flew off with her friend
by her side, once again on the lookout for Persephone,
365 held hostage somewhere on the surface of Trinacria, as both
goddesses would soon discover, aided by the sorceress's
inner compass, which would lead them to Kore's exact
location, pinpointable from the top of Olympus, though
the other gods, sadly, had not been paying any attention.
370 Arethusa, still shedding tears as she bade them goodbye,
returned to the flow of her spring, confident of their success.

Canto XVI

The Euro was running out on provisions and Orpheus was
getting closer to starvation, not to mention an asphyxiating
thirst would overcome him, incapable of being quenched –
water was the one element (along with air) the Apollonian
did not lack, but the salt in it was definitely of no use to him.
As much as he tried to hold himself together, seasickness was
beginning to show, but it was not the kind of ailment caused
by the currents' motions, swerving the oncoming vessels;
it was something worse than not being able to hold a feast
down in the stomach – malnutrition and dehydration,
a fatal concoction which could only be avoided by lying
down in absolute rest while nursed back to nourishment.
The Euronaut was alone aboard a ship with no land in sight;
plus, his senses were progressively abandoning him, enjoying
their ride on Notos' strong blow, driving him to insanity.

The words «food for thought» are so often enounced in the
most assorted situations that one never actually believes
one will need that same repast to prevent a complete brain
meltdown or, in the worst of cases, an irreversible shutdown;
if a body does not meet the requirements to keep functioning,
the soul within will have to abandon it, transcending from
an earthly sort of flesh to an afterlife-like physiognomy.
Whether this living-dead vessel is ferried to Hades's domain,
I know not, for, as far as Orpheus is concerned, he is not
guilty of any crimes, and he is not trying to take his own life.

We all remember he spent a great deal of his journey praying
to the gods, but when it seemed his saviors were not there
for him, he did not question their resolve; rather, he kept

journeying fully trusting the Pantheon, rummaging through his perishables in rations, portions that would satisfy him and still last indefinitely – at least, it seemed to be that way, hoping that at any moment shores would come within range of his eyesight, no matter what lurked beyond the beaches, as long as he could disembark, collect fresh supplies and be on his way, which, to his misfortune, had not yet happened.

Meanwhile, because of the scalding heat spread by Demeter's former state of anger, the kithara fiddler decided he would rather starve for a while, than get intoxicated with putrid foods that had begun to swirl in the air, possibly attracting unfriendly attention, which Orpheus had had plenty of. Albeit his desire to continue his prayers to the Olympians, he could not do it, regardless of how enthusiastic he felt about it, as it was not only his foreseeing abilities that were secluded from Apollo – his plain human sight had begun presenting him with hallucinations; he could not make out what was real, anymore, and the fear that another group of sirens could come aboard and try to persuade him into throwing himself underwater made him look like a madman, telling his visions to go away, while shouting out to them that they were not real, and he would not go anywhere.

Up in the skies, both factions of gods involved in the path Orpheus's fate would take kept arguing that Zeus had no compassion whatsoever for the bard, and that the god's testing of his strength was being pushed too far, generating an even wider chasm between their difference of opinion. Athena and the bearer of the aegis loved each other profusely as daughter and father, respectively, but Pallas had been feeling quite disturbed since the sirens' attack and, thusly, tried to reason with the thunderous god: 'Father, you know

60   I dare not question your judgment and, when I rarely do,
it is because I do not see a fruitful ending to your endeavors.
I beg of you, Orpheus is dying... his madness is nearly
at the top of the ziggurat, and if it does reach that stage,
I am afraid it will be too late to bring him back and have him
65   fulfill his objective; my heart is moved, Zeus – he swore
an oath of love, not just to Eurydike, but to us as well...!
His faith is in us, it is imprudent not to deliver; if the whole
of Greece finds out about his tragic ending, the Hellenes
will start turning their back on us, and you know we need
70   them as much as they need us; flaunting superiority over
the weak will only make them stronger, as they unite against
us by denying us their hecatombs, their prayers, everything
that prevents us from aging or perishing... please, let me
at least provide him with the wisdom he needs to overcome
75   the obstacles you have readied for him – then his destiny
will once again lie in your hands... would you consider
my request if I gathered a majority from our fellow gods?',
Athena asked of her father, confident he would listen to her,
not just on the grounds of being one of his favorite children,
80   but especially because she was indeed the brightest of all
the immortals on the world, wherever or whatever they were.

Reclining on his seat to a more comfortable position, Zeus
attentively listened to the daughter who had literally come
to existence from his own brains, always proud of Athena's
85   eloquence, knowledge, sageness, and wisdom, all of which
she had drained from him, making them both much alike,
which was fortunate for the eternally youthful divinity,
as her influence was sure to make the thunderous god rethink
his approach to certain matters that, otherwise, could end
90   badly, for temperance was one of his weak spots; indeed,
even the gods have them, and not necessarily in their heel.

Part of the weight of Zeus's torso was supported by his right
elbow, having his forearm on the same side fully extended;
his left arm, in turn, was being held up, as his fingers gently
tapped the edge of the marble armchair – putting it all
together, this was the king of gods' usual thinking posture.

After some consideration, Zeus opposed the tip of his fingers
against each other in front of his face while staring at Pallas,
posteriorly intertwining them as he spoke these noble words:
'My loving daughter… always defiant when her mind is set
toward a specific turn to take whenever there's a fork in
in the way, though unfailingly convincing of her bartering…
you ask yourselves why my love for Athena is unconditional,
my children; here is your answer – her wisdom prevents me
from following a path to misjudgment and underestimation.
Very well, then; you may take a vote from those present',
Zeus said, agreeing with Pallas's democratic proposal.

The goddess then turned to the surrounding Olympians,
requesting they came closer and voted either for or against
the following: 'I propose Orpheus be lent a hand from me
as he approaches the Strait of Messene, his vessel steered
under the authority of the almighty Zeus, so that he may
pull his wits together and wisely choose which menace
to face, as he traverses the narrow domain of the creatures
Skylla and Kharybdis, the first of which in the mainland
entrapped, and the latter quenching its immortal thirst
for sea water just off the Northeastern coast of Trinacria.
I, of course, vote aye; is there anyone else who concurs?',
the goddess of wisdom asked the remainder of the Pantheon.

The first to side with Athena was, naturally, Orpheus's
father, Phoebus Apollo, who wanted his half-sister to show

his son the light he could not provide him with from the Sun,
as the excessive heat was precisely one of the culprits driving
the passionate bard downhill toward premature dementia,
for which reason the god stood by Pallas' side, saying «aye».

Ares, on the other hand, saw no reason to vote in favor
of Athena, for, as the god of war, it was his belief that men
had to stick up for themselves and deal with the enemy
on their own; only then, once they had successfully dealt
with the hazard before them, would they be entitled to
the best reward a warrior could ever crave above all other
things – glory and its inherent legendary statute, which is
why the impulsively conflicting god sat and said «nay».

For the time being, there was still all to play for, as there
were two «ayes» and one «nay», with six more votes to cast.
Whichever the result, the decision would have to be quickly
made, otherwise Orpheus would be no more than an easy
prey for either monster; one way or another, the Apollonian
would be swallowed like a ripe fig, though the question was
whether he would sustain a painful or painless demise,
in spite of his reckless mental state, pushing him fiercely
to his death all the same, to Rhamnousia's twisted delight,
something he had sworn not to concede to Nyx's offspring.

Although the queen of gods (as she had stated previously)
had no reason to save Orpheus, who was a member of the
illegitimate side of Zeus's family, Hera did indeed praise
the bard's determination in finding and rescuing Eurydike
from the Underworld, resuming their bond to the wedding
night they had not yet had and, thusly, the ruling goddess
voted «aye», for the sake of loyalty and faithfulness
to true love, making the couple worthy of a second chance.

Poseidon too was called to cast his vote into the celestial
ballot, which he did without even thinking twice, by saying
«nay» and explaining why: 'I have lost too many sirens
to this estranged grandnephew of mine; if we allow him
to proceed, my kingdom will be at risk of experiencing
more losses, no matter which side he may choose to slay,
so, if my will cannot be done, let it be recorded in time
that I opposed the success of this enterprise', the bearer of
the trident said, with only one «nay» away from a draw.

Because no one else stepped forward with another vote,
Athena turned to her blacksmith half-brother and asked him:
'What say you, Hephaestus? Will you not provide us with
your judgment at this hour?', two questions to which
the bronze artisan responded by first reminiscing his days
as a married divinity: 'I used to know what love was about…
it was one-sided love, non-reciprocal, because living forever
does not mean one's eternity will be simple, ever fortunate.
I miss my wife… she betrayed me with my own brother,
and I hate her massively for it, but then again… I wish she
had merely had a slip, passionately coming back to my arms,
only… she was never mine – having a crooked leg and an
ugly face is too hard a barrier to overlook and search for
the beauty within… I am so sorry, sister, but I disapprove'.

Aphrodite, Artemis, and Dionysos were the three gods
the Pantheon had yet to hear from, and so the divinity
of beauty, whose son was the god of love himself, stepped
forward to state her position on the matter being discussed:
'I watched Orpheus sail off the coast of my island, and I felt
an undeniable and unmistakable enthusiasm irradiating
from his soul, as he placed his hope in all of us here today.
Eurydike deserves to be rescued, and surely her husband

is the face she wants to see first, once she leaves the nether
realm... I hereby hand over to Athena my full support',
Aphrodite concluded, much to Pallas's delight, she, who
would normally repudiate the adopted Olympian's lifestyle,
always baring too much for everyone to see, engendering
the bloodiest of rows among men and a great many deal
of approaches from the divine males, which you will remind
yourself of from about nine months ago, when this tale first
began, predictably leaning to both happy and fatal endings,
as is the order of things, pivoting Astraea's scale toward
equilibrium, all the way from where the sky comes to an end.

At that moment, the results were four to three in favor
of Orpheus; should either Artemis or Dionysos vote «aye»,
the last-minute Council of the Gods by Athena summoned
would be adjourned with Zeus's approval and supervision.
However, were another «nay» to be cast, one of the siblings
left would have to overrule one side or the other, unless they
invoked abstention, a perfectly suitable option to avoid
the weight of responsibility, though it would only mean that
time had been wasted discussing someone else's chances
at living on behalf of the almighty and powerful, therefore
giving birth to Politics, inspiring Man to follow the example.

Now, Artemis was a chaste goddess, having sworn to never
yield to carnal pleasures of any sort; of course, this did not
mean the hunting deity was against the union of those who
wished to spend their life with a partner, emphasizing always
the importance of singularity, as she disdained polygamous
practices, of which her father was a reckless demonstration,
forcing her mother to flee Hera's jealousy and wrath, making
her risk both her and her children's lives ever so gratuitously.
In short, it was not Artemis's habit to trust men, whoever

they were, including those of her own family, a profile that
Orpheus fitted snuggly into for being her nephew, Apollo's
son – a heavyweight motive that made her feel broken in two.
Normally assertive, the female archer twin was having issues
as far as expressing herself was concerned, looking down
at her feet, muttering out all of the above reasons as she made
her mind up, declaring the following words, simultaneously
liquifying her guilt through her eye sockets: 'I... I am sorry,
brother... I do not wish your son to perish, but... you know
I have trust issues... how many times have I saved women's
hearts, broken at the hands of men...? And how many have
I killed for boasting their superiority and cruel intentions?
Orpheus may be my own kin, but I find no reassurance at all
concerning his true feelings for Eurydike, once he finds her.
He misses her because they were done apart on their wedding
day, he knows not whether he really wants to be with her;
it is the sense of loss that is compelling him into roaming
through the waters, all the way to Hades's Underworld.
I vote nay... please forgive me, Phoebus', Artemis begged
her twin brother, who only gulped and averted his sight
away from any point at all where his sister could be found.

A moment of silence reigned supreme on Mount Olympus;
the situation had become so embarrassing that no one was
able to look each other in the eye, apart from Zeus, who had
to proudly demonstrate his imposition: 'Well, then... it is up
to Dionysos to rule either in favor or against, so the game
may proceed. What say you? Does Orpheus stand his chance,
or does he lie on his vessel's deck, as good as fodder?', Zeus
inquired the son he had secretly sewn to his thigh, killing his
mother Semele after promising to grant her anything she
wished for (being the splendor of the sovereign god's bolts
her desire and, unfortunately for her, her demise as well).

Rather innocent-looking, the god of thy sweet nectar, who deliberately distanced himself from the discussion to prevent the ending it had come to, precisely, turned back to face everyone staring at him; Athena, Apollo, and Hera held
250 their breath together, fearing an irresponsible decision might come from the patron of inebriation, and even though Zeus was also curious about what his son had to say, the bearer of the aegis lived mostly out of hiding his feelings, seeking always to remain impartial, even a «game», as he put it,
255 was being played, as defiance would not easily be tolerated. However, considering he evidently loved Pallas and had no problem publicly displaying his preference, the thunderous god had allowed this unusually democratic event to proceed.

Clearly under pressure, Dionysos goofily gasped a laugh,
260 attempting to shake the unwanted attention from the top of his shoulders: 'Oh!... I know not what to say...! Indeed, it is an honor – no, a privilege to hold in my power the final word on the matter at hand, but...', he began to say, quickly interrupted by none other than Hera, bearer not of the aegis,
265 but rather little patience for this stepson in particular, whose habits and tendencies were more than questionable (as far as she was concerned, anyway), echoing across the skies these words of disgust: 'Refrain your tongue this instant, parasitic nuisance! You are a disgrace to godship! Had your father
270 failed to conceal you from me, I would have strangled you with a pair of vipers wrapped round your neck! A crucial decision is about to be made, and it all rests upon a drunkard who could not give a toss in the world about anything – lazy chatterbox! Why do you not run along and play with your
275 lunatic Maenads? And while you are at it, have them slit each other's throats – let them bathe in their own blood and cry out «evoe!» as they take the stairs to Hades without

a proper burial and a bribe in their mouth for the ferryman.
Go with them, keep them company and stay there, right by
the bank of the Styx', she said, lashing out at Dionysos,
having no need to pull any punches, averting her eyes away
from him, shaken from the lecturing, to look her cheating
husband in his eyes and intimidate him: 'My king, this child
is not to be trusted. Whatever he utters, whenever he does it,
is bound to take an erroneous path and, thus, influence fate
in a manner the Moirai themselves would not approve of.
I ask of you – be wise, discard his opinion, and break the tie
yourself', the goddess of marriage and family begged Zeus.

In turn, the almighty father of the heavens pushed Dionysos
into making the call all the same, thus undermining Hera's
authority, both simultaneously and implicitly determining
that he, as supreme ruler, would not be overthrown by his
own wife, gifting men (yet again) the twisted power to shame
and belittle women, showing no respect for their opinion
whatsoever – a curse I foresee will take place for millennia
to come, which is a sad, sad truth to speak, let alone sing.
Despite being my verses, absolutely no joy at all do I find
in the enunciation of these words, for it is clear the gods,
the creators of both men and women, desire to maintain
a regime of utter female humiliation to take advantage of.

'Time is running out, Bacchus', Zeus said, leaning forward
on his throne, temperamentally adding: 'Make the decision,
boy! The son of Apollo is closing in on his downfall, and fast.
I will not command Aeolos to provide the winds with new
instructions, so make haste with your choice!', he thundered,
rising from his seat while putting his hands on the map table,
inadvertently placing his palms on both ends of the Strait
of Messene, hiding the two sea monsters from human sight.

Persephone's Fall

'Nay! Nay, nay, nay! There! I hope you are all content!',
310 Dionysos yelled at everyone; as Hera was preparing to run
toward and strangle him with her own hands, instead
of summoning vipers, as she had earlier mentioned, the god
of Bacchanalia threw himself off the clouds and disappeared,
flying fast to the surface of the earth, shrewdly hiding
315 any trace that could lead to his location, one he had not yet
chosen himself, because of the strain he had felt as he evaded
the gods' abode, leaving all other deities in the worst of awes.

As he sat down again, disturbed by his son's childish display,
the bearer of the aegis removed his hands from the board,
320 resting his right elbow on his left palm, while fondling
his silver beard, not quite sure of what had just happened.
Given that Dionysos was nowhere in sight, the members
of the Pantheon present in the assembly all turned to Zeus,
bearing an expression of shock similar to his, though no one
325 dared speak before he decided what was to be done, not even
Hera, piercing her hands with her fingernails, as she clenched
her fists, both distraught and enraged for an Olympian
she could perfectly do without, probably gone to indulge her
in the suggestion of enticing a group of women into his
330 disturbance, something the queen of gods blamed not only
on Dionysos's dead mother, but also on his father, who most
certainly had contributed to the mess the boy's brains
were in, after the electroshock therapy he was given while
still inside Semele's womb, taking after Zeus's frivolity too.

335 Unaware of what he had done, the thunderous father
of the heavens had exerted his strength atop Skylla and
Kharybdis, nearly crushing them both, as he supported
his weight when leaning forward, pressuring Dionysos
as well, though only figuratively, in the latter's case.

340 Once Zeus sat back down in his marble armchair, the aquatic creatures cried out in a fit of pain and rage, feeling provoked. Skylla, on the one hand, was roaring with all its six heads in unison, whereas Kharybdis, on the other hand, was thirsting uncontrollably, whirling as much water as it could, making
345 the sea look irate and unforgiving of whoever had deprived this particular monster from its perpetual quenching, even though it had only taken no more than a minute; still, as per monstrous nature, it was enough to rile them both up.

After another seemingly endless moment of silence, Zeus
350 looked Athena in her eyes and, visibly moved, regardless of his effort to hide his emotions, thus decreed: 'Orpheus will not be assisted at this time, it is decided; my will be done', he finished, standing back up and moving away from the center of the adjourned assembly, hands behind
355 his back, reflecting upon the latest events, choosing not to take part (for the time being) in Orpheus's confrontation.

Whereas the naysayers looked down, those in favor of aiding the bard looked at each other, feeling completely powerless, especially Athena and Apollo (as a caring and loving father).
360 Orpheus was nearing the narrow passage, still with his lyre in his hands, but no music was played, for he had passed out.

Canto XVII

As both goddesses flew side-by-side, Demeter, the Lady
of the Golden Sword, and Hekate, the Moon sorceress,
swept Trinacria's Eastern shore with their eyesight, still
hopeful of finding Persephone somewhere between Syracusa
and Katane, although the eldest of the Thesmophoroi
had done the same when moving from the latter location
toward Ortygia, where she first had hoped to find Kore,
perhaps at the care of Arethusa, sadly realizing otherwise.

After ellipting around for a while, pretending to be Khronos
(and presuming I possess the divine right to play with time
as I sing), the hour in which this tale's subplots are tied again
has arrived at last, not by the hand of the primordial god
of time (let alone myself, for I have no control whatsoever
over cosmologic events), but by Zeus's failure to measure
his own strength, nearly squishing Skylla as if the creature
were no more than an insect, and drowning Kharybdis into
the Ionian, making it disappear from the sea's surface.
Had he been successful in this unintentional enterprise,
the Euronaut would have been in luck, likely beaching
his vessel safely in the sands of his target, despite being
considerably away from Pergoussa, but at least his time asea
would have come to an end and someone would surely come
to his rescue, as per the principles of Grecian hospitality.

However, both monsters were still there, alive and enraged,
prepared to share a treat between them – any living animals
would be Skylla's, and the vessel (or more than just one),
Kharybdis's, taking Man's best traveling means yet invented
down the whirlpool, in an endless spiral toward the bottom.

The moment Zeus lifted his hands from the map centered
in the Mediterranean was the same Skylla and Kharybdis
reacted to the pain unto the both of them induced, signaling
the surrounding areas to learn of their menacing presence
(not that anyone needed to be reminded of their capabilities,
for many had been the men – whether unknowing foreigners
or unfortunate locals – perishing at one monster's hunger
and the other's thirst, wickedly completing one another).

One may wonder how monsters are engendered and given
life to, starting, perhaps, with the same method of conception
between animals, humans, and gods; if one were to consider
Polyphemos to be a monstrous creature, as one would judge
Skylla, then one would realize that such specimens are indeed
created via copulation, granted the cyclops was the result
of a union between Poseidon and Thoosa, though it is rather
unimaginable how the Nereid bore the enormous one-eyed.
Then again, one species may give birth to another, which is
what happened with the Cyclopes, the Giants, the Hundred-
-Handers, and the Titans, who bore their own divinities,
the Olympians, populating the whole of Hellen's domains
with extramarital children; also, we must not forget about
Aphrodite, considered as an Olympian, though she was
the result of Ouranos' slain testicles and seafoam, thus
becoming a member of the Pantheon family, forced by Zeus
to marry into them by recurring to Hephaestus, as we well
remember from earlier stanzas, for which reason I shall not
take each and everyone's backgrounds much further, apart
from Skylla's, as it is of great interest and surely unknown
to most of the Hellenes who have never left the mainland.

The creature living in a cave of the Italic Peninsula had not
been magically created, nor had she always been a monster.

She was the victim of jealousy and consequential revenge; there is some disagreement as to who turned her into what she is today, but one thing is certain – poison was the cause of her transformation into a four-eyed, six-headed, twelve-tentacled monster, having each of her heads gifted with three rows of shark-like teeth, easily severing human flesh. Before, however, she was a beautiful Naiad, a fresh water nymph, who would usually bathe in the waters of her spring; like all beautiful women, mortal or not, Skylla had suitors, among which Poseidon himself, along with Glaukos, also a god of the sea, though obedient to the bearer of the trident. These male deities were coveted themselves by other females, if not already married to them – the case of Poseidon, who had wedded Amphitrite, making her the queen of the seas. As for Glaukos, the sorceress Circe, who had an island of her own to the North, with a view to the Tyrrhenian, was in love with him, which is why she felt something had to be done to put an end to Skylla's beauty, so that no other man would ever want to set his eyes on her, avoiding meeting her gaze at all costs, even if it meant drifting right into Kharybdis's lair, on the insular side of the Strait of Messene, which made the survival of unwary travelers an extremely difficult task.

In short, either Amphitrite or Circe was the culprit, having poisoned Skylla's spring, turning her into a monster uglier than a hydra; aware as she was of her physical appearance when leaning her heads into the salt water, she swore she would devour every man who passed by, showing no mercy.

Neither she, nor Kharybdis knew who boarded the nearing ship (the Euro), but whoever it was, it surely did not matter. Had either creature been told Orpheus's identity, his chances were certain to literally go down the drain, as Poseidon had

voted against Athena's assistance, and Kharybdis, a daughter
of the sea king, faithfully served her father in any occasion.
If, on the other hand, the bard were to be in Skylla's range,
there is no doubt maiming would be the end of him, having
95 his limbs and torso distributed by all six mouths at once.
Eurydike was a nymph herself – non-aquatic, but a nymph,
regardless, and the Apollonian was on a rescue mission
to bring her back from the Underworld alive, naturally
beautiful as she always had been, untouched by the foulness
100 of jealousy, ready to live the married life to its full extent,
whereas Skylla would remain scarred for eternity, never to
taste the flavor of happiness, a fate crueler than death, if you
ask me, like so many other lives across Greece, imploring
the gods for an ending to their suffering, though they did not
105 yield to such prayers; whether these people had a purpose
in store for them, only the gods, precisely, knew about it,
though this did not mean such lives would change for better.

But what is Skylla's parentage, now that I have sung her past
to you, meddled with by an unscrupulous third-party deity?
110 The father is unknown, but the mother… is none other than
Hekate, the sorceress goddess herself, and even though
she carried magical powers within, she could not break the
effects of the venom her daughter had washed in long ago…
inevitably, hatred grew in the heart of the former nymph,
115 as she had hoped her mother would be capable of undoing
what someone who was not a patroness of magic (whether
Amphitrite or Circe, despite the latter being a sorceress) had
apparently done too well for the goddess of necromancy,
who could even prevent people at the verge of Nemesis'
120 clenches from being taken away, never to return to the earth,
though Skylla was unaware of Eurydike's present situation,
let alone of her mother's intervention, which, deep down,

was supported by a good reason, and it concerned Skylla, only not directly – at least, not up until this very moment.

125 The truth is Hekate had nearly perished of grief when her daughter was cursed, despite being immortal, but only to a certain extent – the same with all other gods, who lose their strength when their heart is broken; if we recall how anxious Demeter had become the moment Persephone
130 was raped, we could think she too was preparing herself to die, but that never happened because she swore she would never stop looking, and the fact her friend Hekate brought her news concerning Kore's whereabouts gave her her strength back, heading straight to Olympus to push Zeus,
135 the irresponsible parent, to a point he would have to bend.

The sorceress goddess, on the other hand, was never offered any help with respect to Skylla; there was the unfortunate inability of turning her back into the beautiful nymph she had once been, indeed, together with the consequent severing
140 of ties between them, leaving them estranged for many years. The monster on her outside was barely rational, anymore... she was so constantly irate that all she wanted was to devour sailors, tear them apart and throw their bones to the back of the cave, a rather heinous and unrecommended display.
145 Sometimes, should any sirens swim underneath, she would throw them a few of the remains to be chewed on, though they were mostly fleshless, which made the sisterly creatures growl at her from below; however, Skylla's roars had more sonorous power, scaring them away until the next time.

150 Hekate's motherly-like spirit had not turned up inside her by chance, when both Persephone and Demeter needed her... she did not want to witness another mother and daughter

being pulled away from each other because of someone else,
it was as simple as that, and in the middle of this situation
she saw an opportunity to redeem herself from having failed
to help her child; however, she was not taking advantage
to play the good Samaritan, it was nothing like that – all she
aimed for was reuniting both Mistresses, while watching
Hades closely, vigilant of any harm he may have had in mind.

The question was she saw no malignant intentions coming
from within the Screech Owl (his soul was not completely
clean, of course, but may the one who has never sinned
before cast the first pebble onto the lake's surface and
make it ripple), which is why Hekate was now in favor
of bringing Hades and the maiden back together, setting
the basis of their union on the love they could not refrain
from and for each other; as for Demeter, even though she
was the actual mother, Hekate had felt the need to convince
her of Persephone's autonomy with respect to her happiness,
instead of keeping her manacled, thinking mother knows
best... it just so happens that, sometimes, parents do not.

As for Eurydike and Orpheus, parenthood was not involved
in the goddess of magic's desire to help, but living in Tartarus
made her path cross with the nymph's, which, in turn, led
her to the Apollonian, unfairly turned a widower on their
wedding – it was undoubtedly both appalling and cruel.

Even if Hekate could reunite two couples and a daughter to
her mother, that still would not bring Skylla back – not in
her original physique, not in her deranged cognitive process;
nevertheless, the goddess was helping, by doing good deeds.

And, as protective as she was, the deity of the Moon now

had a rather difficult task at hand – save Orpheus from
Skylla without, however, injuring her (it was one thing to
share no bond whatsoever with her and call her a monster,
as it was another to have given birth to that living being,
despite what she had become because of another's doing).

Hekate knew both were in peril the minute Skylla roared,
after Zeus released her from underneath his hands in heaven;
the last time the sorceress goddess had heard her cry in pain
was the day she was attacked by one of the jealous deities.
After that, the nature of the screaming became animalistic,
which was why Hekate tuned her daughter off, or she would
forever be haunted in real-time, instead of hearing all those
outcries in her head, gruffly lodged as a terrible memory.

The Lady of the Golden Sword realized something was off
when her friend's hand engulfed hers with superhuman force,
far beyond the usual strength a deity can ethereally exert.
They were nearing Náxos when Demeter came to a full stop
in mid-air, without the need to brake and slow down.
As the eldest of the Mistresses looked the goddess of magic
in her eyes, she saw sorrow, anxiety, restlessness, all mixed
together, spreading across Hekate's unrecognizable visage.

The lady of the grain took her friend's other hand to balance
her need to grasp and avoid hurting her any further, asking
in a profound tone of concern: 'What is it, Hekate?! Your
spirit has changed abruptly – was it something you sensed?
Is it Persephone? Is she all right? Let your tongue speak freely
through your teeth, tell me everything!', Demeter pleaded,
fearing the worst had happened to her offspring, bringing
the fight they had had back to her eyes, in the form of tears,
and to her chest, making her heart pound uncontrollably.

'No', Hekate said, hyperventilating, 'it is not Persephone... something terrible is about to happen, but it is not about your daughter...', she went on, breathing heavily, until she held her breath and looked in Demeter's vivid eyes, 'not for now, at least – but we must make haste if we want to save more than just one life', she concluded, inhaling and exhaling loudly yet again, confusing the Lady of the Golden Sword.

Still taking a firm hold of Demeter's hand, Hekate resumed their flight much faster than before, heading East-Northeast. 'What are we doing flying into the sea?!', the lady of the grain asked, adding more questions to her twitching: 'Should we not stay by the shore?! Is... that Messene I see up front? Zeus's beard, why are we moving toward the sea monsters?'.

Hekate looked at her, but with no intention of reprimanding Demeter for the choice of words, as no one knew the truth: 'They are not monsters. One of them is just a temperamental whirlpool, and the other is my daughter', she confessed, looking straight to where the Euro could be easily unveiled. The eldest of the Thesmophoroi obviously had her wits about her and deduced who the goddess of the Moon was talking about, exclaiming no more than: 'Zeus's beard...!'. 'I have never told anyone about it', Hekate said, 'but I guess that would have been the ordinary reaction if I had opened my mouth', she added, as Demeter became rigidly shocked.

It then came to the Lady of the Golden Sword's attention that there was a vessel pointing directly at the strait, about to be destroyed somehow by something (or someone, with all due respect to Skylla, whoever she was, Demeter thought). 'There is a ship navigating between Skylla and Kharybdis!', the goddess of agriculture pointed out, asking her friend:

Persephone's Fall

'What is the plan? Do we save the crew, or do we let them
perish?'; Hekate responded: 'The crew is made of one man,
and he is unconscious – it seems that he is being put to the
test by your family in the skies, even after he prayed to be
kept safe in the course of his mission. The Olympians are
no good, Lady Demeter, they only think of themselves...!
That is why I insisted that you freed the humans from your
temper, helping them instead, just like you always have.
Arethusa certainly agrees with me. I may not have heard
any prayers addressed to me, but I will not let him die.
I need your help, lady of the grain – he is starving and
thirsting, so he will not be getting up on his feet any time
soon; see if there are any remnants of food and water aboard,
make it all fresh again and feed the man while I handle
Skylla', the sorceress goddess explained, letting go of her
friend's hand, telling her to hurry and magically bring
the nearly defunct man back to his old self once more.

Demeter went on ahead, landing shortly afterward on deck;
she swiftly moved to the fallen man and recognized him –
it was Orpheus, the son of Apollo, which made her his aunt.
Now she certainly did not plan on watching him get eaten
or drown, quickly running below to see what she could find.
The rotting stench was the most unimaginable scent she had
ever smelled – not so much of a surprise, given she purified
the fields all year (or used to, for reasons we are aware of),
and was thusly accustomed to the freshest and most mature
crops, harvested under perfect conditions and converted
to bread that rarely went moldy (even if it did, it would take
weeks before turning disgustingly and intoxicatingly green;
the locals from Pánormos knew exactly how to do it, better
than most cities across the whole of the triangular island).
From the crumbs spread all over the ship's floor, Demeter

created steaming wheat for the bard to take a bite and please
his stomach; as far as drinking was concerned, the goddess
of agriculture had a look at the overturned barrels, and not
a drop was left, whether it was water or wine, a problem
she quickly solved under the strain of a required sacrifice
(after all, Orpheus was family, no matter how distant):
the Lady of the Golden Sword grabbed a blade, precisely,
and made a superficial cut on the underside of her forearm,
gushing ambrosia into a small wooden cup she would have
to damp the lips of the bard with before giving him bread,
which, put together, would nurture him back to full health.
Before rushing back up, however, the goddess of agriculture
summarily eliminated all else that had gone rotten, clearing
the vessel from the smell that was embedded in its wood.

As she climbed up the small staircase to deck level once more
with the necessary goods in her hands, the lady of the grain
saw Hekate shielding both the Euro and the Euronaut from
Skylla, who was burning with rage, as she tried to pierce
through the faint-colored barrier her mother had set in place.
At first, she tried breaking through with one head at a time,
deciding afterward that a synchronized ramming of all six
would be more effective, and it was – to a certain extent:
the goddess of magic's sadness for having to prevent her child
from hurting, not only Orpheus, but especially herself,
somehow weakened her powers, as she lacked concentration.

So, there they were, between a rock and a hard place…
to port, the thirsty Kharybdis, enthusiastically whirling
faster and faster, pulling the ship toward her; to starboard,
the roaring Skylla continued to hit Hekate's defenses, nearly
breaking them to pieces, putting herself in peril just as well.
Drifting her face away from her offspring's facial expression,

305   the goddess of the Moon saw the Euro closing in, with
Demeter back in sight, at which point she yelled: 'Milady!
I cannot hold the shield up much longer – I need Orpheus
to get back on his feet and play his golden kithara! Revive
him, quickly!', Hekate begged the Lady of the Golden Sword,
310 who immediately ran and tended to the Apollonian, kneeling
and placing the bread on her lap as she held his head up.

The foreseer faintly moaned, incapable of uttering a word;
he tried to open his eyes, but even the lids were too heavy.
The eldest of the Thesmophoroi addressed him softly, trying
315 not to scare him away from life itself: 'Hush, boy, hold your
peace; I will not hurt you. Here, drink this, it will make you
feel much better, trust me', she said, tilting the cup filled
with ambrosia toward Orpheus's mouth, which was slightly
resistant to moving; Demeter obviously did not give up and
320 supported his head on her right knee, gently opening his
mouth, pouring a few drops of her own blood into his throat.

At first, the son of Apollo naturally coughed up the sweet
ambrosia, but the lady of the grain was ahead of that and
did not waste the precious liquid all at once; it was when
325 he began to react that she felt comfortable enough to drop
larger portions, one by one, giving him time to swallow:
'There you go, boy, easy does it… do not spit it out, it will
make you feel much better', Demeter said, comforting him.

Orpheus's paleness made him look like a ghoul, a soul
330 evading prison in Tartarus, roaming at large on the surface;
however, the ambrosia he drank restored his true colors
and made him open his eyes wide, surprisingly resistant
to sunlight – come to think of it, perhaps it was not so much
of a surprise, considering he was the son of Apollo, the heir

335 of Helios, and the Sun, instead of killing him slowly,
was now helping him rise again, though his stomach was still
in need of attention, and that was where Demeter's bread
came in, addressing him like so: 'Eat, it will give you enough
strength to stand and play the lyre, but hurry – we are all
340 in danger and need you to play a tune; death is getting closer',
the Lady of the Golden Sword told the bard, unaware
of what was going on to begin with, which transpired on his
dazed, confused, puzzled face, just to utter a few examples.

It came to the former Argonaut's mind that he was dreaming,
345 or perhaps even under the spell of another deceptive creature
to the likes of the siren who had disguised herself as his wife,
but the fact is he really did feel better and, reminded of his
faith in the gods, he carried on, convinced it was their work.
Because he had asked for Athena's wisdom and, implicitly,
350 Apollo's guidance, both deities, who had turned away
from the map, incapable of watching the despicable spectacle
that was on its way, were suddenly woken by Orpheus's
prayers, which could only mean one thing – he was alive
and conscious; Zeus did not move at all, and the remaining
355 members of the Pantheon present in the clouds had gone
to their respective palaces – still, they had to tread carefully,
for alarming the bearer of the aegis would be the end of this
new enterprise that seemed to be taking place at the moment.
Instead of moving toward the board, communicated with
360 each other through their minds, hopefully blocking Zeus out,
and decided to concentrate solely on the scene via Orpheus.
A new hope was rising, exciting both the father and the aunt;
as for the father of them all, he was no fool (only when he
wanted to be, anyway), and his omniscience told him his
365 grandson was being assisted by none other than the goddess
of human sustenance and the sorceress, Hades's tenant.

Persephone's Fall

He decided to pretend he had seen nothing, as he was certain
the kithara player's trials had not yet come to their end.

Down below, Hekate battled Skylla, holding on as much
as she could, though it was extremely hard to keep up
without even trying to inflict a bit of damage; then again,
how could she, bearing in mind it was her daughter she was
fighting to protect everyone, including Skylla herself?
Much too tired to go on, the goddess of the Moon glanced
at the Euro one last time, checking if Orpheus was in shape
to begin playing and, for all their sakes, he was, indeed.
Tied to a rope held by the lady of the grain, the bard
was yet again atop the vessel's railing and leaning forward,
so his music could catch Skylla's attention more clearly.

The moment he fiddled the strings of his instrument with
his fingers, playing remarkably right from the first note,
the enraged Skylla (who neither spoke to, nor recognized
her mother, despite the latter's tears) put her irate roaring
to an end, as all six heads hung from their necks fast asleep.

The tentacles, offering support to her sharp attacks, rested
also, loosening their suction; as for the four eyes, they shut
down completely – that sea monster was no longer a threat,
but Kharybdis was still trying to compensate the temporary
loss of her neighbor, whirling and twirling, giving way for
the centrifugal force to produce its effects, but Hekate, free
from her shielding responsibility, hopped aboard the Euro
and turned the helm hard to port, passing as close to Skylla
as she could, painfully mouthing the following words:
'Goodbye, my daughter, my child... I am so sorry...',
sailing the three of them away from the Strait of Messene
at the sound of Orpheus's tune, leaving behind an infuriated

whirlpool whose woodthirst would not be quenched this time around; as for Pallas and Phoebus, watching from the sky via the bard's eyes, quiet celebrating was in order.

Canto XVIII

Having overcome a double threat on his life with the help
of the goddesses of agriculture and magic, Demeter and
Hekate, respectively, Orpheus, the Euronaut, was put back
to sleep by the latter, changing his memory into no more
than a bad dream with a happy ending, in an attempt
to erase traces of divine intervention in human affairs.
The statement is, of course, one to question, as the trial
was supposed to have been the result of the Olympians'
meddling with human affairs, precisely, like they always
did, including Athena's will to provide assistance, but
it just so happened the sorceress goddess did not wish
for Orpheus to know who had been there for him, having
told him to trust himself, instead of hoping for miracles.

At first, Demeter did not understand why it was necessary,
but once they hid nearby, the goddess of the Moon explained
what her plans were for both Orpheus and Persephone,
who was in need of aid herself, but it was up to the bard
to take care of the problem, as Zeus would not allow them
to contradict his authority twice in a row – it was decided.

If there was anything the goddess of human sustenance
did not mind was getting back at the bearer of the aegis
for any reason at all, but she feared her daughter could
be even more at risk than she already was, according to
Hekate's details of the operation set upon Orpheus's head.

The last thing they did after putting him to sleep was moor
the Euro next to an outlet to the West of Messene, in Mylae;
at least the sea would stop its harassment on the poor bard.

Also, he would forcibly need to walk inland to find supplies with which to replenish himself, for Demeter's power boost had deliberately been made temporary, though there were enough remnants to prevent his body becoming weak again.

Once he woke up, Orpheus felt like his head weighed about a talent or so, because of the massive migraine he got from drinking pure ambrosia, straight from the vein of a goddess, without any water to mix it with; never had the foreseer gotten this terribly inebriated, and this was not a poetic metaphor or euphemism, it was a dreadful hangover indeed.

He was lying on the deck, where he had passed out the first time, with his golden kithara under his arm, firmly secured. It took him a while to adapt to the sunlight, which was nearly gone, ceding its place to twilight, as the Moon prepared to emerge under Hekate's orders, complementing the night, commanded by Nyx; for three months, Apollo retired from the skies much later than ever, as the introduction of a new solstice because of Demeter's anger had made it so.

Orpheus rubbed his eyes to improve his sight, standing up with a bit of effort, as if he had been lying on wood for days. He gasped slightly at the first stage, when he leaned forward to sit; then, as he tried to put weight on his legs, they kept failing on him, feeling numb – his body had become havoc. However, after continuously trying to get up while inaudibly cursing whoever had put him through such unimaginable trials, the Apollonian was able to stand at last, though he sought support from the Euro's railing, which he grabbed without hesitation, jerking his limbs out of their numbness.

The sorcerer had not yet realized the ship was anchored,

crying out when he saw the cape heading all the way to shore:
'Zeus's beard…! I have found land! I know not whether it is
my destination, but at least I am somewhere…! I must not
forget, by the way, to lower my tone, despite having a good
reason to rejoice – what happened to me…?', he wondered,
driving his hands to his head, feeling it was somehow about
to fall from his neck, 'My head is heavy as a boulder; it was
either all the wine I had stored that did this to me, blessed
with some sort of a latent effect, or my stomach's crave
for food it has not digested since – well, that is curious…
I cannot remember the last time I feasted; I am surprised
I managed to stay alive this long, Zeus's beard, indeed…!',
Orpheus exclaimed, massaging his entire head abruptly
to see if it would make it feel lighter, and it did (in his mind).

The Euronaut lowered the rope ladder, ending just above
the outlet's ground, as he took a good look at the place
he had come to; the golden chariot of his father was moving
to the right, which meant he was facing South, walking
toward the Northern coastline of a great mass of land whose
corners were not visible from where the kithara player was.
If it was an island, he was not sure, but then again, looking
up, the insurmountable mountain seemed to point in that
direction; Orpheus was admiring it when Enkelados's heavy
breathing echoed from the top, frightening him to death.
Phoebus had told his son before, while teaching him to play,
about the Titanomachy and the Gigantomachy, learning
that his aunt Pallas Athena had thrown Trinacria, an island
in the middle of the Mediterranean Sea, over a fiery Giant.
This meant that the place he was walking on now was
indeed his destination, having to work his way to the lake
in Pergoussa, where the woman his consciousness had told
him about would be waiting for him to guide him into

the domain of Hades, Tartarus; the mountain was Aitne,
there was no doubt about it, and as happy as he was for
getting closer to his lost wife, he knew not how long it would
take him to reach the banks of the fresh water body, having
considered it was probably best to fashion a container
and carry some food and drink on his back, rather than
hoping to find animals to kill or fruit to pick along the way.

The nomadic era was over, thanks to Demeter, and this time
it was her he was praying to, asking her for food nearby.
Unaware she was watching his every move, the goddess
of agriculture asked the sorceress divinity to provide him
with just a small hint pointing him in the right direction.

On top of the entrance to a cave, a small rock glinted like
a jewel, attracting Orpheus's attention to the stony frame.
As he moved closer, so did the cave seem to be incredibly
monstrous as far as its size was concerned; no man would
certainly have pierced into the foothills of the stratovolcano
leaving behind an access the size of a stadium – who in their
right human mind and shape could possibly need that grand
an entrance to the mountain, known as Hephaestus's forge?
Not even the blacksmith god himself would require this sort
of flamboyance, should his forge be there (which was not).

The bard's mind was too confused to discern what seemed
appropriate and what did not, still thinking about a weird
dream he had had aboard the Euro, in which he assisted
two divine women against a whirlpool to the left, and a
hideous creature to the right, charming the latter with his
magical music – it was simply pathetic and he, therefore,
needed to discard all that foolishness and concentrate on
the task he had right in front of him, which was to follow

a signal he interpreted as Demeter's answer to his prayer;
120 rather than fear what might lurk inside the cave, Orpheus
gave his best at assuming a positive posture, believing all
would turn out well after the inferno he had been through
under the scalding Sun, which his father could not prevent,
regardless of his will to tread faster across the dome, so his
125 son would be spared from exceedingly long-lasting days.

Before making his decision to go in the cave, Orpheus closed
his eyes, praying with undeniable fervor to the gods (Demeter
included, asking her to fulfill that one more wish to come out
alive, intact, with fodder in his stomach and, hopefully, fresh
130 water from a spring gushing through the mountain to help
push it down, replenishing him with every bit of strength
he required to proceed along his journey across Trinacria,
heading Southwest, to the great lake, concealing one of the
paths down to Tartarus, where Eurydike awaited his arrival.

135 Watching closely, without dragging a foot away from where
she was hiding next to the goddess of magic, Kore's anxious
mother was hanging on to the Euronaut's every word, rather
putting her faith in him, than making sure she could protect
him, because of the limitations imposed by Zeus; the bearer
140 of the aegis had not spoken to either goddess to reprimand
them, but the Lady of the Golden Sword knew he was there,
as did both Athena and Apollo, who had lost their smile,
once the thunderous master of the skies sat back at the table
to make sure no one would interfere in what he had planned
145 for the son of Phoebus; Orpheus had even said Dionysus
could have his head if he failed to trust the gods would save
him from peril, which means that, if his faith was real in fact,
he would have nothing to fear, the moment he decided
to enter the lair of the unknown, where darkness reigned.

150 Starting at a certain point deep into the cave, the little light
that shone outside kept dimming continuously, forcing
the Apollonian to feel his way by sliding his right hand
on the wall; it both constantly and abruptly changed from
smooth to spiky, and when it felt like the latter, it somehow
155 did not seem natural, as if someone had deliberately hit
the wall in those specific areas, and as Orpheus walked
toward complete absence of light, all the more the mural
kept losing its smoothness, realizing those sections had been
definitely struck by someone – or something – powerful
160 to the likes of a god, most certainly; he was the son of one
and, still, there was no way he could provoke such damage,
let alone with his bare hands, though the spikes in the rock
were spaced both neatly and concavely, suggesting the wall
had not been punched by a human-like hand or kicked by
165 a beast's foot, but rather hammered with the edge of a club,
and a rather big one at that, sending shivers down the bard's
spine, inhaling to the full extent of his abdomen, releasing
the air with a long blow, giving up on the wall as a reference
and holding on to the lyre strapped to his waist, lifting his
170 left arm in front of him, so as not to crash into an obstacle.

Then again, sticking his hand without knowing what lay
within the pitch-black environment might have been a bit
imprudent, for which reason he decided to remove the bow
the people of Tempe had offered him in honor of his father
175 from his back, and fetch an arrow from the quiver held
there as well; he would rather lose a piece of ammunition
than a hand, of course – if he survived (which he hoped
would happen), how would the bard play the lyre again?

As he walked, Orpheus kept looking around, even though
180 his sight was limited, but did not want to give up just yet

on finding a light source, regardless of how dimmed it was. Unsure of how far he had already walked, the Apollonian heard a faint noise and stood his ground, quickly breathing still, but as quiet as he could, waiting to hear the sound
185 again, also closing his eyes to improve his concentration and stop trying to focus on finding a rupture in the dark; there was a considerable difference between a handicapped sight and deliberately shut eyes (the blind, according to Tiresias, eventually got used to it, for as much as they
190 would like to see, having their eyes opened was pointless, allowing the stimulation of all the other five senses, considering foreseers had a sixth, which was the case of Orpheus precisely, despite its uselessness for about half a year, now), so there he stood, figuring out where
195 the faint sound had come from, but it all went silent.

Albeit the clouding as far as his visions were concerned, his sixth sense's other abilities were not failing him this time around, as he could feel the presence of someone (or something, as you have now grown accustomed to) else
200 in that cave; the problem was finding out who (or what...) it was, whether friendly or rude, aggressive or hospitable.

For a few seconds, nothing more took place, and Orpheus stepped forward again, moving even more cautiously than before, when another faint echo was projected across
205 the cave, clearly coming from the right, as the bard's left ear had only caught the dissipation of the sound, fading away as it spread throughout the rocky walls' damaged acoustics (probably a result from all the bashing they had sustained thus far, changing the cave's natural reverbing capabilities).
210 Now, all the Euronaut needed to know was when to turn, but pointing an arrow as an orienting safeguard did not seem

appropriate, for which reason Orpheus put the bow behind his back again, holding only the arrow, which could be used as an improvised weapon, in case he needed to pierce any
215 lurking threats – that was on his left hand, whereas in the right he took hold of the golden kithara, still firmly tied to his waist, and gently started caressing it, as if he were moving the tip of his fingers on Eurydike's visage, imagining her delight as he proceeded with his demonstration of affection.

220 There was naturally a purpose for the event in question, which was to bring out the light of the magical instrument. It was a godly object, so, without much room for surprises, it possessed all kinds of powers, and not all of them were related to Music (depending on the perspective, of course,
225 as the art at hand, gifted to Man by Apollo, was a way to metaphorically find light in the middle of darkness, just like Poetry – hence the heavenly result of their combination).

A few seconds later, the lyre began livening its own golden surface, turning itself into a makeshift torch that spread
230 enough for its proprietor to realize where he was at the moment; even though the ground was hard and thick, mud covered its surface, pressed by enormous feet, judging from the footprints – not only they were lengthy, the space left between them also showed the range the steps of the creature
235 who had left them could achieve, which meant it most definitely did not have the legs of a human being, hence the height of the ceiling, unreachable by the dim light shining from the kithara; Orpheus was not at all pleased with what he had gotten himself into, inflated by a bad
240 feeling about the whole situation, and though it was true he had asked for a sign from the Lady of the Golden Sword, unknowingly provided by the goddess of magic, it was hard

for the bard to keep both his faith and hopes up, constantly disrespecting the instructions he had been given by the voice of his consciousness, a bad enough situation, made worse for conscientiously disobeying those orders, always asking for forgiveness and redemption for questioning his instinct over and over again, as if deliberately begging for negative consequences as far as the enterprise was concerned – luck certainly did not last forever, and the ending was nearing, should the Apollonian choose to maintain his poor attitude.

Shortly after rearranging his thoughts, the Euronaut resumed his cautious walking and stopped rubbing the kithara as he saw the corner he was looking for; because he was closer, the source of the sound he heard not many moments ago also became clearer and, therefore, more frequent, without the need to reverb on the cave's walls with a louder beat.

As for the extinguishing of the lyre, he did not intend to surprise or be surprised, once he revealed himself to who or what was repeatedly producing the noise; in the foreseer's experience, it sounded like chains or shackles were in friction with the rock, which could only mean one thing – either someone was being held a prisoner, or perhaps an animal was restrained (the latter option was actually great, in case the creature felt cornered and wanted to attack Orpheus).

Amid the sound of chains rummaging against each other, there was moaning as well – the bard realized the voice was that of a woman, likely captured by surprise, turned captive in the meantime; Orpheus leaned against the wall, grabbing it like a shield as an aid to his attempt at stealth, quietly sliding his sandals to the corner of the cave, and as soon as he was done with that part, there came the difficult step:

peeking, without knowing yet whether he would be able to
see anything, but it he had to move, as he did not know either
if the monster leaving the insurmountable footsteps on
the ground was already inside the cave, or on its way back
to its lair, which is what that cave was – calling it a home
would be insane, at least with respect to human standards.

Moving the arrow to his right hand, Orpheus took a deep
breath and exhaled with the tip of his tongue between his
teeth, deciding it was time; he gradually turned his neck
to his right as much as his spine would let him and peeked,
holding back the remainder of his visage below the eyes.

A ray of sunlight dimming by the second traversed the high
ceiling through a circular opening, illuminating a manacled
woman, confirming the bard's initial hunch; her hands and
feet were restrained, forcing her to lie on a stack of grass
covered by a dirty cloth to the likes of the one she wore
wrapped around her head, stained with the color of blood.

Clearly wounded, that was why the woman was moaning
in pain, not just because of her head, from the look of it,
but also due to the friction of the shackles on her skin.
Before jumping in a careless manner to the middle of the
path leading down to the prisoner, Orpheus had to think
the situation through, analyzing any detail he could collect
from the environment, whose light was growing dimmer,
therefore increasing the difficulty of what had just become
a rescue operation; the search part concerned food and drink,
but it would have to wait for a while, as the perception of
information was disappearing through the bard's fingers.

Asking himself (on Zeus's beard) what he was doing, his

thoughts drifted to Eurydike, who certainly would not
have been proud of him for abandoning a captive woman,
when he had every chance to both retrieve and free her
305 from imprisonment; after all, was it not that he was on his
way to do? Just because this woman was not Eurydike did
not mean it would not consume him to leave the wounded
woman behind, lying to himself about the true reason why
he had entered the cave, merely scavenging for supplies.

310 It was done, he was going to make his move, quickly treading
on mud and rock, keeping close to the wall, so as to avoid
unveiling his position straight away, for he was not yet sure
both he and the woman were alone, and as he moved, he
thought it wise to grab the bow again and complement it
315 with the arrow he had been holding until then, thus making
better use of it, should he need to tauten the string and strike.

However, and regardless of the amount of swiftness and
stealth involved in his running, the Apollonian could not
help but trip halfway, luckily bringing his arms forward
320 and cushioning his chin on one of them, otherwise he was
certain to have broken his teeth or bruised his skin, to say
the least; an object of some kind had made him tumble.
He was unmistakably getting sick of constantly falling
everywhere, all the literally bloody time – he got up in
325 a grudge and looked back, checking what had been in
the way: it was a bone; he knew not whether it was human,
but bones in dark caves are generally not a good sign.
He tapped around in the dark, looking for more evidence,
until he found more bones of different shapes and sizes,
330 which was normal, regardless of being feral or human, but
when Orpheus picked up what felt like a skull, he feared
its shape, trembling that it could have been a person's.

Closing his eyes again, he held it by the lower jaw, and began
tapping from the back, which was in fact the skull's face.
The Apollonian sensed the teeth at first, but they were not
sharp or big enough to match those of a beast he knew.
Then, he moved to the area of the nose cavity – there was
no elongation that made it resemble an animal's muzzle.
The eye sockets were wide, but not as much as the ones
on the face of, say… a bear, a tiger, or a lion, perhaps.
From there, he slid the palm of his free hand all the way
back until it met the busy hand – the back of that skull
was round; if any other doubts still existed, it all came
to the eerie truth: Orpheus was holding what had been
the head of a human… man or woman, it does not matter,
as he quickly let go of it, breaking its jaw with the fall.

The racket he made when tripping had already been loud
enough, but it was dropping the cranium that caught the
woman's attention, who faintly asked: 'Who… who is there?
Is it you again, you… you monster…? Back from grazing
your precious little sheep, are you? Do us both a favor and
just kill me… I cannot even look at myself properly without
feeling disgusted… I stink of rotten flesh, you idiot…!
Let me go! Get me out of here!', she cried, doing her best
at twisting her limbs, echoing the sound of the chains across
the entire cave; if she kept moving much longer, they would
both be done for and Orpheus might as well have pierced his
throat with one of his arrows – he needed to calm her down.

'Hush, now!', the Apollonian whispered, closing in on her,
'I know not who you are talking about, but I assure you
I am not them. My name is Orpheus, and I came in here
to look for something to eat and water to drink, but I guess
I ran into you, instead. How did you end up here? Your body

is raddled with wounds… what is it that is keeping you
in here? This place is covered with human bones!', Orpheus
silently exclaimed, looking at the woman from above,
blocking the last remnants of sunlight traversing the opening
in the ceiling, which made it hard for her to see his face.
She asked him to kneel, so she could look better at him,
a request to which he obliged, looking back every now
and then, fearing the man-eating creature's sudden return.

'Orpheus… why does that name sound familiar…? Have
we ever met before?', the woman asked; the Euronaut
replied: 'No… no, not that I remember, no…', he said,
in a tone of surprise, looking over his shoulder again.
'It will come to me… I am Persephone. Would you like
me to tell you a funny story? I was on my way to meet
with my mother after an argument we had, when a rather
eloquent cyclops is on his knees right in front of me,
on the beach. Suddenly, a tidal wave covers him completely
and I am caught in the middle. I lose my senses, have no
idea how I got here, and the next thing, I am manacled
in this cave, home to Polyphemos, the same cyclops I saw.
Every day he lives the same routine – takes his flock in the
morning, spends all day out and leaves me here. He does
not say a word. All he told me some time ago was that
he was my new guardian and would never let anything
bad happen to me. You said yourself I am covered in blood.
I feel like I am close to death, judging from the stench,
but, somehow, I have not yet been taken to Hades's home…
our home…', Persephone faintly said, as Orpheus quickly
turned back to face the goddess of springtime, this time
imprisoned for real, in actual need of rescue; still unknown
to him, the bard had just found the woman he was supposed
to look for by the shores of Pergoussa Lake, in Enna.

'Did you just say «our»...', the Apollonian meant to ask,
before being suddenly interrupted by approaching footsteps
that were heavy enough to make the cave tremble, but gently.
A flock of sheep could also be heard bleating between each
step, probably running scared from the shepherd himself.
Persephone told Orpheus to hurry and hide behind a stack
of supplies, or the oncoming cyclops would eat him in
no more than two bites, spitting his bones out afterward.

Some of the sheep came running toward the pile of grass
Kore had been uncomfortably lying on all day, trying to
move slightly to avoid getting bedsores, though nobody
could say that was a bed (not one to sleep on every day,
at least); the goddess of rebirth tried startling the sheep
away, but her wrists and ankles were so bruised that she
was unable to move anymore, giving up and allowing
the animals to take a bite off the only support she had
before becoming hung in mid-air by the chains and shackles.

'Stop it! Leave her alone, you silly ewes!', Polyphemos
roared, once he stepped in, bringing with him a lit torch
he dropped into a recess he had carved for it to stand.
The flame was wide enough to spread a great deal of light
across all three walls (or the dead-end his lair was in fact);
that was the moment the bard, already hidden, saw how big
the cyclops was – he was not just incredibly tall, he was large
in every way, having his back turned, as he drove the flock
into the corral where it stayed overnight (which, by the way,
could use some cleaning, as there were excrements in its area.
They simply had not smelled because they were already dry,
but the place looked filthy all the same, and it was not only
the corral – the whole cave seemed to be a sty; the Apollonian
was surprised the cyclops did not have any pigs, but then

again, he was enough of a pig himself to live in such a place.
Orpheus was positioned on the opposite side of the corral,
hiding behind sacks filled with goods, such as goat cheese,
bread, meat preserved with salt, together with fruit and
vegetables Polyphemos either grew, stole, or exchanged with
other cyclopes, though, again, it was hard to come across
a specimen, probably because of the location they lived in,
to the North of the island, where the sorcerer had been
driven by Demeter and Hekate; it is understandable, once
you think about it – Aitne is like a barrier segregating that
area from the rest of Trinacria, and going around it by sea
meant an encounter with Skylla and Kharybdis, usually
ending bad for those who dared take the risky journey.

When Orpheus came back to his senses, it was nearly dusk,
so any other cyclopes would have probably retired to their
respective homes – whether they were similar to this one,
he could not say, but hopefully they would be cleaner,
to say the least; no one had ever thought these children
of Gaia's lived in abodes with this sort of... presentation.

As he watched, the foreseer lost his focus for a moment
and started looking at all the perishables within his range.
There were even barrels filled with water, wine, and milk;
on the one hand, finding a farmer cyclops was somewhat
useful, but on the other, it still was a cyclops, and the truth
is gazing at food made Orpheus' stomach ask to be fed –
and a bit loudly, at that, which attracted Polyphemos's
attention, jeopardizing the bard's life in a way worse
than thirst or starvation... suppose that, instead of eating
him, the cyclops squashed his brains out just by tightening
the grip of his fist, or painted the walls of the cave with his
blood, beating him all around until he held in his hand either

an arm or a leg... Persephone had to do something before
Orpheus's cover was blown, so she addressed Polyphemos
460 to pick a fight with him, giving the kithara player a chance
of hiding again with food in his hands and something
to drink by submerging his quiver in one of the barrels,
whichever he reached first and, most importantly, without
making any fuss – otherwise, he could just stay where he was.

465 'Hey! When are you letting me out of here? You come in,
you do not even say a word to me anymore, what do you
want from me, you enlarged male beast?', Persephone yelled,
discouraging Polyphemos from taking his inspection further.
He did not look away at once, biding his time smelling
470 the area where Orpheus's stomach had rumbled, now held
with all his strength to prevent any more inopportune noise;
it was like the bard was smothering his own abdomen.

Kore, however, did not give up on the shouting until the
cyclops averted his eye to her, when he finally stopped
475 trying to pick up on the scent of a human intruder in his cave.
'Are you looking at me? You look at me when I am talking
to you, cyclops! I cannot tell whether your eye is set on me',
Persephone said, rattling him at all costs to make him leave
and go break other places in the mountain with the club
480 he had fastened by the waist, hoping Orpheus could do
something about the chains and set her free once and for all.

'Why must you hurt me so, why?!', Polyphemos asked of
Kore, 'Why do you make fun of my appearance?! Have I
not been good to you all this time, nursing and protecting
485 you?!', the cyclops roared, making the cave tremble.
The goddess of springtime then retorted: 'Good to me...?
Are you out of your mind, or is it loose inside your skull?!

Persephone's Fall

Look at me! I am imprisoned in here, getting sore and bruised
all over! How can you claim you have been taking care of me
if you do not let me go?! If you had a shred of respect for me,
you would set me free. Then I might consider becoming your
friend', Persephone concluded, throwing these harsh words
at Polyphemos as if she were spitting on him, a lady or not.

A puerile grudge took over the cyclops, stomping the ground
as he shed tears from his eye, one at a time, agitating the
foothills of the stratovolcano and infuriating its prisoner,
though it is not Persephone I sing about; all the commotion
made Orpheus drop his quiver, which he had taken a chance
to fill with water, quenching his thirst and helping the grub
go down, but as he was still chewing, he nearly choked and
coughed, dropping the bow, the arrows, and the golden lyre.

Normally, the cyclops's racket would not allow the echoing
of other sound, but because the kithara hit the ground, it let
a note loose, which was insufficient to charm Polyphemos,
but enough to draw his attention and confirm his original
suspicions – there really was a human in the cave, and his
one eye had him locked; after a moment, the cyclops grew
enraged and gave his best at crushing Orpheus like a bug.

The bard had to move fast, so he got up, grabbed his bow
again, a few arrows, and the kithara, and ran from the tip
of the club Polyphemos was wielding, which, compared
to a human-sized club, was like trying to avoid a ship
falling directly on top of his head, for some godly reason.
He tried shooting an arrow at the cyclops's eye, but he
did not know how to make use of it, especially under
pressure; the only practice he had with strings was reflected
on his musical abilities, not hunting, despite his father being

Apollo and one of his aunts Artemis, who had not even voted
in favor of him being assisted by Athena, before reaching
the Strait of Messene, which meant that, perhaps, discredit
had taken over the bard, forcing him to adopt other methods.

The golden kithara, with its magical powers, could have
helped Orpheus charm the cyclops into doing his bidding,
but Polyphemos was too focused on trying to kill him to
listen to its notes, played improperly while the bard was
running, of course, driving the enlarged-man close to Kore
to inadvertently break her chains; how they would leave
if successful was another question to ponder upon entirely.

'I knew there was a little rat wandering about!', the cyclops
exclaimed, 'I saw a vessel moored down by the cape, but
you are not boarding it again! Once I am finished with you,
I am turning that ship into firewood! Come here!', he added,
continuously cutting off Orpheus's every hope of escaping.

Praying to his father, Phoebus Apollo, the bard asked for
an accurate shot this time around, tautening his bow as hard
as he could, aiming the other arrow he had taken hold of.
In the skies, night had already fallen, and though Apollo
did not have permission to help him with his marksmanship,
the god inflated his son with trust, hoping it would suffice.
Orpheus, too tired from running, positioned himself right
behind Persephone, pointing the arrow at her head, crying:
'Stop right now or I kill her where she lies!', at which point
Polyphemos halted his pursuit for the Apollonian, confused.

'What are you doing...?!', the goddess of springtime asked
him in a faint whisper; the bard averted his sight to her and
back to the cyclops, as if trying to tell her to trust him.

Persephone's Fall

'You came in here to take her from me! Why would you kill her?!', Polyphemos shouted, slowly lowering his club. 'That is where you are wrong! I do not know this woman.
550 Whatever you do with her is fine by me. I was simply on my way to my destination and needed to resupply the ship you saw outside – yes, it is mine, indeed, and I have run out of food and water. I saw this cave and came in to replenish myself, that is all. The woman is of no interest to me; besides,
555 if she is in chains, she is your prisoner – you deal with her. I apologize for barging into your... home, but once I saw you had perishables in store, I could not help but take some. Now, if you let me go with some food and drink, you will never see me again and she stays alive – do we have a deal?',
560 Orpheus asked the cyclops, to see if he would yield to reason.

After a few good moments, both the bard and the goddess began to wonder if Polyphemos had understood the barter he had just been offered, cluelessly ogling at the cyclops. Then, out of nowhere, he dropped his club on the ground,
565 nearly startling Orpheus off his feet, but he remained calm. 'Very well, take what you want and leave us both alone', Polyphemos told him, stepping away from the cousins.

Exhaling profoundly through his nose, the Apollonian felt both surprised and relieved at the same time, saying: 'Good!
570 Good... I shall forever be indebted to you, my dear friend'. Orpheus lowered his bow and arrow without meeting Kore's gaze at all, concentrating his focus solely on the cyclops. Then, once he got close to the food and drink storage, he grabbed an empty bag and started pouring supplies into it,
575 without really minding what it was he was selecting to take.

Biding his time, the moment the kithara player had been

waiting for arrived at last, which he could confirm based on
the cyclops' shadow, cast by the torch behind – holding a
finger in front of his enormous mouth, Polyphemos told
580 Persephone to stay quiet, turning afterward to Orpheus,
quietly picking up the club that lay at his feet; as the shade
grew bigger by the moment and the cyclops gained enough
momentum to crush the bard to death, the latter shut his eyes
and dropped the bag of goods, unfastening the lyre from his
585 waist, which he began to play, charming the club, instead of
the cyclops, whose hands rapidly came down empty.

Confused, Polyphemos looked to his right, then to his left,
but could not find the club anywhere; only when he saw
Persephone looking above his head did he realize it was
590 floating upside-down, precisely aimed at his one eye.
Turning slowly to face the cyclops, Orpheus kept playing
the kithara, telling him: 'A man's word is a binding contract.
If you cannot stick to it, you can never be trusted again'.
Drawing his attention to himself, the sorcerer commanded
595 the club to go up and come back down in all force, striking
Polyphemos right on top of his head, knocking him down.
As he fell first on his knees, the ground trembled yet again,
tremoring completely when he dropped unconscious, making
Orpheus move out of the way, or the cyclops's eye socket
600 would have engulfed him right where he stood playing.

Somewhere behind the rock walls, the prisoner I sang about
earlier, Enkelados, became so disturbed for having his sleep
interrupted that he exhaled most profoundly, making Aitne
erupt and all its surroundings tremble violently, including
605 the cyclops's cave, which was somewhat lucky for Orpheus
and Persephone, as the chains restraining her were bound
to the walls, partially collapsing and thus setting her free.

Persephone's Fall

Up above, in Olympus, Apollo and Athena rejoiced with
Orpheus' success; even Zeus was timidly smiling, proud
of his grandson, for he had always known he had it in him.
The bearer of the aegis turned to Hermes and told him:
'Wear your talaria, son – it is time to take Persephone back
to the lake; while you are it, take Orpheus with you'.

The messenger of gods swiftly dove from the Pantheon
and flew straight to Trinacria, aiming for the cave's circular
skylight; Demeter and Hekate, who had been waiting
outside, saw the traces of stardust moving down to their
approximate position, at which point Hekate gently said,
holding the lady of the grain's hand: 'It is Hermes – he is
taking Persephone back to Pergoussa. We should follow
him, so you may bid each other goodbye before the restart
of the cycle', the sorceress goddess concluded, as the Lady
of the Golden Sword softly nodded, shedding a few tears.

Inside, both the youngest of the Thesmophoroi and the bard
laughed with joy, asking each other what had just happened,
in utter disbelief; it was incredible how they had managed
to get themselves out of that utterly complicated situation.
Nevertheless, their laughter was suddenly interrupted by
Hermes's arrival, to the surprise of Orpheus and Kore's
realization, being the latter confirmed by the messenger
himself: 'The time has come, cousin… as for you, Orpheus',
he added, rendering the bard' eyes wide open: 'You are
coming with – step forward and join us', which he did,
gulping in awe; Hermes freed Kore from her shackles
and took hold of both her and Orpheus's hands, flying
out the cave the same way he came in, leaving behind
three traces of stardust in the sky; Hekate and Demeter
immediately followed them, headed for Pergoussa Lake.

Fall

Canto XIX

How long for have multiple generations been told the most amazing of stories, beginning terribly wrong at one, unique place, just to finish beautifully right back where they started? Millennia – the world was created so long ago by primordial deities humans eventually forgot about in favor of their descendants that it is pointless to try to be precise by defining a specific number of years, decades, centuries, and millennia, indeed... not all who walk on this earth share adoration for the same idols; I, for instance, gave up on my faith long ago, and for that, I was punished with the severest of penalties. That does not mean, however, I am not happy at present, because I am; I have everything I need right here, by my side.

I should, nevertheless, give you a piece of advice on how to live life (not «your» life, taken that part is for you to decide, but rather on how to live life to its fullest): taking someone or something for granted is one of the worst mistakes you can make as long as you live, but so is assuming you could never have done it, perpetually asking yourself, «but what if...?»; may I add my use of the adverb is deliberate, as even in the afterlife your memory will live on, your soul will keep carrying your consciousness – what you thought was only a part of your earthly body, your brains, does not cease its existence come death; it lingers... now, whether in Tartarus, the limbo, the Elysian Fields, or any other place you believe in... that, I cannot tell you, for it depends on what your faith is, how strong it is, and your being worthy of immortality – not as far as the body is concerned, but the soul and the soul alone, which is what really matters... we all have a body – gods, people, animals, plants, dirt... even dirt is material.

30 It is no surprise to anyone we are born to live (regardless of
how long), so we may die later and join the earth as soil,
seeds, plantation, food eaten by others, still inside their
carnal carcasses... the ashes of a funerary pyre spread by
the four Anemoi to where our physical remains will give
35 birth to something new, exactly to the likes of the legendary
phoenix; it does not matter if it lives up to five hundred years
before catching fire and burning to dust – what is important
is, somewhere, wherever that may be, even the smallest piece
that once was ours will give life to someone or something,
40 always renewing the cycle of life (and death, come to that).

The gods themselves cannot live forever, if nobody prays
to them anymore; we all need each other, and not just as long
as we live – the afterlife should too comprise reciprocity.
Our deeds are our legacy, and their remembrance through
45 generations to come is what allows us to stay alive after
we die, another star sent to the celestial dome, watching over
the earth from the night sky, shining as a sign of protection.
To power of metamorphosis is not exclusive to the gods –
we can all change to anyone or anything we want, as long
50 as we do not abuse of that power, using it only to do good.
Go on and live, live the way you think is best, and achieve
your own glory, not because you played the hero, but rather
because you were happy and made someone else as happy
as you for staying by their side, for better or worse, whoever
55 they are – a wife, a husband, a parent, a sibling, a relative,
or a friend, as being trustworthy is one of the best values
we possess and can display by sharing it with all the others.

As rosy-fingered Dawn gradually became visible in the
horizon, making the transition from Nyx's darkness and
60 Hekate's Moon to Phoebus's golden chariot, about to

depart from behind Mount Aitne, still concealing its light, the horde that had successfully escaped from Mylae, cyclops territory, was now safely back in Enna, traveling Southwest to the lake where it had begun, landing by Pergoussa's shore, approximately the same spot where Persephone had been coloring her flowers, accompanied by Athena, Artemis, and the nymphs, as her mother kept slightly back, taking care of her own chores, never in her eternity guessing what was would happen next… it has been a long year since then.

The Lady of the Golden Sword landed nearby shortly after, alone, as Hekate had gone straight to her earthly cave to prepare everything for Orpheus's departure, who would not be taking the same way as Persephone, about to return home. Her daughter, together with Hermes and Orpheus, had their attention drawn to where Demeter presented herself, gasping in several emotions bursting all at once – Kore's first reaction was to run toward her mother, as the goddess of agriculture did the same, finding each other at the center of their path.

'Mother!', Persephone exclaimed, holding Demeter with all her strength, while sobbing on her shoulder, telling her how sorry she was for storming off from Katane without saying another word, adding: 'I went back looking for you shortly after, but you were not there anymore… I did not know what to do, and then this cyclops stood in the way and took me to his lair, but I am sure I was knocked out before he saw me', she concluded, while her mother held her strongly as well, telling her it was all right, that she knew about everything, that it was over at last, and that Apollo would be there soon.

When Persephone asked her how she knew about it, Demeter told her: 'Hekate explained it to me; I have had her help all

this time, especially as far as figuring out a few details is
concerned, such as... realizing my daughter is no longer
a little girl, and that she should be free to be happy the way
she wants to be, as opposed to what her mother or anyone
95 else want or just think is best for her – it is only up to her
to make such decisions', she said, looking Persephone in her
beautiful emerald eyes, caressing her hair with both hands.

With respect to knowing about her daughter's perilous
situation in Polyphemos's cave, the lady of the grain said:
100 'There was nothing Hekate or I could do... Zeus wanted
Orpheus to be tested at all costs, and we had already aided
him at sea, joining him in his fight against a couple of sea...
menaces, so to speak, for which reason he forbade us to
assist him again. He saved you on his own, without any
105 divine intervention whatsoever involved; Hermes only
freed you when he proved Zeus how worthy he was'.

'But... why did he have to be tested, anyway? Who is he?',
Persephone asked her mother, who replied in the form of a
question: 'Orpheus? Do you not remember him?'; Kore's
110 answer was a slight shoulder shrug, conveying she had no
idea, but Demeter quickly reminded her: 'He is a half-
-nephew of yours, son of Apollo and the muse Calliope.
Half a year ago, he married one of his father's daughters,
Eurydike, an oak nymph, but she was killed on their wedding
115 day and now he is on his way to Tartarus to try to bring her
back, though Hekate told me he is not going with you.
Hades might think he was too lazy to take the regular way,
the same the dead take themselves, including Eurydike,
despite not being dead in the usual sense of the word and...
120 well, never mind that, it is much too complex – just make
sure you talk Hades into freeing the girl, so they can be

together again and live for as long as possible, but do not
say a word before he reaches the palace', Demeter adverted.

The first rays of sunshine were beginning to show from the
125 back of Aitne, meaning it was time for them to say goodbye.
Holding each other again, Persephone enounced her words
as sweet as honey: 'I will miss you, Mother... so very much'.
The lady of the grain complemented by saying: 'I will miss
you too, Sweetheart... I know not how I will spend my time
130 without you close to me, but... Hekate will be sending news.
I love you', the mother told her daughter, who echoed her
in her words and feeling: 'I love you too, Mother, so much'.
As they held, Persephone's wounds were gradually healed
by Demeter's motherly love, restoring the maiden's outlook
135 to what it had always been – extraordinary, divine beauty.

It was hard to let go, but they had to, looking and smiling
at each other, as Persephone walked in reverse a few steps,
facing afterward the expectant Hermes, who gave her his
hand; before going through the entrails of the earth, though,
140 she turned to Orpheus, smiled at and told him: 'I guess I will
see you soon', closing her eyes, as the messenger of gods
held her by the waist and dove for the bottom of Pergoussa,
momentarily leaving a few remnants of molten rock behind.

Orpheus was more than confused or puzzled – bedazzled
145 might actually be a more appropriate term to define his
state of mind; the lady of the grain was about to start crying,
as were the skies, when she called the bard and told him
to come closer, adding: 'It is your turn, boy – let us move'.
Demeter drove him inside Hekate's cave, looking over her
150 shoulder one last time, dropping her first tear at the same
time the first droplets of rain came rushing down the sky.

Tiago Lameiras

Fall had arrived once more, quenching the thirst of both Gaia and the Hellenes, who sent Demeter their prayers.

Canto XX

'Orpheus, this is Hekate, a goddess and a friend', Demeter told the bard, introducing him to the sorceress deity inside the latter's earthly lair, further explaining: 'She lives in the realm of death, Hades's domain, where Persephone has just gone, but because you could not go with her, you will have to take the same path the dead do as soon as they leave this world', then having Hekate complete her words: 'It is the same path Eurydike took when she disappeared from the place she had fallen on, and though she was not really dead, as you may have already heard, the ferryman Kharon took her anyway across the river of souls. Should he refuse to fare you, remember to stick to your wisdom and convince him – he is a creepy creature and will turn down passengers for no reason at all, so be prepared. That is all I am allowed to say. I will take you to the shore of the Styx that is still a part of the world of the living, then it is up to you, and let me stress this for as long as it takes – trust yourself, trust your gut, do what you think is right', the goddess of magic highlighted, a goddess whose voice seemed to be somewhat familiar to the Apollonian, which is why, when he was about to ask Hekate if she had anything to do with him fulfilling his enterprise at all, she laid her right index on his lips, sealing them while simultaneously telling him: 'Some other time – now focus!', she exclaimed, as both vanished, leaving a trail behind (not of stardust, but rather dark smoke, which quickly disappeared); Demeter, having stayed, wished him Godspeed on his new journey, hoping he would come back.

About a minute later, Orpheus found himself beached by the river, feeling he was going to be sick because of the ride.

30 Flying with Hermes and Persephone had scared him, but due to the fresh air of the evening, the bard was still able to hold his food down, the same he had grabbed in Polyphemos's lair; now that he had gone through the heated entrails of Gaia, however, he did not know whether he would manage
35 to equal his prior feat, trying to stand as slowly as possible. 'Honestly, how many times can a man tumble, be knocked out and get back on his feet…? This entire journey has been an incredible laughing riot of a metaphor for life', Orpheus said to himself aloud, drawing attention from someone near.

40 The beach was foggy by the stream, becoming completely invisible all the more one walked inland, deliberately forcing those who arrived there to focus on the river, faintly crying every now and then, which eventually aroused the bard's curiosity as to what flowed in those waters; Hekate had told
45 him she would only take him to the river of souls, so that was probably it – souls trapped in a spring, cyclically gushing to the sea and back for eternity… as the kithara player got closer, a barge was on its way as well, concealed in the fog.

Easily yielding to temptation, the Apollonian bent his knee
50 and drove his hand to the surface of the Styx to stir the dirty water and clear his sight; the moment he wet his palm, his wrist was taken hold of by a traveling soul whose appearance was that of a fleshless woman, carrying nothing more on her skeleton than skin – all the muscle was gone, including the
55 eyes, as the enlarged, empty sockets showed rather well. The speed at which she grabbed Orpheus's wrist startled him, impulsively making him cry out and grab the wizened wrist to release himself, but he only ended up captured by the soul, pushing him with an incredible strength as she
60 screamed to his face with a rotten breath: 'Get me out!

Get me out of here! Now! I did nothing wrong! I want to
live! Pull me, little boy! Pull me! Pull me now!', she kept
on going, though it was Orpheus who was being pulled.

He tried striking his feet in the sand to generate friction,
but the soul was dragging him in all the same, submerging
his forearms at that stage, which became as raggedy as her
entire «body», if I may use that vocable in this context.
His face would soon be underwater, burning both his eyes
and hair; it was what the Styx did to people, it corroded
their crooked bodies as an act of purification, keeping
their souls as a reward to add to the endless collection.

The water was turning red from the loss of blood and flesh,
and the bard's nose was only about a iamb away from
melting; fearing the worst, that it was the end and he would
not be able to rescue the nymph after all, he gnashed his teeth
and uttered: 'I love you, Eurydike... please... forgive me...'.
It was then that a strong breeze was blown to the bard's face,
followed by a striking sound; the screaming soul pulling him
into the water had been hit in the head with an oar held by
a skeletal character aboard a sober barge – it was Kharon.
Once he realized he was free, the Apollonian pulled his arms
back from the water and, as he did, his blood and flesh were
restored; it was, nevertheless, as painful a procedure as being
corroded or eaten alive by a lion with sharp claws and fangs.
Unable to hold it in, the dinner he had coveted for so long
ended up in the water, disputed by the traversing souls.
It was definitely not a pleasant picture to save for the future.

'What the hell was that?', Kharon uttered, incapable of
changing between expressions, though the tone was helpful
as to understand what he meant every time he spoke.

Gasping for breath, Orpheus looked up to the moving skull, asking him: 'Are... are you the... the ferryman', a question to which Kharon replied like so: 'Yes, I am. Who is asking?'. The foreseer proceeded: 'I am... Orpheus... son of... of the Sun-God, Phoebus... Phoebus Apollo. I am here on... on... please excuse me', he begged the ferryman, trying to catch his breath again, so he could speak without interruption. 'I am here on a mission – about six months ago you ferried an oak nymph by the name of Eurydike. She was sent here by mistake. She is in your master's domain, right now. Alive. The gods have entrusted me with her retrieval back to earth'.

Kharon looked at Orpheus for a while (though the bard could not realize it, because he too was missing his eyes. Suddenly, the most unexpected reaction burst through his jaws – he was laughing; no such myth had ever passed between generations... the ferryman – laughing; it had to be a sordid joke, especially when describing the movement of his lower jaw, wagging against its upper counterpart.

As he began wheezing in need of air, despite the lack of lungs, he approached Orpheus's face and said: 'You are disturbed, friend. I have no idea what you are talking about. Also, if you are not dead, I cannot take you anywhere. Either stay on the beach or throw yourself in the river of your own accord. Being pulled into it does not count. You will have the ride of a lifetime – literally', he concluded, widening the gap between his face and Orpheus's once more just to sit down in his barge and remain still; it was much too peculiar that such a character existed in fact, despite all other creatures sharing the earth with Man... this assembly of bones beat all of them put together and no mistake. The bard thought he had experienced enough awkwardness as it was in little over a day, so he decided to push on.

'Hey! What if we barter? Will you take me across the river
if I pay you?', the Euronaut asked the resting ferryman.
125 'You are not dead, boy. If you are not planning on letting
the river devour you, just stay there for, say… about three
weeks – then you will be dead. I will even give you a proper
burial by feeding you to this miserable scum scratching
the hull of my barge with their finger blades', Kharon said.

130 Much too tired to deal with further obstacles, he showed
the ferryman his lyre: 'Here, take a look at this – solid gold.
Unique in all of Greece, given to me by Apollo himself,
and worth a lot more than all the obols you have collected
so far'; looking interested, Kharon asked the Euronaut:
135 'Have you any idea whatsoever how many poor devils
I have ferried ever since the end of the Titanomachy?
What makes you think I do not already own that kind
of fortune, if not much more?', the ferryman said, in a tone
of confrontation, but Orpheus would not be so easily
140 discouraged from his intent, asking Kharon again: 'Final
offer, ferryman. Either take the kithara, or I will play it
as long as there is air in my lungs – the same tune, repeatedly.
What is it going to be?', unsparing of his wisdom in trickery.

Kharon was stubborn himself, and so he decided to push
145 the ridiculousness of the situation – just a bit further:
'I would actually appreciate some sort of entertainment.
Why do you not give me your best? I might grow to like it'.
Pushing the kithara against his chest for support, Orpheus
put his fingers on the strings, however adding these words
150 before playing: 'Your wish is my command, my good friend'.
The moment notes reverbed from the magical instrument,

Kharon's lower jaw dropped to its maximum limit – he had
just been successfully enchanted, hopping off the barge and
kneeling on the sand, showing his allegiance to the Euronaut.
Bowing down his skull, the ferryman addressed Orpheus:
'Please, my Lord – it is your wish that is my command'.
The sorcerer replied: 'Good. You shall be commended
for your resourcefulness, my dear ferryman. Now, would
you be so kind as to take me across the river to the gates
of Tartarus?', a request that Kharon promptly fulfilled,
saying: 'But of course, my Lord! Anything you ask of me'.

The power of the kithara not only benefitted Orpheus with
respect to the ferryman, but it also kept away souls that
otherwise would have attempted to swamp the barge.
The first part had almost been too easy, as the saying goes.
It was what lurked ahead, beyond the fog, that was worrying
for the son of Apollo and Calliope, the human prodigy.

Canto XXI

By the gates of the Underworld, petting Kerberos, was none
other than the ruler of the domain, Hades, the Screech Owl.
Judging from the look on his face, he looked rather anxious,
but, then again, what man would not feel nervous, awaiting
the arrival of the woman of his dreams, six months later?
A lot had been left unsaid, but, as both him and Persephone
eventually came to agree, they needed the time to understand
what it was they felt for each other; the Master of Death had
no doubts – it was either Kore the guardian of the gates
to his heart, or for eternity they would remain slam shut;
bluntly put, only the goddess possessed the key to opening
a much-secluded treasure no one else thought was real.
The maiden gave him the chance others would have easily
refused at face value, for Hades was not regarded as a god
to be idolized or adored, but rather feared, hence the death-
-related epithets he was mostly known for across Greece.

The three-headed dog had his six eyes open, which meant he
could not see, rolling over on himself, happy about all the
cuddling his master was giving him, while the latter spoke to
him, as if confiding in someone who could not only perceive
the language of men, but also reply in it: 'I miss her deeply,
Kerberos... do you think she had the time to think about us
as a couple? She has changed me so much... sometimes, I find
myself smiling for no apparent reason, though it is her I am
thinking of. Even the prisoners have noticed it – they look at
me with disgust because they think I am taking pleasure from
their punishment, picturing me as a wicked demon having
fun with other people's disaster, can you believe it? If they
are in said situation, it is because they had been calling it

upon themselves for far too long, thinking they could cheat death… you remember Sisyphos, do you not?', Hades asked the dog, who, in turn, replied affirmatively with his barking.

'Never have I ever seen such perversity and depravity in one man alone, tying me up in my own chains. You would think by then I should have already been used to humans' deceit, but he was daring… and cunning – with respect to tricking me, that is. Boasting he was smarter than Zeus was certainly the worst sentiment he could be proud of. He was a king, so his subjects owed him respect to begin with, but if he wanted to stay in his throne while loved by his people, he had to be worthy of it, he had to deserve continued adoration, instead of scaring everyone by making a habit out of killing to assert his rule. To be fair, my brother is very much alike him, but he is the immortal supreme leader, and nobody can be more powerful than him. At least Zeus's vanity was useful… it put Sisyphos in his place. How frustrating it must be to spend an entire revolution of the Sun pushing a boulder up a cliff, just to come rolling straight down near the top. Hubris is a fine sentiment… until the Erinyes send their harpies in search for the malefactor – that is when the criminal finally bows', Hades mumbled, lost in his discourse; Kerberos had been listening to his master quietly, resting his heads on his paws, until he eventually fell asleep with his eyelids still open.

For a human, it was a rather creepy image to behold; as if the three heads were not already enough, the fact the dog's eyes were visible, though they could not see themselves, was inconceivable, which is why this feature of his was so useful, in case the dead tried to escape by fooling his noses off their trail, whereas having his eyes closed was perfect as far as preventing other sorts of trickery was concerned.

Persephone's Fall

Having realized Kerberos was somewhere else because of
the sudden silence in his panting, Hades left him asleep
and moved back inside, closing the diamond-encrusted
gates behind him, unaware of the time, as Apollo could
not send sunlight to a place where flames were the only
source of luminescence, so he just kept walking toward
his palace, hands behind his back, in a pensive posture.

Then again, he did have a reference with respect to the
time of day – Sisyphos himself; he was still in the early
stages of pushing the boulder up the hill, meaning the
Sun had probably already risen, and it was still early in
the morning; the equinox must have been underway,
but it was impossible to be as precise to the minute.
Sensing Persephone was getting closer made Hades's heart
nearly jump out of his chest, as it put a smile on his face –
a somewhat timid smile, may I add, feeling quite silly
for embarrassing himself like that, because, if that was
his reaction to thinking Persephone was on her way, how
clumsy would he get once he stood in her divine presence?
Some men are reluctant to admitting the woman they love
make them feel this way, but they need not say anything.
A heart that is in love is an open book – readable in its whole.
The surrounding prisoners, sentenced to excruciating pain
for eternity, thought they were being made a mockery of,
gnarling as the warden walked by, smiling to himself.

A few more steps later, with the palace already in sight,
feminine voices could be heard in a tone of happiness.
Also, a ray of light fading toward the Underworld's ceiling
indicated a god was leaving – Hermes, from the look of it,
as there were gold particles falling on the palace's roofs;
that was it, Persephone had returned at last – and the other

woman talking to her must have been Eurydike, of course.

Without wasting any more precious time, unknowingly
avoid the same mistake Demeter had made for the past
95   six months, Hades ran for the entrance to the palace, and
there she was... Persephone, in all her splendor and grace.
She had her back turned on the door; it was the nymph
who was facing the entrance, noticing Hades after a couple
of seconds – her joyful stare, together with her smile,
100 made the goddess of rebirth look over her shoulder to see
what Eurydike was staring at, though it was not what,
it was who: Hades, unrecognizable since the last time.
There were tears in his eyes, but certainly not of sadness.
The love of his eternity was back and facing him, slowly
105 turning around, dressed in a white tunic held by her right
shoulder; if her nude back had already caught his attention,
seeing her visage after all that time, timidly smiling at him,
was the best feeling in the world, from the underground
to the stars of the night sky, absolutely no doubt about it...

110 It could have been just him, but she looked so much more
beautiful... it was likely the result of allowing love to enter
her heart, letting down her guard; her dark hair was loose,
resting on the same shoulder holding her gown together,
absorbing the surrounding light, becoming fairer, as usual.
115 Her almond-shaped eyes were fully green, incomparable
to the void that had once invaded them, fading their shine
away for constantly crying, feeling imprisoned right there,
in that palace, staying there against her will, but now...
she was not back just because of the Moirai, that much
120 was clear – no, she wanted to be there, as one could tell
from her confident walking down the hall, as Hades walked
in the opposite direction, toward her, rushing his step.

Once they met, roughly at the center of the hallway, neither
of them knew what to do; they just kept shimming their sight
sideways, carefully observing every detail on each other's
visage, until their eyes finally met for a few seconds, both
laughing of embarrassment and timidity shortly after.

Putting together all the boldness he could find, Hades was
the first to speak, candidly enouncing those same words
everyone hopes to hear after they have been gone for a long
time: 'I have missed you. Not just today. Not just for the last
six months. I have missed you my entire life', he earnestly
confessed; Persephone, smiling back at him, threw her arms
around his neck, placing her heart on top of his own,
whispering unto his ear: 'Do you feel that? My heart beating
together with yours? It says I have missed you too, every
single day I was away from here, realizing my real home
is where my heart pulls me to – you', she too confessed.

Hades smiled, lovingly kissing her neck, after she had done
the same; a few steps away, by the statue of the goddess
of rebirth, the one the Screech Owl had purposely built
for her, Eurydike crossed her hands over her own heart,
hoping she would soon be in the arms of her husband,
on his way across the Styx for her, according to Kore;
she simply could not wait to live a moment like that,
as much as Orpheus, though I am forced to add his
impatience was slowly taking the best of him – for the worst.

Canto XXII

The Styx's riverbed must have been the widest in the world, Orpheus thought, as he could not see land in sight, no matter how much he tried; the continuous presence of fog, of course, was of no help, either, but he sure hoped Kharon's barge would reach the Tartarus bank soon, as his fingers were starting to get callous – some even felt like they would burst at any moment, bleeding out, in which case the bard would likely be in serious trouble, as the ferryman was locked inside his subconscious and was not aware of what he was doing, or how servile the Apollonian had made him (not even Hades was persuasive enough to make him that obedient, so, that on itself was another feat of the son of Apollo's to be told to future generations, should his tale be spread across Greece).

The bard had the impression he was somehow reliving his time aboard the Argo, traveling to uncharted territory as he charmed souls (instead of sirens) to stay away from the frail barge, even though they accompanied the vessel as it crossed the river, which would normally become agitated because of the spirits flowing within, precisely. The Styx was one of the most temperamental bodies of water in existence, as it was an entrance to the Underworld from overground (to the likes of the Acheron, for instance), and if a human or any other living creature with reasoning abilities dared venture their chances upstream, it was likely they would not return, similarly absorbed by the waters like Orpheus almost was, had it not been for Kharon, weirdly polite without yet being enchanted by the lyre.

Every now and then, the former Argonaut looked over

his shoulder, just to make sure the ferryman was possessed
in fact, and was not planning any counterattacks, such as
throwing Orpheus overboard himself, making his apparent
death wish come true, in the end; however, there was nothing
to worry about, for Kharon was still under the power of the
kithara, bearing a smile on his face – considering he did not
have a «face» at all, he could have been evilly smirking
without ever giving his game away, thus duping the duper.

Orpheus just did not seem to learn from his mistakes; worse
than that, he kept ignoring the advice provided to him
by everyone he came across with along his way and wished
his success, which was clearly Hekate's case, the goddess
that had inspired him to set sail, helping him for the entirety
of his journey, even when thought he had only dreamed of
encounters at sea with wicked monsters of all sorts, including
a hybrid between a ketos and a hydra, or a live whirlpool.

He thought his lack of confidence in himself would become
his demise, eventually, which was counterproductive, raising
his self-awareness on how he could not and did not trust
himself, paradoxically enough... he wasted too much time
lost in this kind of thoughts – when you think about it,
it sort of resembles an act of hubris, because, by doubting
himself, even though a deity told him repeatedly to hold on
to his trust, Orpheus is defying the resolve of the divine,
and when someone does that, sooner or later death is due
to arrive; of course, for someone who had decided to face
a cyclops, rescue a woman he did not know was a goddess
(let alone family), and had sailed (to begin with) from
Europa, in Greece, across the Aegean Sea, into the
Mediterranean, the Ionian, and last, but not least,
the Tyrrhenian, while looking for his prematurely dead

wife, whose hopes of coming back to the world of the living were still there to play for... well... it really had to be either a death wish, or a love quest, and it was, it definitely was.

Orpheus had already lived enough risky adventures next to Jason and the Argonauts, cannibals (just to mention a few examples), which is why he had no reason to leave his home, go out to sea and get lost, killed, or a combination of both. It was Eurydike who drove him to continue; should love stay out of the equation, he could do whatever he pleased by making use of his magical powers – he needed not work, make money, in short, a livelihood as common as any other. He did not think himself big for being the offspring of Apollo and Calliope, both divine; part of him was that of a demigod, indeed, but he never abused his power, directly confronting that of the different members of the Pantheon, quite the opposite – all he wanted was to live happily, with his wife, and he was on his way, closer than ever – one last leg to go.

Again, the Apollonian was in luck, as the fog started to dissipate, clearing the view in front of the barge; land was coming up – he had made it, he had reached Tartarus. Now, all he had to do was get inside, bring Eurydike with him, cross the river again, and emerge back to earth. What could possibly go wrong, with such a scenario in sight, already pointing to the greatest of successes?

Now, because he had sensed Kharon's barge approaching, Kerberos began closing his eyes, so as to see who it was, though he still felt sleepy; as Orpheus came closer, he saw the three-headed dog getting up on the beach, turning bigger at each of Kharon's strokes – he would likely make a good pet companion for Polyphemos, whose size was undoubtedly

90   proportional to the hound's (not just that, they could
     complete each other as far as the cyclops's lack of eyes
     was concerned; then again, a dog that size would likely
     make the sty Polyphemos already lived in much worse).

     Considering Tartarus was a large-scale underground piece
95   of architecture, any louder noise ended up reverbed in
     soundwaves traversing the environment, which means
     Kerberos quickly became involved in the spell of the lyre,
     just as Orpheus was about to stop playing and rest his hands.
     Still in awe, the bard was approached by the canine
100 and licked from the feet up, nearly falling and dropping
     the golden kithara in the water, and once in the wrong hands,
     who knows what it could be used for (a mass breakout)?

     The bard turned his head halfway to the side and asked
     Kharon: 'Ferryman, what is this thing?!', and the rower
105 happily obliged him: 'Why, it is Kerberos, my Lord,
     the hound of Hades, guardian of the Underworld gates'.
     Still trembling in fright, Orpheus replied: 'Thank you,
     Kharon', who, in turn and with the nicest of inflections
     in his voice, responded: 'By all means, my Lord. Glad
110 to be of service', the ferryman concluded, subservient.

     Making sure he was undeniably harmless, the Apollonian
     cautiously stepped out of the barge, with Kerberos right
     by his side, panting and waiting for Orpheus to give him
     a command, which he did: 'Kerberos', he said, making
115 the dog happily bark with his eyes closed, 'open the gates
     for me, would you?'; the hound promptly obeyed and
     patted with one of his anterior paws the gates, prying them.
     For some reason, Orpheus felt the need to bow to him,
     and went in, still playing the kithara with worn-out skin.

Persephone's Fall

120 The moment the foreseer stepped out of range, the gates closed behind him, sealing all sight and sound that came from the outside; even if he had continued to play the lyre, which he did not, the instrument's effect over both Kharon and Kerberos ceased immediately, leaving them both dazed.

125 The dog was unaware of what had just happened, but the ferryman... he knew something was off, suspecting the boy from the opposite bank of the Styx was behind it.

Canto XXIII

'Before you arrived, Eurydike was telling me how nice you have been to her all this time, my Dear', Persephone said, as she sat down in the dining room of Tartarus Palace, next to Hades, while the nymph sat opposed to them, giving both
5 deities their deserved space, so they could be close to each other, holding hands, losing themselves in the other's eyes, every now and then; Eurydike was so embarrassed she felt she should either go outside or retire to her chambers...

'Oh!, nonsense', Hades exclaimed, 'I am the one who owes
10 you an apology for making you feel like... a third wheel', he added, timidly giggling along with Persephone, who was progressively assuming the role of Queen of the Underworld. Trying not to be rude, the goddess of rebirth resumed her conversation with Eurydike: 'I am glad you felt welcomed
15 in this home, I really am, but the good news is Orpheus is on his way right now! You must be so excited... his chivalry is undeniable – marrying him was an excellent choice. To think he did not recognize me, had no idea who I was... he could have left me in that cave to die of my wounds,
20 either because of an infection (which I believe I was close to, in the middle of that filth), or due to exsanguination... my ambrosia, repeatedly pumped out of my body by my anxious heart. No, seriously, he was so cunning, so brilliant. That boy does not only play music, he does absolute wonders
25 with his golden kithara', the goddess of springtime said.

Eurydike was very much happy to hear such good things about her husband, but Hades had only just now picked up on the chat, and seemed confused about Kore's storyline.

'What is this about, then? A cave…? Dying?! What happened to you, my Love?', the Screech Owl asked his… girlfriend, as I may well put it now; Kore briefly mentioned the row she had had with her mother, who was unaccepting of her daughter's feelings for him, therefore provoking a clash between the two, resulting in their separation for the entirety of the time they were supposed to have spent together. However, because of the sweetness in both her heart and her mother's, they soon started looking for each other, but she was the one with the worst luck, captured by a cyclops and held prisoner, under the excuse he would always protect her from harm's way, and that he would not lose her again. Polyphemos had probably suffered a great loss in his lifetime, trying to compensate the event by finding another woman – herself, in this case; Hades was shocked and appalled, mostly because he knew who the cyclops was: Poseidon's child.

'I swear I could have gone to war with him, had his son done any more harm to you than he did', the Screech Owl said, visibly disturbed by the idea of losing Persephone. Nevertheless, she was quick to comfort him, fondling his beard and assuring him she owed her very life to Orpheus, a moment she saw opportune to further explain why the bard was expected to arrive at the palace at any moment.

Hades, however, already knew about it, making it his turn to do some explaining: 'Hekate came here as frequently as she could, but there was a time she kept busy, though she would not tell me why. I assumed it was not my business, anyway, but I figured it had something to do with you and Demeter. Nevertheless, before her schedule became cluttered, there was one last thing she did, precisely the day you left. She saved Eurydike's life from the maids who used to serve you food and clean your bedroom, the Danaids.

Persephone's Fall

They had a foul plan to cleanse themselves, even though
they had been sentenced for that to never, ever take place:
I ordered them to help Eurydike wash in the same purifying
water they carried day after day, by filling one of the tubs
in the lavatory – if only Eurydike were to bathe in it, there
would be no leakages, so that is when they realized that,
if they forced our nymph here to stay underwater, their
life could be restored or, at least, their sins erased, giving
them a free passage to the Elysian Fields', he concluded.

Persephone could not believe what she had just heard,
but Eurydike nodded, confirming every word, adding:
'They even told me Hades had promised to release them
as well, like he had promised me, accusing him of lying
to them… never in my short life had I ever seen someone
being so deceitful… worst of all, it was not just one, it was
the whole group! One sister short of fifty! Unbelievable…'.

'Well…', Persephone restarted, 'I am sure your husband
will not allow anything bad to happen to you from now
on… I know you were almost killed on your wedding day.
Just thinking about it makes me shiver in terror… do you
remember what happened, exactly?', a question which
the oak nymph struggled for a while to answer, doing
her best to recollect that day's memories: 'It was both
the worst and best day of my life, of course… the reasons
matching each of those feelings are obvious, but the minute
we accepted each other as a spouse, we celebrated all day
long… everyone was so happy for us – the Argonauts
for Orpheus, the people of Tempe for me. In the end,
we all were family. But then, there came the moment…
a satyr, baring his depravity like all others of his kind,
came for me, running much too fast for my bare feet

on his goat legs and hooves... it made me distance myself from the village, having no idea where I was going, as long as he just... disappeared and left me alone, but he would not. So, I came across a viper hiding in the meadows, it attacked me, and when I recovered, I was walking down the staircase to the riverbank on the world of the living's side, jumping in the ferryman's barge without even paying him. It turned out I was not really dead, or, rather, I am not dead, not at all'.

Meanwhile, Orpheus had already crossed several solid rock bridges connecting prisoners' areas between themselves, and was getting closer to the palace, which could be seen from his current position; the horrors he had witnessed so far, together with the heat of the flames, the reeking stench of putrefaction, the painful screaming that did not cease, no matter how hoarse the inmate was... it did not surprise him no man had ever tried to enter Tartarus alive. Who in their right mind would want to see such a display?

Some of the prisoners had even addressed him, asking what the kithara was for, if it was magical, if it could release them; only one or two seemed to be interested in who he was and what he was doing in hell without being dead, for they could detect Orpheus's complexion was different from theirs. Though the bard was visibly scared, he tried his best to keep a straight face and move on undisturbed, but there were a lot of angry people down there willing to dismember him, so he would stop boasting his being alive and able to walk freely, despite his not saying anything to provoke them.

After a few more moments crossing over bridges that did not seem to end, Orpheus finally approached the palace and entered the house of Hades and Persephone, heavily panting

and wheezing, drawing Eurydike's attention before he
collapsed on the marble floor, right by the entrance.

The oak nymph hurried down the hallway crying his name:
125 'Orpheus! Orpheus! What happened, my Love?!'; the rulers
of the Underworld followed shortly after, worried about
the bard's condition, knowing not whether he was dead
or alive, though neither suggested either of the hypotheses –
Eurydike would have certainly felt even more disturbed.
130 However, to everyone's relief, he was breathing in a much
calmer manner, catching his breath back as he tried to get
up (no wonder he was tired of falling everywhere he went;
he was also exhausted from trying to get back on his feet).

Carefully supporting his weight on his forearms and elbows,
135 Orpheus looked up and saw his wife's visage, displaying
concern for him; even with her worried expression, she was
exactly as beautiful as he remembered her from the day
of their matrimony, the same accursed day that had
provoked all of his trials, so he could prove his love for
140 Eurydike, precisely, she, who smiled to tears when the bard
uttered her name and said: 'Heaven... I am in heaven...
my mission is accomplished... now I embrace you, Nemesis.
Take me where you must – I am ready at last', fainting after.

The nymph's tears of joy quickly turned into a doubled
145 stream of preoccupation, looking at both Persephone and
Hades in despair, trying to get them to do something
for Orpheus, which they did – it was the Grecian way,
tending to xenia at all times, no matter who showed
in front of Hellen's descendants and their illustrious gods.

150 The king of the Underworld lifted his grandnephew with

a sleight of hand and rested him on a lounge in the living
room, asking Persephone to serve him a cup of nectar.
'Worry not', Hades told Eurydike, 'he will be just fine'.
Similarly to what Demeter had done before, the daughter
155 followed the mother's steps and helped the bard swallow
by carefully holding his mouth open, without however
choking him, naturally; the nymph was in a frenzy,
holding her hands against her chest to prevent her heart
from bursting through, or it would all have been in vain.

160 Fortunately, a few moments later, Orpheus started to react,
rapidly blinking his eyes, trying to become aware of where
he had been taken to; when he saw Eurydike right by his
side, however, crying of joy once more, holding his hand
and caressing his hair, he uttered: 'Am I dreaming again…?'.
165 The nymph shook her head in denial, saying: 'No… no,
Darling… you are alive and well… I am by your side, now,
and will never leave you again. Come, it is time for us to go
back home and live our tale', she added, kissing his forehead.

Eurydike turned to both Hades and Persephone, thanking
170 them for everything they had done for her and Orpheus,
making one final request: 'Is there any way you could please
take us to the gates…? My husband is much too exhausted
to walk back'; Persephone volunteered and took them.
Hades agreed and smiled – the only queen Tartarus would
175 ever meet was by his side, and she loved him for real;
there was no way he would ever let go of her, the treasure
he had been looking for throughout his entire eternity.

When the three arrived at the gate and it opened, Kerberos
immediately came chasing them, but Persephone stepped
180 in front of the couple and lifted her hand, forcing him to stop.

'You have a mistress, now. You obey me as much as you obey Hades, is that clear?', the queen sternly told the dog. The three-headed canine moved away, whining as he walked, far more submissive to Persephone than his original master.

185 Then, she turned to the ferryman, still waiting on that side of the river to get back at Orpheus for his duping trickery: 'Be so kind as to take this couple back to the other side'. Kharon, disdaining of his new queen, made a forced bow and told her: 'Of course, Milady. Anything you say'.

190 Finally, Persephone faced Orpheus and Eurydike, held them both simultaneously, kissed them on their cheeks, bade them goodbye and said: 'Good luck, nephew. Good luck, my friend. Good luck to you both and Godspeed'. She withdrew back to her new domain, and the gates
195 closed, setting the barrier between both sides of the wall.

Kharon looked at the couple, one spouse at a time, saying at last: 'Well, hurry up, then. There is a life to go back to'. His regular tone was eerie, but those words sounded worse. Orpheus was still slightly shaken from all the horror seen
200 inside Tartarus, and though the rulers had been kind enough to him and Eurydike, he was still not feeling reassured.

The ferryman began to row, taking the bard and his nymph back to the world of the living; because the fog never ceased, there was no telling where in the riverbed's width they were.
205 Taking advantage of the poor sight, Kharon induced a vision into Orpheus, without having Eurydike notice anything; he was under the orders of a god and had to fulfill his task, otherwise, instead of faring souls across the Styx, he would become one of them, fed to the angry criminals flowing

210 in its waters, craving for revenge for how he had behaved
in the past, turning them down and suggesting they threw
themselves in the corroding stream to relieve their pain.

Rather feverish, Orpheus trembled with the sight in his mind:
a satyr was hiding in the meadows, carefully observing
215 the surrounding area; he was being instructed by a young
man dressed in a purple tunic, wearing an olive wreath
on his head, displaying wiggled locks all over its surface.
The bard was able to hear what the man was telling the
half-breed: 'Give her the impression you are chasing after
220 her for the kill and force her to run as fast and far as possible.
It is likely the rest of them will start chasing after you once
they see you, so do not waste any time and finish her'.
As the satyr nodded, the youth hid behind a tree in the nearby
forest, patiently waiting for the planned events to unfold.

225 A girl was happily dancing in the middle of a village square.
Orpheus recognized both the location and the girl – it was
Tempe and Eurydike, dressed in her wedding gown, with
an oaken crown ornamented with fresh flowers on her head.
The bard was watching the day of his own wedding from
230 a third-party point of view – what he was supposed to have
seen in his mind on that day precisely had only just invaded
his head now (with an extraordinary six-month delay);
he knew then it had to be deliberate, that someone powerful
enough had had to cloud his foreseeing abilities, preventing
235 his timely intervention in the killing of the satyr before
pushing Eurydike into the wild, where a viper would bite her.

Because of his realization, the slaying scenes were skipped;
the vision returned to the forest, where the young man was
still standing, visibly disturbed – the outcome of his plans

240 had gone wrong, at which point he said to himself aloud:
'Who would have thought... saved by a snake... you may
have won for now, Hera, but this will not last much longer';
Closeup, Orpheus gasped at the ugly truth – the youth was
none other than Dionysos, the god for which he had founded
245 a cult, one of his patrons; he was the one responsible for the
killing of Eurydike (or, rather, attempted murder, since the
snake had been put there by Hera to simply make it look
like she had died, despite the disappearance of the body).

The bard's heart was beating much too fast, as if it were
250 trying to rip through his ribcage and the muscle covering it.
The scene quickly dissolved and advanced in time, to just
a few moments before his and Eurydike's exit from Tartarus.
Dionysos, who had visited the Underworld before to bring
his mother Semele back to life, knew how to easily get back
255 there via shortcuts unknown to the ferryman himself, whose
exclusive means of transportation between banks was his
barge; the young god was talking to him just by the water,
threatening him with his demise, as I have sung earlier.
Kharon still tried to resist the coercion, retorting: 'If you
260 kill me, your uncle will hunt you down and bring your
mother back to this realm – your efforts will have been
in vain', but Dionysos did not let himself be intimidated:
'If I kill you, your only purpose will come to an end and
my uncle will find someone new to do your miserable job,
265 without ever finding out about the truth, because I assure
you he will not go looking for you in these filthy waters.
Truth be told, he does not even like you – you sass too much,
and I completely agree with him. Getting rid of a nuisance
like you might actually come in handy for Hades... in fact,
270 if he were to find out I had something to do with your sudden
disappearance, he would probably thank me. What do you

think, my skeletal friend?', the god of wine asked him, clearly
at an advantage as far as blackmailing was concerned.

If he had a throat, the ferryman would have gulped for
having no other choice, asking Dionysos: 'What do you
want me to do?', and the god replied: 'Your job, it is that
simple. You take Orpheus and his little wife with you to
the other side, under the condition of not looking over
his shoulder to confirm if she is right behind him, not once.
Make him swear on my name he will do as he is told –
he either leaves your barge and sets both feet on the ground,
or the girl goes straight back to the Underworld and stays
there for good. Do I make myself clear?', and Kharon
nodded, having just one more question to ask: 'What about
the girl? If she speaks, he will know she is still aboard'.
Dionysos briefly replied: 'Leave it to me. I will make sure
neither she utters a word, nor he plays a note', and having
said that, the god went away, together with the visions
entirely, bringing the fog back to Orpheus's eyes, in tears.

All he could hear was the sound of the oar in the river,
pushing the barge forward; Kharon had no need of telling
him anything, as the foreseer had seen and heard enough.
Orpheus sought to stay still and quiet as much as he could,
even holding his breath at times, hoping he could hear
Eurydike move, but the rippling in the water was all.

A few moments later (which had seemed an eternity to
the kithara player), the fog began to lift, and the riverbank
of the world of the living was visible once more; each iamb
the barge moved forward was an undeniable torment for
Orpheus; as the bow touched the sand, Kharon spoke
clearly: 'We have arrived'; the Apollonian nodded gently

and replied in a slightly elevated tone, so the ferryman could hear him without turning around: 'I see... thank you...'.

As he prepared to leave the barge, his breathing got faster;
305 Orpheus lifted his left foot first, and stepped on the sand (one of the things he had wanted to do so much had just become a burden he could not bear, but he had to push on). Then, he lifted his right foot, putting his body weight on his left leg alone, standing precariously; he chose his fate
310 when he tried to be more cunning than both the ferryman and Dionysos put together by turning his left foot inside while his right leg was still hanging, hoping it would not count as still being inside the barge... alas, whether it was relevant or not, standing on sand on only one foot is
315 a recipe for disaster, and Orpheus eventually fell back inside, turning his head back and, as he did, he saw his wife, Eurydike, bound by oaken branches, twisted around her body, preventing her from moving or making a sound. In a fraction of a second, she turned to dust and was sent
320 back across the river, dying for real, never to return again.

Orpheus still tried to grab her by extending his arms fully, but all he took hold of was air; Kharon stood where he was, looking at the bard's misery, throwing frozen words at him: 'You were warned... it is all your fault. Get out of my vessel'.
325 The kithara player rolled over and fell on the sand, crying his eyes out, pulling his hair, and scratching his entire body.

Canto XXIV

    Years later, you may wonder what happened to the main
    characters of this tale, bound to be retold for millennia...
    well, I shall indulge you and tell you now, but only the
    short version of it, as is customary for a play's final act.

5   Beginning with the Underworld, Persephone became Hades's
    lawfully wedded wife, officially taking over the role of Queen
    of Tartarus, and not just «consort», wielding as much power
    as her spouse, who loved her truly and deeply, entrusting her
    with full authority in a home that was also hers; every six
10   months, as per decision of the Moirai, Kore was bound to
    return to the upper world, therefore rebirthing Nature and
    renewing Gaia, shedding her snow-coat as soon as she met
    her mother, goddess of agriculture, crops, harvests, and
    human sustenance, Demeter, who always waited for her
15   by the shores of Pergoussa Lake, in Enna, near the center
    of Trinacria, enjoying their time together and recurring
    to their metamorphosis abilities, leading farmers back to
    the field, where they would once more sow their seeds
    and grow their crops, harvested just before Persephone left.

20   Naturally, the goddess of the Underworld would also spend
    time with her friend Hekate, consoling her for not being able
    to visit her own daughter up-close, Skylla, still dismembering
    and ripping the flesh out of men sailing through the Strait
    of Messene, leaving the vessels for her neighbor Kharybdis.

25   Although she would like to visit her sisters in Olympus,
    Persephone preferred staying on her island, asking them
    to dive from the skies and be with her, Hekate, and Demeter.

The thought of having to face her father and stepmother,
two people she could not care less about, was enough
to make that decision, although she did take great care
and interest in asking how Apollo was coping, ever since
the dastardly tragedy that had taken his son's life, saddening
not just him, but Calliope as well, like any loving mother.

Now, this is the part I have not yet sung to you about;
even when the end is near, you never know when a surprise
is bound to come and still do some stirring in the plot.

Back in Thrace, after Orpheus's latest and final expedition,
the one he lost his wife Eurydike to, the kithara player swore
never to fall in love again; though he was still young, he had
had enough and, therefore, gave up socializing with women
(or men, even), deciding to live the quiet life of a hermit.

Because of the misadventure he had gone through in the
Underworld, the gods fell foul of him and were never
worshipped by Orpheus again – all except for one: Apollo,
the Sun-God, his father and teacher, caring also for Calliope.
As much as his parents tried to liven up his spirit, all the bard
could sing were mournful tunes, knowing Eurydike's soul
was treading right below his feet, in the earth's entrails.

Now, in Thrace, there were several tribes, being one of them
the Kikonians, whose female members were followers of
the bard's former patron, Dionysos (making them Maenads).
Because they all wanted to have a go at getting to know
Orpheus better, though he kept resisting and pushing them
back, one day, the women, entranced by their god, became
violent, throwing sticks and stones at the Apollonian, but
none of the throws would hit him because of the golden lyre.

Persephone's Fall

So, induced into a Bacchic frenzy by Dionysos himself,
the women, impervious to the magic effect of the kithara,
threw themselves at Orpheus and, as they performed one
of their usual orgies, dismembered and killed the bard.

Despite having been literally torn apart, his head still lived,
perpetuating the same mournful songs as the lyre played
itself; eventually, both head and kithara ended in the river
Hébros, flowing back to the Aegean Sea and ending up in
Lesbos, where Hephaestus was raised, as you may recall.

The locals took care of the head and buried it in Antissa,
to the West, building a shrine on top of it in his honor.
For years, people from the whole of Greece visited his
shrine, from which Orpheus perpetuated his foreseeing
gift, becoming an oracle even the Babylonians consulted.

As for the golden kithara, the Muses (Calliope included)
took it to the skies, transforming it into a bright star.
Not only that, they collected every single bone of Orpheus's
body and built a grave for him by the foothills of Olympus,
a place no less than enchanting, as birds would stop to pay
their respects, especially nightingales, singing for him.

Being a foreseer, I already know what has yet to happen:
there will come a day the river Sys will flood my grave
and my bones will be moved from where they lie now;
once I am laid to rest for eternity, my soul will wander
the earth no more, returning to the Underworld at last,
where my lovely Eurydike still to this day awaits my arrival,
so we may be eternally, perpetually rejoined as one.

Biography

Tiago Lameiras was born in Lisbon, Portugal, in 1990.
He has a Bachelor's Degree with Honors on Theater – Acting, from the Higher School of Theater and Film of Lisbon.
He is currently completing his PhD on Communications, Culture, and Arts – Cultural Studies Specialization, at the School of Arts and Humanities of the University of the Algarve, Portugal.
His list of publications includes: *Portvcale – A Epopeia Portuguesa da Contemporaneidade* (October 2010), *Viagem ao Centro de Ti – Romance Trovado* (January 2012), *A Mão de Diónisos* (November 2013), *Actor Being: A Role in Mankind* (March 2016), *Utopian Ambition: Constitution of the 2100 Atlantian Republic* (September 2016), *Sonata* (May 2017), and *Epistulæ* (November 2017), as well as poetical collaborations in Chiado Editora's Poetry Anthologies *Entre o Sono e o Sonho* (2012, 2014, and 2015) and Sinapis' *Enigma(s)* (February 2015).

Printed in Great Britain
by Amazon